Strategic Industry-University Partnerships

Strategic Industry-University Partnerships

Success-Factors from Innovative Companies

Edited by

Lars Frølund

Massachusetts Institute of Technology, Cambridge,
MA, United States
Aarhus University, Aarhus, Denmark

Max F. Riedel
Siemens AG, Munich, Germany

ACADEMIC PRESS

An imprint of Elsevier

Academic Press is an imprint of Elsevier
125 London Wall, London EC2Y 5AS, United Kingdom
525 B Street, Suite 1650, San Diego, CA 92101, United States
50 Hampshire Street, 5th Floor, Cambridge, MA 02139, United States
The Boulevard, Langford Lane, Kidlington, Oxford OX5 1GB, United Kingdom

British Library Cataloguing-in-Publication Data
A catalogue record for this book is available from the British Library

Library of Congress Cataloging-in-Publication Data
A catalog record for this book is available from the Library of Congress

ISBN: 978-0-12-810989-2

For Information on all Academic Press publications
visit our website at https://www.elsevier.com/books-and-journals

Working together
to grow libraries in
developing countries

www.elsevier.com • www.bookaid.org

Publisher: Candice Janco
Acquisition Editor: Scott Bentley
Editorial Project Manager: Susan Ikeda
Production Project Manager: Mohana Natarajan
Cover Designer: Mark Rogers

Typeset by MPS Limited, Chennai, India

Contents

List of Contributors

Najib Abusalbi Corporate University Relations, Schlumberger Limited (Retired), Houston, TX, United States

Manuel Martínez Alonso Ferrovial, Madrid, Spain

Kate Barnard University Research Liaison, Rolls-Royce Plc, United Kingdom

Ciro Acedo Boria Ferrovial, Madrid, Spain

Søren Bregenholt Novo Nordisk Research and Development, Bagsværd, Denmark

Alessandro Curioni IBM Research − Zurich, Zurich, Switzerland

Rajiv Dhawan Samsung Semiconductor Inc., Milpitas, CA, United States

Natacha Eckert Siemens AG, Munich, Germany

Nicole Eichmeier BMW Group, Munich, Germany

Lars Frølund Aarhus University, Aarhus, Denmark; Massachusetts Institute of Technology, Cambridge, MA, United States

Mark Jefferies University Research Liaison, Rolls-Royce Plc, United Kingdom

Karsten Keller Nitto Denko Avecia Inc., Milford, MA, United States

Alberto López-Oleaga Ferrovial, Madrid, Spain

Max F. Riedel Siemens AG, Munich, Germany

Chris Sciacca IBM Research − Zurich, Zurich, Switzerland

Hans Ulrich Stilz Novo Nordisk Research and Development, Bagsværd, Denmark

Mirjam Storim BMW Group, Munich, Germany

About the Authors

Lars Frølund (Editor)

Dr. Lars Frølund is a development manager at Aarhus University and the incoming director of research of the MIT Lab for Innovation Science and Policy. In 2005 he established one of the first units for university–industry collaboration in Denmark. Since then, he has worked intensively to develop strategic collaborations between research and private companies.

His research focuses on the success factors of university–industry partnerships in innovation ecosystems and the role and value of intermediaries. He holds a master's degree in philosophy (2004) and a PhD in corporate programs for university engagement (2017). He has received Aarhus University's Gold Medal for outstanding academic achievement and was a Fulbright Scholar at MIT Innovation Initiative in 2016/17.

Max F. Riedel (Editor)

Dr. Max Fabian Riedel is a senior consultant at Siemens University Relations. His daily tasks include consulting Siemens businesses in all aspects of university cooperation, ranging from developing a partnering strategy over finding suitable research partners to fostering long-term strategic cooperation. He joined Siemens in 2012 as a management consultant at Siemens Management Consulting (SMC), the internal consultancy of Siemens.

Max holds a PhD degree in physics. At the time this book is published, he is delegated to the University of Ulm to support the ramp-up of the Quantum Flagship initiative, one of the European Commission's most ambitious long-term projects to bring technology from the lab to the market. Before this assignment, he was the key account manager for two of Siemens' strategic partner universities.

Najib Abusalbi

Dr. Najib Abusalbi is currently a director of corporate university relations for Schlumberger Limited, the world's largest services and technology provider for the oil and gas sector. His current responsibilities include oversight of activities with leading global universities. These activities include developing and recruiting talent globally, and providing support for both education and research programs in the energy sector, with focus on building capacity and boosting technology innovation. In this role, he reports to the Schlumberger

Executive Vice President of corporate engagement. He joined Schlumberger in 1984 following 3 years in academic roles in physics and chemistry. Since then, he held multiple product development and operations management positions in several exploration and production domains.

He holds a PhD in atomic physics from Louisiana State University and is recognized as a scientific advisor in the Schlumberger's Communities of Practice, where he has led several communities including management disciplines, project management, and knowledge and information management, where he has held the role of an executive management sponsor since 2012.

Kate Barnard

Kate Barnard (Rolls-Royce) is a manager in the engineering and technology group with accountability for maintaining and developing strategic academic partnerships around the world. She interfaces with government agencies, academics, and students to promote collaboration, focus strategic direction in line with corporate and national needs, and ensure a diverse talent pipeline for the future. She has led multiple national and international research programs, having worked for the company for 20 years.

She is a chartered engineer with the Institution of Mechanical Engineers and a professional program manager accredited by the Association of Project Management.

Ciro Acedo Boria

Ciro Acedo Boria is an experienced professional with an entrepreneurial and innovative mindset and head of Open Innovation Ecosystem at Ferrovial. His work involves boosting, improving, and making the entrepreneurial ecosystem stronger (startups, accelerators, VCs, entrepreneurs, universities, etc.).

He has managed and coordinated international teams with a strong enterprise focus and has a deep experience as project manager for innovative projects. He has an extensive international experience, and he has lived and worked for more than 1 year in Paris (France) and Seoul (South Korea). He has also become an entrepreneur himself, developing the project Waash. green, and hosting the FuckUp Nights event (an informal event for startups and entrepreneurs focused on learning from mistakes) in his hometown, Seville.

He holds a MSc degree in telecommunication engineering from the Universidad de Sevilla, and an executive MBA, with a concentration in entrepreneurship, from the IE Business School.

Søren Bregenholt

Søren Bregenholt is a corporate vice president and head of R&D external innovation and strategy in Novo Nordisk, responsible for securing access to external innovation, through licensing, university collaboration, and public—private partnerships. In addition, he is responsible for global R&D-based PhD and postdoc programs in Novo Nordisk. He has more than

15 years of experience from various senior management positions in the biotech and pharmaceutical industry.

He graduated from University of Copenhagen in 1995, and received his PhD in biomedical research in 2000 from the same university. He did his postdoc training at the Pasteur institute, Paris, France. He is the author of more than 50 scientific papers.

He is an advisor to the dean of the Faculty of Science and honorable industrial ambassador at the Faculty of Health and Medical Science, both at University of Copenhagen and serves as a chairman of the board in Medicon Valley Alliance, a life science cluster organization.

Alessandro Curioni

Dr. Alessandro Curioni is an IBM Fellow, vice president of IBM Europe and director of the IBM Research Lab in Zurich, Switzerland. He is also the Watson IoT research relationship executive.

He is an internationally recognized leader in the area of high-performance computing and computational science, where his innovative thinking and seminal contributions have helped in solving some of the most complex scientific and technological problems in healthcare, aerospace, consumer goods, and electronics. He was a member of the winning team recognized with the prestigious Gordon Bell Prize in 2013 and 2015.

He received his undergraduate degree in theoretical chemistry and his PhD from Scuola Normale Superiore, Pisa, Italy. He started at IBM Research, Zurich, as a PhD student in 1993, before officially joining as a research staff member in 1998.

Rajiv Dhawan

Rajiv Dhawan received his bachelor of science degree from Simon Fraser University in suburban Vancouver. He then moved on to get his PhD from McGill University in Montreal, Quebec, followed by a postdoc appointment at Stanford University. He started his career at DuPont Central Research & Development as a research chemist and moved to the university relations function and managed several programs, including the ~ 100-year old DuPont Young Professor program. He joined Samsung Semiconductor in 2016 and is currently a director of Strategic Planning and Business Development. In this role, he manages university relations for Device Solutions America and the key activities include collaboration management, technology scouting, and PhD recruiting.

Natascha Eckert

Since 18 years, Dr. Natascha Eckert is active in various leading roles within corporate research and innovation at companies like Siemens and Osram. She has a long-year experience in the university-industry cooperation, currently managing Siemens' global strategic partner programs with universities and research institutes.

She has a long-year history in Siemens' international technology and innovation management and was responsible for expanding Siemens Corporate Technology's footprint to Asia and Russia. For many years she has coordinated the company's engagement in manifold external research and innovation organizations and bodies, for example, Bayerische Forschungsstiftung, Stifterverband, Forschungsunion, acatech, and DAAD.

She holds a PhD degree in BA from Ludwig Maximilians University of Munich and had worked for several years as a strategic consultant for various companies.

Nicole Eichmeier

Nicole Eichmeier works for the strategic talent management department as head of future talent management and strategic university cooperations within the BMW Group.

With a network of colleagues, passionate about innovation, she is setting up initiatives and research projects in defined target and research fields.

She studied industrial engineering. She is working for BMW since 2000, the first 12 years in different positions in R&D and purchasing in Munich and Asia, the past years in the strategic talent management area.

Mark Jefferies

Mark Jefferies (Rolls-Royce) is a senior manager in the Rolls-Royce corporate technology strategy group, with extensive experience in leading and developing complex industry—academic collaboration. He is accountable for leading the overall effectiveness, delivery, and strategic development of key academic research partnerships for the Rolls-Royce Group. This includes the company's highly successful network of University Technology Centres, engaging hundreds of academics and over 500 doctorate students at any one time.

He is a chartered engineer, a fellow of the Institution of Mechanical Engineers, a fellow of the Royal Aeronautical Society, and a senior member of the American Institute of Aeronautics and Astronautics.

Karsten Keller

Dr. Karsten Keller is the director of technical innovation and improvement management at Nitto Denko Avecia, USA. Previously, he was 19 years with DuPont, USA, as a corporate technical manager in the science and innovation department and was leading the effort of 400 + university relations globally. He was responsible for the global innovation strategy which includes the aspects of data analytics, benchmarking, portfolio, project planning, leadership, and external relationships (M&A, venture, start-ups, and universities). He has broad working experiences in materials, agriculture, biotechnology, chemistry, food, and pharma.

He received his chemical engineering degree from the University Karlsruhe, Germany. He is teaching as an adjunct professor in process development and innovation at the University Freiberg, Germany.

Alberto López-Oleaga

Alberto López-Oleaga is innovation and processes director of Ferrovial.

He graduated in industrial engineering from the Universidad Politécnica de Madrid and has an MBA from IESE Business School. Before joining Ferrovial, he had developed his professional career in other companies like Empresarios Agrupados where he worked as an estimator engineer and British Petroleum where he worked as IT director.

At Ferrovial, he has held several positions in the organization, human resources, and IT areas. In March 1999, he was appointed as an IT director of Ferrovial Agromán, participating in the integration of Budimex. Later, in September 2003, he was appointed as an IT director of Ferrovial Servicios, participating among other projects, in the integration of Amey, Cespa, and Swissport.

In 2008, he was appointed as an architecture and business processes director of Ferrovial, until 2010 when he was asked to become innovation and processes director, encompassing the Center of Excellence of Assets Management, the Centre of Excellence for Intelligent Transport Systems, innovation management, and alliances.

Manuel Martínez

Manuel Martínez is an open innovation manager at Ferrovial. He is a pro bono contributor to Bankinter's Foundation of Innovation and a part-time teacher at Deusto Business School. He regularly participates as a mentor in programs on innovation and entrepreneurship at large corporations, business schools, and foundations.

He began his professional career in 1999 in the R&D department at the Spanish High Speed Rail Operator Renfe. He has also worked in the consulting area of the IT sector and later launched an online advertising startup where he served as director of operations. In 2003 he was appointed as a director of software marketing for Spain and Portugal at Sun Microsystems, American multinational company, where he also served as head of Web 2.0 and open source business development.

Since 2008, he has been leading the foundation of Ferrovial's innovation ecosystem, aimed at creating competitive advantages and developing new business opportunities, as well as promoting the innovation culture within the company. He was responsible for the design and launching the employee-ideation program Zuritanken, the urban startup laboratory Madrid Smart Lab and the corporate intrapreneurship itinerary Shuttle. In 2009 he cofounded the innovation center for intelligent infrastructure.

He holds a MSc in engineering sciences from the IC, Comillas Pontifical University in Madrid, and has been a student at SGMI, IESE, and MIT.

Christopher P. Sciacca
Christopher Sciacca is the communications manager for IBM Research in Europe, Middle East, and Africa. He joined IBM in 2001 and has worked and lived in New York, Austria, Czech Republic, and Switzerland.

He has a bachelor of science in advertising degree from the New York Institute of Technology where he graduated Cum Laude.

Uli Stilz
Uli Stilz is a vice president of academic partnerships at Novo Nordisk A/S. In this role, he is globally responsible to access external innovation through university collaborations and public–private partnerships. Furthermore, he oversees Novo Nordisk's R&D-based PhD and postdoc programs.

He graduated with a master's degree in organic chemistry from ETH Zürich. He then moved to the Max Planck Institute in Martinsried, where he received his PhD in biochemistry in 1990. After postdoc studies at California Institute of Technology, he joined Hoechst AG where he held various positions before he was appointed as a vice president of the newly established innovation unit within the Diabetes Division at Sanofi. In 2014 he joined Novo Nordisk A/S in his current role as vice president academic partnerships.

He was appointed as an adjunct professor at the University of Frankfurt in 2012. He serves on various editorial boards for international peer-reviewed journals, is a member of scientific advisory boards in Europe and North America, and represents Novo Nordisk A/S at trade organizations (EFPIA). Between 2012 and 2014, he had been the president of the European Federation for Medicinal Chemistry.

Dr. Mirjam Storim
Dr. Mirjam Storim works for the production strategy department at BMW Group, Munich, Germany, as the head of make or buy steering and production partner management. Prior to that she holds functions at Oliver Wyman, at the Eberhard von Kuenheim Foundation of BMW AG and within the BMW Group. Starting 2011 she relaunched the university cooperation strategy of the company and built up several strategic partnerships with universities in Europe, the United States, Asia, and China. She studied in Freiburg, Ioannina (Greece) and Munich and holds a PhD in philosophy from the Ludwigs Maximilian University in Munich.

Foreword

We are living at a crucial moment in history as we enter the age of the fourth industrial revolution. New technologies are merging the physical, digital, and biological worlds in ways that create both huge promise and potential peril. The speed, breadth, and depth of this revolution are forcing us to rethink how countries develop, how organizations create value, and even what it means to be human. It is differentiated from previous revolutions in terms of speed with which innovations develop and diffuse.

Universities and industry alike are important drivers of these innovations. Fundamental research in universities is laying the foundation for radical scientific and technological breakthroughs in fields as diverse as materials science, neuro- and biotechnologies, and artificial intelligence, among others. Industry is equally shaping this revolution by putting these breakthrough technologies to work and engaging in research and development efforts of their own. Their effective cooperation will therefore be fundamental in assuring that the fourth industrial revolution will evolve in a way that supports and accelerates human progress rather than challenges it.

As humanity undergoes and adapts to deep transformations with the advancement of technology, universities must focus on training students to lead in a new world where computer science, artificial intelligence, and other emerging technologies will become as pervasive as electricity. Collaboration between academia and industry is a good step in that direction, enabling implementation of theoretical ideas, translating basic research into useful products, and providing students with experience in the private sector. But the private sector also has to take responsibility for the effects of technological change on society. As universities and industry partners develop agendas for strategic collaboration, it is important to do so within a wider systemic approach that balances opportunities and risks.

This is a most timely opportunity to intensify the exploration of success factors for strategic industry−university collaboration, as the contributions to this volume set out to do. I believe that collaboration between industry and academia can play a crucial role in solving many of today's challenges. Educational institutions can ensure the transfer of lessons learned from previous industrial revolutions. As such, they are ideally placed to serve as a bridge between the past and the future. The world can only improve if we meet across boundaries and create space for the discussion of big issues that increasingly emphasize the academic, scientific, and research components of addressing global challenges.

By sharing insights from leading global companies on how they work strategically with universities, this book offers the keys to building a better future.

Klaus Schwab
Founder and Executive Chairman of the World Economic Forum

Acknowledgements

There are many people we would like to thank for making this book possible. First and foremost, we owe a great debt of gratitude toward the people who have written the chapters in the book: Nicole Eichmeier and Mirjam Storim from BMW; Ciro Acedo Boria, Alberto Lopez-Oleaga, and Manuel Martines Alonso from Ferrovial; Alessandro Curioni and Chris Sciacca from IBM; Karsten Keller from Nitto Avecia; Søren Bregenholt and Uli Stilz from Novo Nordisk; Kate Barnard and Mark Jefferies from Rolls-Royce; Rajiv Dhawan from Samsung; Najib Abusalbi from Schlumberger; and Natascha Eckert from Siemens. Thank you so much for your willingness to share your expertise.

We would also like to thank the entire university relations team at Siemens and especially Natascha Eckert for her ongoing support and encouragement of the book. Deep and long conversations with Prof. Fiona Murray from MIT were instrumental for synthesizing the insights into the university partnership canvas. We would like to thank Todd Dawey, Thorsten Kliewe, and Arno Meermann from the University Industry Innovation Network (UIIN) for giving us the opportunity to further develop the findings of the book during the yearly UIIN conference. The realization of the book would not have been possible without the patience and enduring support of Anette Miltoft and John Westensee from Aarhus University.

At Elsevier, we would like to thank our editor Scott Bentley for believing in the book, and Susan Ikeda, our production manager, for bringing us with great expertise toward a publication.

Finally, we would like to thank our families for their support and patience.

Copenhagen and Munich
May 2018

Introduction

"It is hardly possible to overrate the value (...) of placing human beings in contact with persons dissimilar to themselves, and with modes of thought and action unlike those with which they are familiar (...) Such communication has always been, and is peculiarly in the present age, one of the primary sources of progress." (John Stuart Mill, "Principles of Political Economy", 1848).

As Prof. Klaus Schwab points out in his foreword, the fourth industrial revolution is transforming our world at a speed that was previously unknown. We live in times of steadily increasing pace, where product life cycles become shorter and shorter, where knowledge and skills become outdated quickly and where disruptive innovations are revolutionizing whole industry branches in only a few years. In these times, innovative companies cannot anymore rely solely on in-house resources but must work together with external partners to stay competitive. Universities are power-houses of innovation where new technologies are developed, new trends are formed and fresh talents are educated. Partnerships between universities and corporations are thus a fundamental driver of economic progress and an important catalyst for finding solutions to our societal problems (Etzkowitz & Leydesdorff, 2000; Etzkowitz, Ranga, & Dzisah, 2012).

However, partnerships between corporations and universities are also challenging because of the different goals and cultural norms of academia and industry. There is a large amount of research and governmental reports on the challenges in industry—university partnerships (Bruneel, D'Este, & Salter, 2010; Lambert, 2003; *The Dowling Review of Business—University Research Collaborations*, 2015). Against this background, it is tempting to say that to have successful partnerships we must strive to take away the differences between universities and corporations. This would be a mistake. As John Stuart Mill mentions, one of the primary sources of progress is placing dissimilar people in contact with each other. We must be aware of the differences and the challenges they create for successful collaborations, but we must at the same time acknowledge that successful industry—university collaboration is not about taking away the differences, but managing them in a way so that the differences becomes an opportunity and not a problem.

The companies contributing to this book acknowledge the differences between themselves and universities and strive every day to make them an opportunity for innovation and economic progress for the company, the partner universities and society. In doing so, they are not only confronted with the intrinsic differences and challenges on the project-level of university–industry collaboration but also the differences and challenges that become apparent when looking beyond the single project at the overall collaboration portfolio with often hundreds of projects. The result is a change from an ad hoc approach with many individual, uncoordinated collaboration activities to a strategic approach, which is characterized by a professionalization and institutionalization of *university relations* of the company.[1] These units and people, sometimes called university relationship managers, are often situated in the R&D organization of the company, which bears witness to the fact that companies today depended on external knowledge to stay competitive.

Many authors of this book are heading such units. They give insights into their daily work and what they consider the most important success factors for strategic university collaboration. Each chapter starts by a short introduction to the company and an overview of its university collaboration approach. Then, the authors focus on one specific success factor, describe the challenges they face and their approach to solve them, and give actionable recommendations to the reader.

During the several workshops preparing this book, five success factors for strategic industry–university collaboration became apparent:

1. Select the focus areas of your university partnerships in alignment with your business goals
2. Select your primary university partners in a systematic way
3. Select collaboration formats that match your focus areas and business goals
4. Have dedicated people, processes and organization to support your university partnerships
5. Regularly evaluate your university partnerships, using suitable key performance indicators

---

1. This, by the way, is a trend not only at the company but also the university side, where we have witnessed an institutionalization and professionalization of support functions for industry collaboration like the technology transfer offices (Boardman & Corley, 2008), and industry liaison offices (Lee & Ohta, 2010), just to mention a few. Important drivers of this development on the university-side have been (and still are) innovation policy frameworks on national and international level with clear incentives for universities to engage in multistakeholder collaborations that follows the triple helix model (Etzkowitz & Leydesdorff, 2000) and importantly focus on the application of research results to specific societal challenges—also known as modus 2 research (Nowotny, Scott, & Gibbons, 2003). Recent examples are EU's Horizon 2020 program that promotes research projects with a strong industry involvement both in the work packages of the projects and in the governance of the research projects.

SELECT FOCUS AREAS

A central task for innovation management is to find the right balance between activities driven from the expert level (bottom-up) vs activities driven from the management level (top-down). For university collaboration, this means to find the balance between partnerships initiated and steered by individual development departments and academic research groups vs collaboration or programs on a company/university level (often called "strategic partnerships," though, as we will see later, we prefer to use the term "strategic" differently). Bottom-up initiated partnerships are usually smaller and with a narrower focus and time horizon than top-down initiatives. They are therefore normally more agile, closer related to everyday business and have a higher probability for short-term impact. On the other hand, they often use the academic partner as an "extended workbench" (Perkmann & Salter, 2012), which is often not looked upon favorably at universities and which limits the chances of achieving breakthroughs through unexpected research results. Top-down initiatives have the advantage of addressing a bigger picture and leave more room for creativity. However, business impact is usually expected only on a long-term and company-wide scale and very often unsure at the beginning. In the extreme case, such initiatives address grand challenges of society and set high-risk, high-gain targets.

Unfortunately, there is often an inherent mistrust between the expert level and management level. In the worst case, this leads to bottom-up activities being questioned by management as "pet projects" or top-down initiatives lacking support from the experts. When implemented well, top-down initiatives bundle existing, related bottom-up projects and expand on them and new bottom-up initiatives complement the existing top-down programs.

In the chapter about BMW, the authors show how the selection of focus areas for university collaboration can happen trough balanced bottom-up and top-down processes that connect the innovation topics of the whole company to the topics for university collaboration. BMW has established a "University Strategy Circle" which aligns university collaboration projects with their seven research clusters and preferred partner universities and selects the best proposals for cofunding.

SELECT PARTNERS

Choosing a suitable collaboration partner often goes hand-in-hand with choosing topics for external collaboration, and it is not an easy task. Are you looking for the world leader in a certain field, even if you have never worked with this group, if it might be located far away from your research center or if it expects very high resource and money commitment from the company? Alternatively, do you want to work with the researchers you know and value from previous (maybe even personal) experience, which are located close-by, but who do not attract the best students or whose expertise does not match your problem well? Or, to formulate it differently, are you looking for great researchers or great collaborators? As always, the answer depends on your collaboration scope and goals, the desired degree of interaction, potential interaction of the research group with your competitors, available budget and many other factors. Unfamiliar top researchers should be approached with small projects to test if they are also good collaborators—familiarity might then develop over time. On the other hand, familiar research groups might be encouraged to adopt their focus or might gain international reputation through the industry partnership and thus attract better talent.

DuPont outline in their chapter how they help their project leaders to make well-thought-out decisions about their research partners. DuPont has created an online tool in which researchers enter their partner requirements and project goals. The tool then suggests best suited partners, based on a data analysis of global research expertise, previous relations, contractual situation, and other factors.

MATCH COLLABORATION FORMATS

Many different ways exist how companies and universities can collaborate but which one to choose depends greatly on what one wants to achieve with the collaboration. For example, contract research, where the company finances the university in return for research results and often intellectual property rights, is well suited for extended workbench types of projects. However, it often requires long contract negotiations and might restrict thinking outside the box as it usually fixes clear milestones to reach. As another example, student idea contest and hackathons are great to get to know young talents, but contrary to common belief, they most often fail at creating new ideas with business impact. The best format to choose for a certain topic also depends on the university partner. For example, most ivy-league universities will not give away IP rights and are quite expensive to work with. On the other hand, they offer some of the world's best talents, professors and labs and are eager to work on problems with large societal impact. This makes them good partners for addressing long-time and large-scale challenges but not well suited for extended workbench projects.

IBM and Novo Nordisk show in their chapters the large variety of ways how they work with universities and give examples for successfully matching cooperation formats to their business needs. IBM takes the reader on a time-travel through the last 50 years in which it has even developed a completely new field of study to educate students with exactly the skills needed by the company. Novo Nordisk describes how the different formats are closely connected to the different strategic needs of the company and the different stages in the translational drug development process of a big pharma company.

DEDICATED PEOPLE, PROCESSES, AND ORGANIZATION

Collaboration and partnership does not work without good personal relations. Nevertheless, they can also impede judgment of the involved people, for example, when choosing familiar collaboration partners even if there are better researchers and collaborators available, or when evaluating project progress. Some formal governance and processes to steer the collaboration portfolio strategically is therefore necessary. But how much is required and even beneficial for the overall company's aims and when does bureaucracy start to become a burden? One way to address this challenge is to put people in charge of governance and managing the processes who are not bureaucrats. Instead, they should be incentivized by the overall performance of the collaboration portfolio and at the same time have a large personal network within the collaboration projects.

Rolls-Royce and Siemens describe in their chapters how they govern their strategic university partner networks and the important role that dedicated people play in this. Rolls-Royce shares seven learnings on what the authors consider a collaboration's most vital ingredient—human relationships. Siemens highlights the value added by dedicated university account managers on the company and the university side and on management and working level.

REGULARLY EVALUATE PARTNERSHIPS

Regular evaluation of partnerships is essential for steering the company's collaboration portfolio. But what evaluation criteria are best suited for university—industry collaboration? What is the right balance between quantitative and qualitative KPIs, on what level should one evaluate and how to find the balance between necessary control and needless bureaucracy?

Schlumberger and Ferrovial give insights in how they evaluate their relationships with universities in general and the success of long-term collaboration projects in particular. Using concrete examples, they give advice on the KPIs, the evaluation process and the subsequent decision making process (Fig. 1).

The authors of this book offer to the reader best practice methods, concrete examples, and actionable advice. At the same time, it is important to realize that there is no "right" solution, no "recipe" to follow, which fits each company and each collaboration. This is also reflected by the great variety in the way the chapters are written: While some authors share a lot of personal anekdotes or stories form their company's history, other authors use a more formal language. Some include photos, others graphics, or tables. We decided to explicitly allow for this variety in style, as it often reflects the company's culture and importantly the success factor the authors elaborate on.

FIGURE 1 The five success factors for strategic industry—university collaboration.

Nevertheless, one thing became clear in the preparation of this book: while the particular approaches of the featured companies differ significantly, what makes them excellent is that they are closely aligned with the business goals of the respective company. This seems like a trivial insight at first, but it is often forgotten in the literature on this topic. Therefore, when we say "strategic" cooperation, we do not necessarily mean high investment,[2] but rather continuously and systematically aligned with the overall company business goals. The final chapter of the book summarizes all learnings from the individual companies and synthesizes them into a *university partnership canvas* in which the business goals play a central role. We hope that we can thus provide the reader with a useful tool to benchmark and further develop his/her organization's approach to university—industry relations.

REFERENCES

Boardman, P.C., Corley, E.A., 2008. University research centers and the composition of research collaborations. Res. Policy 37 (5), 900—913. Available from: https://doi.org/10.1016/J.Respol.2008.01.012.

Bruneel, J., D'Este, P., Salter, A., 2010. Investigating the factors that diminish the barriers to university—industry collaboration. Res. Policy 39 (7), 858—868. Available from: https://doi.org/10.1016/j.respol.2010.03.006.

Etzkowitz, H., Leydesdorff, L., 2000. The dynamics of innovation: from National Systems and "Mode 2" to a Triple Helix of university—industry—government relations. Res. Policy 29 (2), 109—123. Available from: https://doi.org/10.1016/S0048-7333(99)00055-4.

---

2. The university collaboration approach by DuPont, for example, is deliberately moving away from few large projects with high investments to more smaller projects with can be closer to the business needs.

Etzkowitz, H., Ranga, M., Dzisah, J., 2012. Whither the university? The Novum Trivium and the transition from industrial to knowledge society. Soc. Sci. Inf. Sur Les Sci. Sociales 51 (2), 143–164. Available from: https://doi.org/10.1177/0539018412437099.

Lambert, R., 2003. Lambert Review of Business–University Collaboration. Retrieved from ⟨http://scholar.google.com/scholar?hl = en&btnG = Search&q = intitle: Lambert + Review + of + Business-University + Collaboration#7⟩.

Lee, K., Ohta, T., 2010. Formal boundary spanning by industry liaison offices and the changing pattern of university–industry cooperative research: the case of the University of Tokyo. Technol. Anal. Strategic Manage. 22 (2), 189–206. Available from: https://doi.org/10.1080/09537320903498538.

Nowotny, H., Scott, P., Gibbons, M., 2003. Introduction: "Mode 2" revisited: the new production of knowledge. Minerva. Available from: https://doi.org/10.1023/A:1025505528250.

Perkmann, M., Salter, A., 2012. How to create productive partnerships with universities. Mit Sloan Manage. Rev. 53 (4), 79–88.

The Dowling Review of Business—University Research Collaborations. (2015). Available from: https://assets.publishing.service.gov.uk/government/uploads/system/uploads/attachment_data/file/440927/bis_15_352_The_dowling_review_of_business-university_rearch_collaborations_2.pdf.

Chapter 1

Overlapping Broad Innovation Horizons With Business Relevance: How BMW Group Defines Topics for Strategic Collaborations

Nicole Eichmeier and Mirjam Storim
BMW Group, Munich, Germany

BMW Facts and Figures (Fiscal Year 2017)

Company name:	BMW Group
Headquarters in:	Munich, Germany
Annual revenue:	EUR 98.7 billion
Number of (R&D) employees:	~130,000 (~14,000)
R&D budget:	EUR 6.1 billion
Average number of University R&D collaborations p.a.:	>250
Industry branch(es):	Automotive products and services Product examples: passenger vehicles, services as DriveNow, financial services

For automotive manufacturers, innovation is key—and cooperation between industry and universities is gaining importance and momentum as a result. The following article outlines how to ensure the ideal fit between

Strategic Industry-University Partnerships. DOI: https://doi.org/10.1016/B978-0-12-810989-2.00001-1

university—industry cooperation projects and a company's strategic and R&D needs. Taking the BMW Group as an example, it outlines the process of determining topics and scope, and establishing essential criteria for sustainable partnership structures.

1.1 UNIVERSITY RELATIONS AT THE BMW GROUP—AN INTRODUCTION

Unique mobility experiences by the BMW Group have been inspiring people around the world for the last 100 years. Throughout its history, the company has reinvented itself time and again, shaping change both within the automotive industry and in mobility more widely with pioneering, new technologies. Today, the BMW Group is setting standards with its new corporate strategy, NUMBER ONE > NEXT. Launched in 2016, the BMW Group's centenary year, NUMBER ONE > NEXT represents a roadmap into a new era that will see us transform and redefine not only individual mobility but also the entire automotive sector for good.

In its mission to deliver unique customer experiences, our company builds on innovative technologies, digitalization and sustainability, and embraces the opportunities that emerge as our industry is transformed. As different industry sectors meld, their mutual influence is increasing, with digitalization, for example, giving rise to disruptive technologies and services that are putting established R&D and traditional innovation management to the test.

Against this backdrop, the BMW Group is set to develop its technological expertise over the coming years and decades to enable it to enhance interactions between individuals, vehicles and services, and drive progress in sustainable mobility. The approach we are taking comprises six strategic strands: brands and design, products, technologies, customer experience and services, digitalization, and profitability. At first sight, these solutions seem simple, no more than a list of familiar terms. But an automobile is one of the most complex products in mass production. A single vehicle requires more than 10,000 parts and components to be invented, designed, produced, and assembled to create a final product that befits the brand in every respect. All this is done in close cooperation both within the broad matrix organization that is the BMW Group and beyond it, with the thousands of suppliers who are our partners worldwide. For this to work, a functional networking environment and capability are crucial. Our approach to networking infrastructures is reflected in the architecture of our Research and Innovation Center in Munich, called the FIZ. Built in the 1980s, the FIZ has a honeycomb layout with short distances between engineers, designers, and production experts. This supports faster, more intensive communications between the different departments.

To this day, the FIZ continues to serve as a model for our stringently focused, holistic approach to R&D—but at our company, we also understand that disruptive trends in the wider world require action as well. For this reason, we operate a network of R&D scouting locations around the world, in Mountain View, Woodcliff Lake, Beijing, Shanghai, Tokyo, and elsewhere. And, for this reason as well, we like working with universities, all over the world.

A particular characteristic of our R&D work is that it is based on our belief that research and development happens not only in our R&D departments but also across many other disciplines and divisions of the company. Our marketing team, for example, requires an in-depth understanding of our customers, which in turn requires a detailed knowledge of social media—we will point that out in one of our project descriptions later. This knowledge must be based not only on current phenomena but also on trends that will shape the future and that form the basis for the BMW Group's own work in the research and development of new digital channels, applications, and interfaces. Another example from a completely different field is the use of simulations in business management. Simulations are widely used to solve complex, real-world problems by virtual means but have not yet been used to develop business models. In the 1990s, we used engineering simulations as the basis for its model initiative. Today, in the digital age, business simulations are enabling smarter, faster business decisions—something we are working on intensively.

Overall, demand at the BMW Group for a broader based approach to R&D that encompasses every discipline has grown over the last few years, especially since the launch of Strategy Number ONE in 2007. At that time, we faced the challenge of evolving from an automobile manufacturer to the leading provider of premium mobility products and services. This transition resulted in the first ever premium electric vehicles: the BMW i3 and i8. It also gave rise to our initial concepts for mobility services, which now form a portfolio that includes the car-sharing program "DriveNow" and "ParkNow," an app that helps urban drivers to find parking spaces in crowded cities. Both of these services come in response to societal changes, urbanization, and new customer requirements around the world. Since 2016, the shift that was commenced under Strategy Number ONE has been continued under Strategy NUMBER ONE > NEXT. Today, mobility is about more than merely vehicles: we now operate in the services market—an entirely different business from that of manufactured products and the kind of seismic shift that requires a well-prepared R&D division.

Tackling the day-to-day challenges of innovation takes a variety of perspectives and skills—and it is a well-known fact that we have them. But which role do universities play in this context? Well, collaborations with universities allow it to learn from others continuously, and to keep an open mind as it forges new pathways into the future. So when it comes to generating innovations over the longer term, solid university contacts are highly constructive.

University collaborations have a long tradition at BMW Group and are highly diverse, ranging from joint research and collaboration projects to research contracts and cooperation projects that foster the skills of younger people. Our company has hundreds of university contacts that have grown from former projects, personal contacts, and partnerships in specific areas. University—industry collaborations have frequently been described as informal in nature and decentralized in structure. Increasingly, however, companies are adopting a more strategic approach to them (see Perkmann et al., 2011: How should firms evaluate success in university—industry alliances, p. 203). We have done so with considerable success, and we now operate a three-tier system that identifies three types of university—industry cooperation projects.

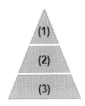

BMW Group university cooperations are subject to a three-level hierarchy:

(1) Strategic partnerships

(2) Cooperations based on individual strategic goals

(3) Individual contacts.

At the top of the hierarchy are our strategic partnerships, which have a special status within BMW Group. Why did we decide to put strategic university partnerships at the top of its cooperation hierarchy? When Strategy Number ONE was implemented in 2007, it became clear that a top-down focus on new, less well-known topics was needed. A review of university contacts at the time concluded that most R&D cooperation projects were based on long-standing contacts in Germany. A solid network of university contacts is constructive, of course, but did not appear to be the best approach to advance the BMW Group's transition from an automobile manufacturer to the leading provider of premium mobility products and services. We recognized that the simple fact of leaving the comfort zone of well-known ideas and university partners might be a value in and of itself. Further on, to give a simple example out of strategy: if you identify next urban mobility in megacities as one central business field in the future, you have to reach out for university partners in megacities—which are not necessarily in Germany, but instead in Singapore or China, for example. To better prepare for the future, we had to identify additional strategic partners of international renown with an established reputation in relevant fields of research and, with respect to the story of megacities as an example, in strategically relevant parts of the world.

How do we organize these partnerships and make them run? Each of the strategic partnerships is jointly coordinated by a dedicated mentor at our

Munich headquarter and a contact based locally near the university. The willingness and interest to shape a successful cooperation, passion for innovation, and a good internal and external network are the success factors for mentors and local contacts. Together, they provide transparency over the skills and opportunities offered by the university and act as the main point of contact to the BMW Group. Strategic partners are closely involved with the BMW Group management members in our University Strategy Circle, a committee of several heads of specialist divisions (e.g., head of production, R&D, and marketing innovation) from across the relevant areas of the company. The University Strategy Circle monitors ongoing cooperation projects, especially with strategic partners, and is focusing on R&D projects but also future talent management activities and education policy. The circle meets two times a year to discuss and determine which future research topics will form part of the joint R&D projects. The process is controlled and coordinated by an independent function that evaluates and balances the different objectives. A typical meeting meant for selecting future research topics is organized like an elevator pitch as we know it from innovation management or accelerator ecosystems. The coordinator of the research cluster—we will explain in the next chapter, what this is—gives a short presentation on his ideas, connects them with the company's overall strategy, and argues why this project should be done with his preferred strategic university partner. Not an easy job as the audience is completely mixed in roles, mind-set, background, and responsibilities, and the coordinator has to deal with lots of questions out of his "home" department with its specific and well-known mentality and rules. On the one hand, this has been practiced within automotive companies over years, as the car has always been one of the most complex mass production products of the world and has always required alignment across different functions. But on the other hand, this requires the openness for interorganizational learning, as we talk about visionary projects for the future, beyond the product named "car" as we know it today.

To reflect the importance of this type of specific partnership and facilitate cooperation projects for both sides, the BMW Group and its strategic university partners negotiate a framework contract or master agreement. Then, a special purchasing system ensures that projects are launched swiftly and directly; rather than the usual bidding process with at least three possible suppliers, the key factor underlying innovation partnerships is compatibility and shared interests. Where projects fulfill the exact criteria outlined in Section 1.2, additional financing may also be provided.

In conclusion, it is understood that the best university partner must be selected on a case-by-case basis, depending on its suitability for the project, program, or initiative in question. This brings us back to our original question of which topics are best handled in university partnerships, or, in other words, when and on what topics do we cooperate with universities rather than other partners, such as engineering service providers or suppliers?

1.2   THE IMPORTANCE OF DEFINING RESEARCH CLUSTERS AND IDENTIFYING SUBJECT AREAS

Relevance is key in business, and based on this simple fact, one can say that every topic handled in cooperation with a strategic partner university has to show its clear connection with strategically relevant questions and research fields. Considering when and why universities are the preferred option for handling certain topics, let us begin by outlining briefly the BMW Group's system of research clusters as the starting points for detailed research topics.

As an organization, the BMW Group is structured as a series of product or market-related functions and departments that approach a single topic from a variety of angles. Mobility, for instance, is the focus of various departments whose approaches differ according to their remit. In the interests of university partnerships, however, topics such as these must be viewed holistically, with clearly defined project content and targets, and results being shared. Our functional setup was clearly not compatible with such a view, and an alternative system was therefore needed that would allow us to combine the different disciplines successfully into our projects and communications with universities. For this reason, we developed what we call "research clusters."

These clusters are aligned with the CEO's corporate strategy department to ensure their relevance and reviewed annually in the light of new challenges and influences. In other words, there is a direct pathway from corporate strategy and its annual "strategy radar screen" of trends and challenges worldwide to the management of topics within the strategic university partnerships. The relatively broadly characterized research clusters allow to look left and right of one's well-defined role within the highly segmented company, and on the same time they are well linked with mid- and long-term strategic targets of the company. The clusters are

- **Society, market, and customer:** These three points drive and inspire our everyday business. Projects in this cluster focus on gaining insights into our markets and customers so that we can optimize our business by enhancing our interfaces to the customer. The issues explored here include the norms and conventions of human interaction, human needs in an increasingly complex society, and the potential effects of changing social values on the automotive industry and our products and services.
- **Dynamic powertrain:** Projects in this research cluster focus on flexible architectures for different drive concepts (including conventional engine power, battery packs or hydrogen). They investigate regulatory standards and customers' needs.
- **Automated driving:** Research in this area concentrates on new technologies and concepts that will minimize accident rates and enhance driving safety. Efforts in this area aim to facilitate driving by providing situation-dependent support.

- **Connected vehicle:** This explores the importance of connecting driver, car, and surroundings to enhance vehicle systems on the basis of intelligent driver assistance and digital services.
- **Smart production and logistics:** This research cluster consists of projects dealing with new trends in manufacturing and future challenges along the purchasing, supply, and value chain. It also investigates how energy efficiency and storage in plants can be adapted to make energy cleaner, more economical, and safer to use.
- **Mobility solutions:** This research cluster explores every aspect of mobility, from personal transport to multimodal solutions.
- **Business (r)evolution:** Work in this area aims to identify and develop growth opportunities for the BMW Group by exploring new markets, business opportunities, and target groups for mobility products and services.

One of the greatest challenges facing our company is the "silo mentality" found within so many companies. However, by structuring research clusters as outlined above, company-internal barriers can be overcome, making research and development relevant for numerous departments, rather than merely for R&D.

A key factor in the success of the various research clusters is the people carrying out the work. Their tasks and skills are clearly coordinated by highly reputable and experienced managers who not only set the strategic focus of the cluster but also collate the various research interests and topics of the divisions and find the partners they require. Their task can be challenging, as coordinators of research clusters are not the supervisors of those who contribute their research interests and topics.

The role of a coordinator is an additional role besides their daily business. Ideally, they are responsible for concept or strategy issues related to the particular research cluster. For sure, it is challenging dealing with such a wide scope of topics. Although they are not the specialists for the research topics they have to understand the content and target of the project ideas and evaluate them in relation to our business respectively our strategy before presenting in the University Strategy Circle.

Research clusters and strategic university partners are the two basics that have been defined when we started our strategic university cooperations. As soon as we had defined the research clusters, we were looking for the best universities to cooperate in those clusters. The two basics are creating the framework we are working in this organization. The coordinators exchange experiences and ideas in their cluster in regular networking meetings, synergies can be identified easier. In addition, work is carried out in innovative groups that allow new ideas to grow and allow the existence of errors. Since cooperation across departments and divisions and a healthy attitude to error are crucial to innovation, these university projects could inspire a new approach toward the organization of learning across the company more widely. This assumption is confirmed by research on university–industry cooperation projects suggesting that alliances of this kind may indeed result in concrete, directly commercially relevant deliverables, but that their more important role is "in stimulating interorganizational learning" (R.M. Cyert and P.S. Goodmann, in: Perkmann et al., 2011: How should firms evaluate success in university–industry alliances, p. 206).

Selected projects conducted with one of the BMW Group's strategic university partners are eligible for special cofunding from a budget that is centrally controlled by the University Strategy Circle. In order to secure funding for the coming year, research clusters must provide annual updates on their cofinanced projects and fulfill certain criteria. These include

1. Demonstrating significant potential for saving costs and enhancing quality, technology, flexibility, etc.
2. A degree of openness around the nature and usefulness of results.
3. The contribution to our company's strategy.
4. Fulfillment of at least Technology Readiness Level 4, as shown in the following chart (see Readiness Level).

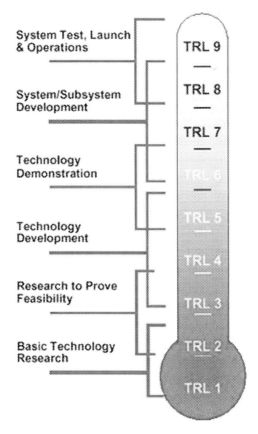

The above chart was originally developed by NASA in the 1980s and is still used today in various industries and in the European research program Horizon 2020. The BMW Group has been using it to structure its production innovation projects and research department for several years, and it is now the standard for our projects with strategic university partners as well.

So, having outlined our system of research clusters, central budgets, and applicable criteria, let us return to the central question posed above: when and on what questions do we cooperate with universities rather than other partners, such as engineering service providers or suppliers?

It has often been said that university collaborations result in an outcome-impact gap: "Promising outcomes of university projects often fail to translate into tangible impacts for the companies involved" (Pertuzé et al., 2010: Best practices for industry–university collaboration, p. 83). From a practical, business point of view, this is indeed true. Successful expectation management is therefore crucial when setting up industry–university cooperation projects. We have found that topics suitable for university cooperation projects—and for strategic university partners in particular, as opposed to "extended workbench" projects (as defined by Perkmann and Salter, 2012: How to create productive partnerships with universities, p. 80, among others)—can be characterized as follows: on the one hand, they should provide sufficient space to define a research hypothesis with unexpected results, on the other, their business relevance should be such that clear targets can be set. And, last but not least, there must be a clear idea of how to benefit from the results of the research project: how mature will outcomes need to be? Which department—or engineering service provider—will continue to work on findings ready for series development?

1.3   THREE EXAMPLES ON HOW WE DEFINED TOPICS FOR STRATEGIC COLLABORATIONS

The first example is focusing on the shift in strategy toward the target of becoming the leading provider of premium mobility products and services, the rising challenges out of disruptive technologies and digitalization, and the increasing significance of megacities as the location for future mobility. With all these facts, it has become clear that there is a significant need for new cross-functional innovation—what a usual supplier is not able to cover. The University Strategy Circle discussed and confirmed the need for a new research place to be. They quickly came to the conclusion that these broad questions and trends can neither be outsourced to any supplier, engineering provider, or something like that nor be concentrated on an own BMW Group R&D center elsewhere in the world. They agreed that Singapore can be seen as the perfect place to do research on all this: it is limited in space, can be seen as a laboratory for future mobility, is cutting edge in managing and monitoring traffic, and has continuously introduced high regulatory standards for passenger cars. And they agreed that we would need independent and strong local partners to understand what we are looking for.

Singapore has famous universities, among them the **Nanyang Technological University (NTU)**. To cover all our broad interests and address our various questions across different departments, we launched a joint research facility called the Future Mobility Research Lab, together with the NTU, in 2013. This investigates and works on key topics around future transportation and contributes to several of the research clusters outlined above: a focus on advanced battery materials supports work in the field of "dynamic powertrain," and advances in the human−machine interface contribute to both "automated driving" and "mobility solutions." The lab also explores how research findings can help meet the needs of the Asian market. Being based in a densely populated, highly urbanized megacity with a sophisticated, tech-savvy population, NTU is in the ideal environment for a study of this kind.

At launch, the Future Mobility Research Lab was staffed by dedicated professors, researchers, PhD and bachelors' thesis students, and BMW Group associates, one of whom was a guest associate professor overseeing the R&D efforts in the lab. To support collaborations and help NTU students to gain a clearer understanding of the difference between academia and industry, they are invited to spend up to 6 months on an internship in manufacturing in Munich. In addition, students on a BMW Group talent program with one of NTU's partner universities can attend NTU as academic exchange students and participate in projects in the Future Mobility Research Lab. This exchange adds an important dimension to the lab's activities and helps to attract future students for the lab and potential employees for our company.

Under the ambit of advanced battery materials and human−machine interfaces, the cooperation project between the BMW Group and NTU aims to meet key transport needs by developing the most sustainable solutions possible. Efforts concentrate on electric vehicles, where the ecocredentials, safety, and efficiency are of paramount importance. In addition, the project investigates mobility solutions for megacities with particular regard to consumer behavior in relation to multimodal transportation and car sharing. One aspect of this is the development of advanced routing algorithms that make daily commuting more convenient. After 2 years of intensive research, the Future Mobility Research Lab has already made some significant findings, and all of them have found their way into the headquarter's central functions and projects:

- **Advanced battery:** Experiments are currently being carried out on new battery materials, such as high-voltage cathodes and anodes (the positive and negative poles of a battery). These have the potential to double the energy density of battery packs and consequently to extend vehicle range and speed up charging times.

- **Human—machine interface:** Current sensor technologies are able to tell if the driver is sleep or alert. They can also detect whether a vehicle is on course for a collision with another road user based on speed and direction data. However, at present, these two sensor systems are not linked, so the driver's state has no effect on the safety functions that are operating. For this reason, a driver enhancement system is now under development that will adapt to the driver's condition and increase or decrease the range of assistance technologies being deployed for support. It is based on parameters such as the driver's state of alertness, attentiveness to events on the road, and traffic density around the vehicle.
- **Mobility solutions**: A newly developed mobile application offers more accurate estimated arrival times by better predicting traffic conditions. It is based on an intelligent routing system that takes into account an individual's driving style and the current traffic situation based on real-time traffic information. It also has a search function that analyses the parking situation in the vicinity of the destination.

The technology readiness level of all these projects was at about 4—this means, the projects have all been around technology development. Based on this good first experiences, BMW Group and NTU launched a new electromobility research program within the lab in 2016. This program involved the all-electric BMW i3 and plug-in hybrid BMW i8 sports car, which runs on electricity and petrol—and again, we have chosen Singapore and the NTU as the best partner for that because of its character as a laboratory for future mobility and the chance to have surrounding conditions within Singapore that support these innovations.

Global developments such as climate change, dwindling supplies of natural resources, and ever increasing urbanization are bringing change not only to the world but also to the realms of personal mobility. As calls for a new balance between the needs of the planet and the desires of individuals increase, demand for more sustainable mobility is growing, and the BMW Group is responding through BMW i, EfficientDynamics, and ConnectedDrive. For this reason, a further research program has been launched, supported by combined funding from the BMW Group and Nanyang Technical University worth S$1.3 million in addition to the initial S$5.5 million originally provided for the Future Mobility Research Lab in 2013. New research will focus on two new areas within the defined research clusters: electromobility in Asia and smart materials. Work on the Lab's original three research topics will continue.

The scientists at the lab will use the two BMW i vehicles to conduct real-world research on driver behavior and collect detailed data on vehicle performance. The cars will also be used for on-road trials of new technologies, such as a mobile application that can accurately predict traffic and end-to-end traveling times.

Previous projects and the additional research extended to cover electro-mobility in Asia and smart materials, even more invaluable discoveries are expected. Findings will be shared with Singapore's academia and lead to a broader technical understanding of modern-day all-electric and plug-in hybrid vehicles. By ascertaining how drivers interact with BMW i vehicles out on the road and developing an improved understanding of their behavior, research into electromobility in Asia will provide the basis for future enhancements to electric and hybrid technologies.

By conducting this research in a densely populated, urban city state like Singapore, the team at in the lab will gain insights into how electric vehicles can be made more relevant for global megacities. Other issues under investigation include how consumers will be affected by emerging technologies such as fast and wireless charging and smart assistant driving technologies. In addition, the current proliferation of touchscreen interfaces in cars is giving rise to a growing need for a better understanding of how their surfaces might be made more tactile. Research into various kinds of shape-memory materials and dielectric polymers are already allowing scientists to develop technologies that will allow buttons to appear on interactive surfaces and touchscreens when required.

What we have learned so far at this place and project: The research topics have definitely been the right ones, strongly linked with strategic targets of the company and still cutting edge for BMW Group. And Singapore has been the best place for doing research with universities on these topics! But beware: We have over 10,000 km to fly from Munich to Singapore, and we have different cultures of working together and dealing with projects. An eco-system of disruptive technologies and trends requires fast and transparent communication pathways. So, it still has been a challenge for us to steer the partnership in the one direction and to hear their ideas (in the other direction).

The **second** example of a BMW Group university partnership project involves the **MIT Sloan School of Management** and addresses the "society, market, and customer" research cluster.

The MIT Sloan School is home to numerous experts from across the MIT community, who together form a single, powerful network addressing the challenges we face. They help organizations to push the boundaries of current management knowledge and adopt better business practices which a supplier, e.g., marketing agency is not able to do. This is why the coordinator of the research cluster "society, market, and customer" addressed them with their questions and hypothesis, not exactly knowing what they could find out together. This has been the background for our project with the MIT: With the rise of social media, conversations about companies are started not by the organizations themselves but by individual consumers, who often do not appreciate interventions from the corporation concerned. This development is forcing change upon marketing specialists, even in companies that are used to being talked about.

The BMW Group has some 14 million Facebook followers, who make more than quarter of a million posts a day. A BMW-related tweet is sent around the world every 7 seconds, and more than 2 million images of our vehicles have been posted on Instagram. These figures are impressive and can easily give a company into a false sense of security that what they are doing is right. However, clicks and figures are not what social media is about. Far more, the burning question for any corporation must surely be: What are we worth, and how do clicks and figures impact people's behavior and attitude toward our brand(s)? Another point to consider, of course, is whether or not these communications help to sell a company's products. In the automotive world, this question is certainly relevant, as car buyers tend to carry out extensive research before making their purchase.

The challenge for a company like the BMW Group lies in refraining from influencing conversations and posts. When consumers talk about what they like or dislike in a product, their exchanges are usually very open and tend to happen in places other than corporate websites or fan pages. Such conversations can have little connection with the company's official message, and often even contradict it, which causes many companies attempt to monitor them and become involved. However, this is a process fraught with danger, especially for those who are too intrusive; rather than being empty "marketing promises," communications by consumers are real. For this reason, the BMW Group aims to ensure that its communications are genuine.

When it comes to communicating with customers, new technologies such as microvideo and mobile sharing are opening entirely new opportunities. In a quest to learn more about our customers, our marketing innovation group began discussions with MIT to launch an experiment in consumer-to-consumer marketing. The goal was to ascertain the effects of the BMW Group's own attempts to shape conversations in mobile social networking. For several years, we have been producing a video series called The Hire, in which famous directors create short films starring the likes of Mickey Rourke and Clive Owen, who perform feats of derring-do in BMW cars. We are now in the process of finding out whether its fans would make such high-caliber movies about the cars—using their smartphones.

Working in conjunction with the MIT, the team has been exploring the use of Hollywood-caliber storyboards around ordinary events, such as buying an ice cream, going hiking for the day or reading a book. The aims of the project are threefold: first, to obtain data about the brand impact of consumer-to-consumer marketing; second, to test microvideo as an emergent technology; third, to learn about how consumers share on their smartphones as opposed to on social media. On this basis, MIT is developing a special driving-themed storyboard with a template video featuring BMW cars that will be made available to 160 students at the MIT Sloan School of Management so they can create their own similar films. If the experiment is successful, it will be extended to a sample of 1500 non-BMW owners with tablets or smartphones and an interest in luxury vehicles.

Social media has extended the reach of businesses by far, which may or may not be positive. As consumers view and share their experiences on social media, our first collaboration explored the persuasive power of their stories. Research suggested that stories "cocreated" by the brand and the consumer are more persuasive than those created separately. This raises the questions of which aspects of cocreated stories are most effective and whether these would differ depending on the source of the story.

In summary, it can be said that for BMW Group, marketing mobile social networking is an emergent platform on which it already enjoys a significant presence but in which it would also like to become involved. The storyboard experiment is allowing new ideas to be tested and responses to be gauged, ultimately with a view to increasing sales—or, failing that, as a method of assessing the suitability of social media networking as a means of approaching and communicating with customers and fans.

The interesting question at this stage is: Would we have been succeeded to a similar extent if we had decided to work with a professional supplier out of the consumer and market research sector? We would clearly deny this. In the field of "society, market, and customer," we are used to cooperate with agencies and suppliers but based on traditional methods from an industry perspective. The pathway of discussing and shaping the experiment design during this MIT cooperation has been completely different from a supplier engagement and gave different new impulses for our communication via social media.

The **third** example of a university partnership project involves **MIT's CSAIL (Computer Science and Artificial Intelligence Laboratory)** and focuses on the field of "smart production"—an area in which the BMW Group is advanced. With the future of manufacturing in mind, the partnership project represented a step toward a new type of collaboration.

When our robotics innovation team applied for this project in the University Strategy Circle, the goal was clear but the means of attaining it was not. This productive uncertainty was convincing the members of the circle. We wanted to know more about human–robot interaction to enable them to deal with each other more naturally in the future. Rather than approaching robots from the "either ... or" perspective—i.e., the idea that robots will replace workers, which dominates so much of the discourse today—we wanted to explore the advantages of each. We wanted to ascertain what robots do best and for which tasks employees are the better option. Some of our employees have worked for BMW Group all their lives and consequently have considerable knowledge and experience of building cars. The question, therefore, was how their expertise might be supported effectively by robots to allow them to produce their best cars ever. In an attempt to set up the project, the team first explored all the different sections of MIT before finally choosing to CSAIL, whose research matched our needs. CSAIL focuses on integrating robots into teams of people to carry out physically demanding, safety-critical tasks—as does much of our own research in manufacturing and assembly. Although it was apparent from our first meeting that CSAIL knows little about automotive manufacturing and more about aerospace, the enthusiasm of the team and the overlap between the fields of automotive and aerospace were sufficient to merit the launch of a project. More than that, we even saw it as an advantage that the team members of CSAIL haven't been deeply involved in automotive manufacturing and can therefore consider the task from a completely different perspective without the prejudice we have in our minds. From the first meeting onward, a joint research project was crafted that would advance our shared vision for human–robot collaboration in manufacturing.

Final automotive assembly requires employees to perform a wide variety of tasks with a range of tools and materials. As a result, time is wasted as workers move between the assembly line, tool carts, and stocks of materials. Since walking between positions offers no value-add, it was proposed that mobile robotic assistants be deployed to transport tools and materials back and forth in final assembly in order to enhance efficiency.

Project work began with a visit by MIT to our plant in Munich. Here the team explored the assembly line environment and learned more about some of the specific challenges they faced: an assembly robot of the kind being considered would have to be able to navigate both on and off the production line. In final assembly, much of the floor of the hall is fixed, allowing robots to move easily across it. On the line itself, however, certain sections of the floor move, requiring robots to be able to straddle, cross, or travel with them. Moreover, with space at a premium, layer upon layer of complexity added to the challenges around the robot's control capabilities.

Moving around in the assembly area also means robots must be capable of sharing space with employees. At present, they remain housed in cages and are perceived as a danger. Removing them from their cages and allowing to travel across the factory floor requires interactions to be reliably safe, appropriate, convenient, and predictable. For human–robot interaction to succeed, people must feel safe and trust the technology that is moving among them.

After their initial meetings, the research teams began to hold biweekly conference calls to share their findings and coordinate activities. While the BMW Group team focused on hardware design, MIT was to develop control algorithms. The first milestone was to deploy a prototype robotic assistant in Munich for testing over the summer. Specifically, MIT was tasked to make this robot exercise on the CSAIL treadmill. Once the algorithms had been transferred from simulation to hardware, preparations were complete for a technology transfer. The MIT team then visited our plant in Munich to see how the product of the collaborations works in the context of a real assembly line.

Before robotic assistants finally become a widespread reality, the MIT and the BMW Group still have some way to go. However, there is already a clear sense of the road ahead and a follow-up in the real plant environment makes sure that the results of the project will find their implementation.

A very important learning for our strategic university cooperations! Working in close collaboration on the factory floor is exciting, and one of the most successful aspects of this project so far has been the intensity of technical collaborations. MIT and the BMW Group share equivalent hardware, software, and infrastructure, and each have their own lab space to accommodate their counterparts when face-to-face meetings are necessary.

Cooperation projects of this kind are fundamentally about openness, courage, trust, and about a shared vision goal. Both the MIT and the BMW Group agree that industry–university cooperation projects are mutually inspiring and introduce new environments and issues. Projects are developing by themselves as they forge ahead.

All of our strategic university cooperation projects have one thing in common: they provide sufficient space to define a research hypothesis and allow for unexpected results. They are also sufficiently business-relevant to allow specific targets to be set. In addition, it is interesting to note that projects and topics are not always instigated by the BMW Group. Far more, university partners play an important role in open innovation processes, and not every undertaking stems from the company's ideas. Universities are a valuable catalyst for the automotive industry and help us to think "outside the box" and generate new innovations.

1.4   CONCLUSION AND RECOMMENDATIONS

With regard to the success factors explained in this article—defining topics for strategic university collaboration—our key findings and recommendations are as follows:

1. Ensure a project offers sufficient space to define a research hypothesis and allow for unexpected results. Strategic university partners are part of the academic system, which differs markedly from the industrial system, and it is the discrepancies between them that offer significant potential for innovation. For the BMW Group and its projects with strategic university partners, these different structures have not always been easy to work in, but they allow new research approaches and unexpected results, as exemplified by the MIT marketing project described above.

2. Retain a strong focus on the strategic and business relevance of the project for the company. Topics for collaborations should not be generated out of the need to adhere to and support the company's strategic pathways. According to a study carried out by MIT in 2010, 60% of a sample of over 100 projects carried out in 25 multinational companies resulted in outcomes that were not adopted for products or processes and had no influence on company decisions (Pertuzé et al., 2010: Best practices for industry–university collaboration, p. 84). This demonstrates clearly the importance of linking university partnerships closely to the corporate strategy.

3. Ensure follow-up—because without it, any innovation born out of a university project is useless. For this reason, depending on how mature the result is, follow-up activities should be determined beforehand to be carried out an implementing entity—in our case the BMW Group itself or a supplier. In addition, companies should have a well-defined in-house organization for managing university collaborations, with strong, high-level mentors at the helm, as is the case with the BMW Group's University Strategy Circle.

4. Use strategic collaboration projects to stimulate interorganizational learning. The organization of research clusters and strategic university cooperation projects at the BMW Group allows knowledge to be shared conveniently between different topics. It also allows synergies and fosters innovative group work in a culture that is accepting of errors and allows ideas to develop more freely. Moreover, because some ideas are highly specialized—and sometimes even inconvenient for the company to implement—special processes may be required, such as the purchasing process outlined above.

5. Secure commitment. Research projects live from the commitment of the people who work in them. A significant success factor for strategic collaborations is to ensure that their research is closely linked to recruiting and talent management, as described in the NTU example above.

REFERENCES

Perkmann, M., Salter, A., 2012. How to create productive partnerships with universities. MIT Sloan Manage. Rev. 53 (4), 79—88.

Perkmann, M., Neely, A., Walsh, K., 2011. How should firms evaluate success in university—industry alliances? A performance measurement system. R&D Manage. 41 (2), 202—216.

Pertuzé, J.A., Calder, E.S., Greitzer, E.M., Lucas, W.A., 2010. Best practices for industry—university collaboration. MIT Sloan Manage. Rev. 51 (4), 83—90.

Readiness Level. See ⟨https://de.wikipedia.org/wiki/Technology_Readiness_Level⟩ (accessed 07.05.18).

Chapter 2

DuPont's Global Collaboratory: Selecting University Partners Globally and How Does Industry Track University Relations for Success

Karsten Keller[1] and Rajiv Dhawan[2]

[1]Nitto Denko Avecia Inc., Milford, MA, United States, [2]Samsung Semiconductor Inc., Milpitas, CA, United States

---

Box: DuPont Facts and Figures (Fiscal Year 2016)

Company Name:	DuPont
Headquarters in:	Wilmington, DE, USA
Annual Revenue:	US$24.6 billion
Number of employees:	46,000
R&D budget:	US$1.6 billion
Average number of University R&D collaborations p.a.:	>400
Industry branches:	Agriculture, Performance Materials, Industrial Biosciences, Nutrition & Health, Protection Solutions, Electronics & Communications Industry
Product examples:	Pioneer® seed products, crop protections for insect, weed, and disease control solutions, plastics, polymers, resins, biomaterials, food enzymes, biofuels, food ingredients, Corian® solid surfaces, Kevlar®, Nomex®, Tyvek®, electronics, printing and package printing, solar and photovoltaic materials

---

Strategic Industry-University Partnerships. DOI: https://doi.org/10.1016/B978-0-12-810989-2.00002-3
19

2.1 INTRODUCTION DUPONT

Founded in 1802 on the banks of the Brandywine River in Delaware, DuPont has grown in size, product lines, and geographies. DuPont has transformed over two centuries to remain one of the most successful and sustained industrial enterprises in the world. Today, it aspires to be the world's most dynamic science company—pioneering the development and application of science and technology to meet global demands for food, energy, and protection—demands that continue to be driven by population growth. The global population reached 7 billion in October, 2011 and it is estimated that the population will grow to 9 billion by 2050. It is becoming increasingly important to focus research efforts on meeting the needs of this growing population. As a result, DuPont scientists and engineers focus their efforts on inventing and innovating in new ways to feed, protect, and provide sustainable energy and materials to society. Approximately 85% of the R&D budget is directed to these megatrends.

DuPont is a science company dedicated to solving challenging global problems, while creating measurable and meaningful value for its customers, employees, and shareholders. Our dynamic portfolio of products, materials, and services meets the ever-changing market needs of diverse industries in more than 90 countries. As of end 2016, DuPont had around 46,000 employees and generated US$24.6 billion in revenues. DuPont R&D expenditures in fiscal year 2016 were US$1.6 billion (7%). In August 2017 DuPont merged with Dow Chemical to become the largest Chemical Company in the world.

2.1.1 A Global Approach

DuPont believes that by working together, with more people in more places than ever before, it can find new and better ways to solve global challenges and provide for the food, energy, and protection needs of the world's growing population. DuPont leverages the strength of the global R&D engine to address these needs on a local basis.

Over the past 30 years, DuPont has continued to evolve its business footprint so that today more than half of the company's revenues come from outside North America. At the same time, with local demand increasing for products, DuPont has developed relationships within countries through recruitment and training of local talent. It is equally clear that by strengthening its local presence, DuPont better serves the needs of customers in-market. Indeed, more than a decade ago, DuPont developed a strategic plan for R&D that has resulted in placing scientists and engineers on five continents across the globe in mission-specific centers to identify and develop ideas for local markets. The model has now delivered both integrated R&D centers and market-specific innovation centers, both of which are connected electronically to core capabilities around the world.

The first interdisciplinary laboratory established outside of North America was the Meyrin, Switzerland site, which has been successfully serving the entire European market since 1987. DuPont has also opened new integrated sites in Shanghai, China in 2005, in Hyderabad, India in 2008, and in Paulinia, Brazil in 2012.

The Shanghai site has been so successful that it went through its second expansion. Home today to over 300 professionals, including 70 PhDs, the Shanghai center boasts state-of-the-art applications development and customer tailored technical service capabilities with extensive networking throughout the Chinese academic community.

The DuPont Knowledge Center in Hyderabad, India, closely follows this model. Today it houses more than 400 employees focused on developing science solutions for the Indian market and leveraging India's science talent to global programs.

The most recent global R&D center is now growing in Paulina, Brazil. It too, is based on this same model. A key benefit is the ability to tap into creative scientists who understand local cultures/markets, and who are well-networked with thought leaders in regional universities and public labs.

This model becomes even more powerful with the addition of partnerships and collaborations with academia, governments, and other institutions around the world to generate innovations that meet local needs, in what DuPont refers to as "The Global Collaboratory."

Globalization, collaboration, and scientific innovation have therefore been intricately entwined at DuPont and are essential to DuPont's ability to successfully evolve as it enters into its third century as an organization.[a]

2.1.2   University Relations

DuPont collaborates globally with over 400 academic groups every year and spends in excess of US$30 million on these collaborations. For this reason, it is essential, within a corporate function to provide oversight of these collaborations. The University Relations team is a corporate function and as such, focuses efforts on how to bring value to each Business unit in the corporation. It actively engages in external university relationships to amplify the internal science and market capabilities. In order to develop differentiated technology for our customers, a significant effort was focused on the area of "Integrated Science." This term refers to DuPont's goal of finding technology at the nexus of disciplines and markets in which we operate. For this reason, there was a great emphasis on initiating programs whereby multiple business units could derive value through a connection from the UR corporate function. The team

---

a. IP as the new business normal: why every business must focus on IP to secure its future, Douglas Muzyka, Senior Vice President and Chief Science & Technology Officer, DuPont, AIPLA mid-winter conference January 31, 2013.

understands the broader needs of DuPont Science & Technology, as they report into the CTO's office. The number of individuals in this group averaged between three and five over the past many years, though there is a much larger network of individuals around the corporation. The global university relationship team is built through a network of DuPont's business units and functions and it is charged with maximizing the business impact of external collaborations for DuPont. The team leads PhD recruiting and research collaborations with universities worldwide. The DuPont University Relations team also sponsors corporate research programs, like the DuPont Young Professor Program and special research proposal calls. The team, which has a global network, has created tools, policies, processes, and communication materials for enabling and supporting strategic collaborations with universities and provides the infrastructure that facilitates research proposal calls, reviews, awards, and ongoing relationship management. As mentioned previously, DuPont collaborates with hundreds of universities and understanding and managing all of these interactions to capitalize on synergies is a difficult undertaking. For this reason the University Relations team built a global web-based database around university relations activities to increase alignment, and knowledge sharing within DuPont.

2.1.3 DuPont Young Professor: The Oldest University–Industry Program in the US

The DuPont Young Professor Program forms a key element of the University Relations Strategy for the Corporation and facilitates interactions between faculty and corporate researchers. The experience from DuPont has shown that it is essential to have a University Relations team with a budget that can be utilized to catalyze relationships between the corporation and academic partners. Some of the budget for these activities is held at the non-business unit level, as many times businesses shy away from making the longer-term investments that a corporate function can make. The corporate funding is not meant to replace business investment; rather, it can be utilized as a leverage point, whereby businesses can be encouraged to invest in longer-term research/relationships. In many cases, the corporate funding can be from 50% to 100% of the investment made in an academic interaction (50% for a collaboration program or 100% for the DuPont Young Professor Program). It is inarguable that long-term investments are essential for the future health of a company and these investments function as a means of encouraging "good behavior" on the parts of the business research leadership, whose first inclination is to focus on the shorter-term efforts. Besides the moral obligation, that is corporate philanthropy, programs like the DuPont Young Professor Program have tremendous value for a university relations group as a tool for building connections with leaders of tomorrow. The program provides a means by which nontenured faculty members can receive critical funding for opportunities that would otherwise go unfunded. This grant has been used in many cases for high risk/reward programs that could not get government funding, but allowed the professor to set herself/himself on another research trajectory. The DuPont Young Professor competition also serves as a tool to allow researchers to engage the best and brightest in academia and learn about future trends in disciplines key to DuPont's future. This provides an opportunity for the corporation to connect with researchers in our domain and learn about what the top young academics, trained at top institutions, see as future trends. This enables additional connection points that feed into our database that we can target as internal needs develop. The DuPont Young Professor program will celebrate its 100th anniversary in 2018. It has supported over 700 young processors worldwide with funding exceeding US$50 million dollars.

2.2 SELECTING UNIVERSITY PARTNERS GLOBALLY

To select a university partner globally, to a great extent, depends on the company's business goals. While in the following example DuPont is presented, the result might be very different with other companies. The following selection approach can be seen as adaptable and universal to other companies' businesses goals. A company could use the same approach and fill in their own goals. On the other hand, it provides insights for universities as well, elucidating how companies make their own selections on university partners. The first question a company should ask is:

2.2.1 Why Should We as a Company Collaborate With a University in First Place?

Not every company sees the necessity to work with universities. However, to answer this first question, a company might want to first define what business or technical challenges can be solved by collaborating with universities. Business or technical challenges are changing rapidly in companies and therefore the university collaboration needs to be flexible and adaptable. DuPont employs three general criteria when deciding whether to work with a university or not: (1) Business Perspective; (2) Talent; and (3) Technology & Research. In the 215-year history of the DuPont Corporation, Talent and Technology & Research were the dominant driver for collaborating with universities in the beginning of the 20th century. To get the right Talent, the efforts were relatively constant over time, while the importance of Business Perspective is prevailing in the university selection today. Other priorities have shifted in importance, depending upon many different factors. For instance, when DuPont was moving from a black powder company towards the upcoming area of chemistry, significant investments were made to train chemists in academia to fill the pipeline from which DuPont could hire from. When DuPont strengthened its interest in industrial biotechnology, collaborations were increased with academia and acquisitions were also made. Throughout these times, universities have always played a critical role in our research and development strategy.

DuPont has changed their approach in the recent years regarding university relationships to increase their business impact. Over the last decade or so, DuPont sponsored large and long-term research alliances like the DuPont MIT Alliance or the Global Climate and Energy Program with Stanford, which were purely driven by a science approach. The goal was to utilize these programs to source talent, improve perception, and bring insight useful to DuPont researchers to develop new internal programs. The lack of tangible benefits from these investments resulted in moving away from this approach. Furthermore, concurrent to this, internal changes within the corporation diverted greater research & development budgets to the businesses rather than DuPont Central Research & Development (the long-term R&D Center of DuPont). By their very nature, businesses have greater focus on "Development" than to the longer-range "consortia type" program. Today, university selection is driven with business perspective, focusing on increasing business impact for the company in the next 2−5 years.

A more recent trend is for large companies to do less fundamental science internally, than what was done in the past, as the focus is generally on shorter-term business goals. Companies, pressured by shareholders to create more business impact, have thus shifted to sponsoring the critical longer-range work to academic institutions. The reason for this is two-fold. First, shareholders, sometimes unfairly, focus on fundamental research conducted in corporations as an example of corporate excess and a sign of poor research productivity. Second, overhead costs for doing research internally, are significantly greater than sponsoring longer-term projects in an academic setting. If universities are able to transfer more fundamental research into commercializable technology through developed intellectual property or technology spin outs, industry may be willing to increase collaboration budgets in the future.

To improve business impact, DuPont created a clear and concise approach to select university partners for open innovations projects with the purpose of improving understanding and the who, what, why, where, when, and how questions in relation to engagement in universities collaborations. Subsequently there is a second question every company has to ask:

2.2.2   How to Select a University/University Professor?

Overall, DuPont's interest is in collaborating with top professors at key universities around the world. Ultimately, the goal is to work with the professor/group that can most quickly enable the organization to accelerate its goals. The general preference is to have these professors come from a list of our key partner universities. This is done for an array of reasons, including familiarity with research agreements at particular schools/terms, proximity to our R&D facilities, master agreements, etc. The decision will always be to work with the university faculty member that can most quickly allow the completion of the collaboration project, but if two university faculty options are similar, the decision will be made to go where there is past history.

2.2.3   How Do We Measure Success With University Partners?

The following section should help provide a clear guide to finding the right university–company partnerships. It should also help define engagements for success between universities and companies, which can be achieved by three criteria based on DuPont's systematic and data driven approach. The three criteria are Business Perspective, Talent, and Technology & Research with many additional subcategories. The following sections will provide further insight on science dating between universities and companies, but also offers new opportunities to optimize the collaboration with universities in a new Industrial Venture Collaboration (IVC) model.

2.3   CORPORATE UNIVERSITY RELATIONS DATABASE

Measuring success of university relations will very much depend on what criteria the company is using. A university database is an option to measure and track successes with the universities and therefore provides guidance for the selection of universities for future engagements. For a small company with few university collaborations, the database can be executed in a simple excel sheet. In DuPont we built a database on an internal website. The database includes many different types of information, all based on the three criteria. Having a database on an internal webpage offers transparency to all internal stakeholders, business units, and functions.

While there are over 400 different universities that DuPont collaborates with, there are thousands of universities with which DuPont does not engage with. This brings the question, with whom should the company collaborate with, so that the engagement is with the best fitting universities? How does a company discover white spaces in technology and benchmark different universities? DuPont's database cannot be used only by tracking existing university relations, but it allows for discovering new options for collaborations. At DuPont, these white spaces are really defined by the concept of Market Driven Science. The research & development community (technology fellows, leadership, etc.) along with Business Marketing define possible areas that are aligned with DuPont's core competencies, market access, and future goals. The research leads in conjunction with the University Relations teams search for the most credible partners to conduct this work. Decisions to collaborate are made by the businesses based upon the strengths of the university research group and alignment with the programs mission, overall cost of the program, IP conditions, and lastly the possibility of hiring talent. Fig. 2.1 shows the overview of a global database on a website. The university relations information is presented on a map where the university is located. By clicking on the university flag detailed university data are available.

Large companies spend tens of millions of dollars with universities every year. The amount is approximately 1%−2% of the annual R&D budget. Pharmaceutical companies tend to fall on the higher end, while commodity companies are often below the 1% mark of total R&D spending.

Establishing and investing in such a database tool makes sense for larger companies, with many university interactions. Fig. 2.2 provides an insight of typical university data which are directly linked to the website.

2.3.1   Using the Website, Matrix, and Roadmap

The website is a way to track all existing university data relevant to the company. By collecting university activities and data, one can maintain an ever-green process of internal university information. Therefore, the website provides insights to the company on how the university programs are performing and what strategic decisions need to be executed to improve overall impact with university partners. The website with the database provides the framework to manage all the different university data. The three major criteria Business Perspective, Talent, and Technology & Research with many additional subcategories are brought together as a matrix in Fig. 2.3.

The matrix, which encompasses the many ways by which a corporation can work with academia, contains external and internal data with approximately 50 subcategories. All the input of the data are compiled by adding them from various stakeholders and the interactions with the university. In addition, external university data of public sources are used. DuPont developed this matrix to find ways to be more impactful and also to find the right university partners. The three major criteria are influenced by the company, university, a combination of both, and several third party information. Every company can list their own matrix based on the importance of fulfilling their business goals. Here are some simple scenarios for different company approaches. Company A is focusing on Talent at the moment. It selects the most successful matrix points and compares them between the universities. For example, Company A learned over time using their database that "school location," "program size," and "on campus events" define the best success to gain the right Talent. Therefore Company A is making strategic decisions with whom to engage and what other universities would fit in the similar pattern. Company B is focusing on the Technology & Research side. Due to their business model of open resources, intellectual property rights are not an issue. They are selecting based on third party information but also based on

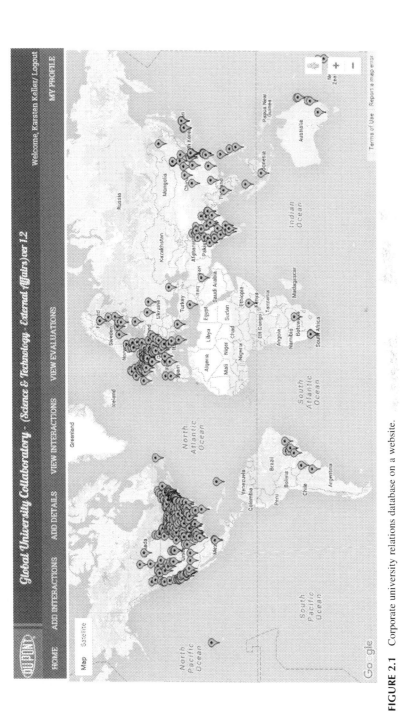

FIGURE 2.1 Corporate university relations database on a website.

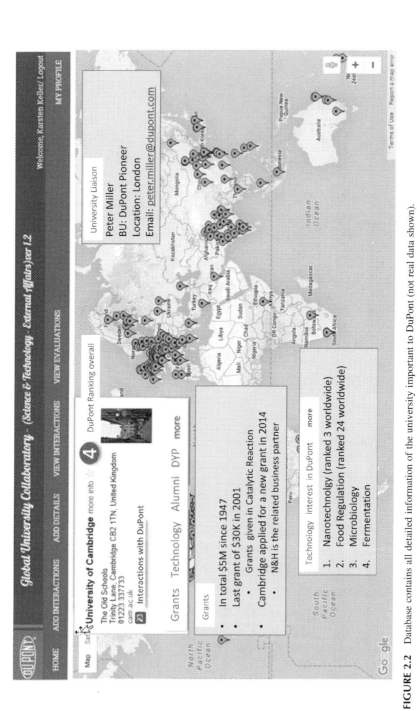

FIGURE 2.2 Database contains all detailed information of the university important to DuPont (not real data shown).

DuPont's Matrix and their criteria

Talent
On Campus Events
Career Fairs
Campus Interviewing
Information Sessions / Networking Events/Symposia
Partnership Programs
Interns/Cooperative Education Programs
Undergraduate Scholarships
Support to Student Organizations / Projects / Events
Continuing education partnerships / Development courses
University Information
Focus of Program(s)/Majors offered
Size of Program(s)
Location of school
Diversity of Graduates
Demonstrated Talent/University Compatibility
Quality of Program(s)
Quality of students
Alumni at DuPont / Success of school's in DuPont / Retention of school's
Hiring talent from multiple colleges/departments within the university
Prior recruiting success
Competitive environment / Interest of school's graduates in DuPont

Business Perspective
Master Research Agreement
IP, Licensing, In-Licensing
Regulatory Affairs /Policy
Strategic interaction planning
Philanthropic Support
Ease of Doing Business
International University Program
Comprehensive University Visits

Technology/Research
Sponsored Research
Named faculty positions
DuPont Young Professors
Research Center
Consortium Membership
Grants
Quality Indicators
Research Output, Quality of Faculty, Quality of Education
Impact and collaboration factor
Science quality
Key Discoveries being made (Strategic Interests)
Technology Indicators
Collaboration Indicators
Grand Challenges
DuPont's technical areas
Business Unit's relevant
Current Collaboration on research or Business Unit's projects
Graduate Level Fellowships/Scholarships/Awards
Symposium/Conference/ Seminar Support
Advisory Boards
Adjunct Professors
Guest Lectures
Joint federal proposal development
Network collaboration
Joint Proposal writing
Third party government funding
Scientific Visits
Scientific Communication
Transactional Services
Contract/ Fee for Services
Utilize Shared Facilities or Equipment
Unsolicited Requests for Collaboration
Request from University
Unsolicited University Requests (Funding, Technology)

FIGURE 2.3 Example for a Matrix to select and judge university relations. Talent − University driven, Technology/Research − Company driven, Business Perspective − University & Company.

their own experience in Technology & Research. They might have high impact through "named faculty position," "third party government funding," and "business relevant topics." By collecting and tracking data Company B is able to make better choices over time. Company C often sees that the research outcome with a university has very little business impact. Through their database and tracking business impact, the most successful combination is "IP rights with master agreement," "consortium memberships," and "comprehensive university visits." As an example of all university relations, DuPont plots the success for different scenarios (technology, hiring, and business) as an outcome of the database in bubble chart diagrams, Fig. 2.4, where the size of the bubble defines the success. The size of the bubble signifies the number score of the DuPont−University interactions. Based on the evaluation needs, it reflects the sum total of the possible categories from the matrix shown in Fig. 2.2 (i.e., number of interactions, number of students hired, amount of joint IP produced, etc.) or a chosen subcategory. The large bubble around the headquarters of DuPont is the University of Delaware.

By plotting different results for all three criteria, a company is able to make deliberate decisions on who and where the right university partners are, what is important, and when and how much engagement will bring

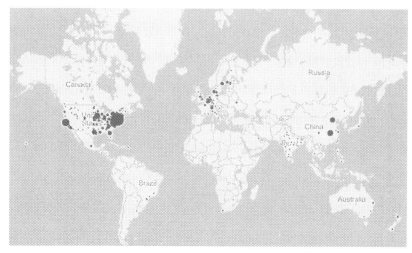

FIGURE 2.4 Bubble chart of success defined by company's matrix.

further success and impact. University partnership changes over time can be seen, too. When decisions need to be made, typically at the Business Unit Level, the University Relations group provides input on which schools we have interacted with in the past and the success we have seen. The numerical value of the past successes can indicate the likelihood of getting preferred IP terms, access to talent, etc., which is the reason a lot of emphasis is placed on it.

In practice, these data provide guidance and options of DuPont collaborators to select successful universities based on real data. Often the business unit comes to the university team and wishes to collaborate with a certain university. The data now provide potential better options to work with other universities. In some cases, the university team rejected to engage with certain universities. If the business unit insisted to collaborate, the university team did not support the engagement.

The simple company scenarios are examples. As DuPont works with many hundreds of universities and is using a more complex matrix, the outcomes are not so predictable. In the following sections of this book the different companies have different approaches and goals to collaborate and select universities, leading to the selection and success with universities being much different.

Senior leadership often asks what the top 10 universities are for the company. This systematic and equalizing view on real university data can lead to unexpected results. Depending on the company's matrix, the top research universities might not necessarily be the most impactful ones. The top-tier universities (i.e., Harvard, Yale, MIT, Princeton, etc.) have a lot of strengths in science and engineering, but companies may find less favorable factors like intellectual property rights and licensing or access to Talent to be less favorable than, say local State universities.

Some might argue that this approach is quite complex and takes a lot of effort. The DuPont database with the website was created in less than 6 months with an intern. The database is like a big Excel sheet and automatically ranks, compares, and selects universities in real time with new data entries. The data entry fields are prepopulated (e.g., hundreds of lines of university information, company matrix, technical areas, and business information related to universities) and university activities can be added in less than a minute. As an output, the database provides a *University Assessment* with a percentage fit to the company. For example, based on all the data, University A has 76% rating to the company, University B has 60% rating, and University C has 49% rating. A full score, 100%, would ultimately be the theoretical maximum for the company, which is the ideal but not practicable to reach. The database also provides a *University Engagement*, based on all university company activities, which describes how well the company is engaging with the university. In the same example, University A has an engagement level of 23%, University B has an engagement of 67%, and University C's engagement is 46%. Again, 100% would be the ideal engagement score a company could have with a university. In this example University A is assessed as a very well-fitting university to the company (76%) but the engagement level is only on 23%. The database provides precise information of what the strategy decision should be to increase the engagement with University A by selecting subcategories from the matrix and acting on them. DuPont learned by using the database that they collaborated with some universities too much while other universities needed an increased engagement.

To create company-specific university rankings and to make smart collaboration selections, the database must have two internal features. The first feature is that the matrix items, Fig. 2.3, need to be weighted based on the company's assessment of importance. DuPont used a simple 1−5 scale to weight the matrix items, for example a career fair is weighted differently than a multimillion dollar grant to a university. The weight feature of the matrix is flexible and can be adjusted based on the company business needs, for example, if the company decides that next year more recruiting is needed, the matrix items relating to Talent would be scored higher to find the best universities in this category. The second internal feature of the database is that all the data needs to be normalized. Normalization in the database is executed with the best university in the class of the matrix item being set to 100%. All other universities receive lower percentages based on the best in class. If University A received the largest grant (US$1 million) from the company, and University B only US$800,000 grant, University A would be normalized to 100%, while University B would have a score of 80%.

The current DuPont database is still a simple and self-made way to execute the selection of a university. In the future more sophisticated big data analytics and Artificial Intelligence (AI) systems will replace these self-made approaches. In the planning stages for database development, there were no commercially available programs to process information and to aid in selecting universities for company goals. The hope is that even more sophisticated solutions will be developed commercially.

Once the university selection is made, the actions and activities the company will take will become apparent. DuPont's approach to this is to create a roadmap in which activities to be accomplished over the next 1−3 years are agreed upon. The roadmap is sponsored and led by the university team. The liaison teams (comprised of alumni and champions of the university) from the company work with the universities to execute the roadmap to improve success based on the company's matrix. Building a great relationship with the university is most important to make progress.

In summary, if a company decides to work with universities it should define the measurable success in their own matrix. The next steps for the company is to decide on the weight factors to all the matrix items. By filling in the university's information the company can now track the data of university assessment and engagement. For a small company this task could be completed in a simple excel sheet, but if the company works with many universities, a web-based database is recommended, as shown. By knowing the university assessment and engagement score the company can set up action items in a roadmap with the university to reach the business goals in collaboration with the university.

In general, to select university partnerships globally, it is often emphasized that it is all about relationships, relationships, and relationships. If the company is not able to properly define the business challenges and how universities are able to help, the relationship alone will not make the collaboration successful. A database with the matrix helps to describe what success could look like with real data. In the literature and in university relations conferences, there is also a common mindset of a partnership continuum[b], starting with a simple first step of university engagement towards a holistic partnership with many different engagement categories as a final goal. The shown matrix approach is much more practical and is not dependent on an end goal of collaboration. In some circumstances, the approach might lead to large alliances with universities to collaborate as it is described in the partnership continuum. In our circumstance at DuPont it led to terminating large alliances and favoring opportunistic and flexible approaches to select the right university partners. This decision was based on real data in our

---

b. Partnership Continuum, Jeff Southerton, Geanie Umberger, Goran Matijasevic, Scott Steele, Wayne Johnson, University-Industry Demonstration Partnership UIDP, 2012.

database, which showed that large alliances did not have the needed business impact to justify renewal.

The database approach with the matrix was presented from a company perspective. What is the take-away for a university? While companies, like DuPont, assess strengths of their partners through understanding of their future directions and core competencies at the universities, the academic institutions should similarly build their own databases to select the right companies that align with their strengths and perceived company needs. Science dating should be a means by which the needs from universities and companies are addressed simultaneously. At DuPont, plans in place called for a deep dive into the areas where we expected the greatest amount of research & development to occur. With an understanding of these areas and paying attention to adjacencies, we would in turn utilize internal knowledge and data science capabilities to select key partner universities/professors. Both parties would subsequently be brought together to discuss possibilities of collaboration.

2.4   SCIENCE DATING: AN OUTLOOK TO THE FUTURE

Matching university capabilities and business needs with that of a corporation can be considered, science dating. Universities should engage with companies (i.e., to find out what their matrix is) and what is important for the company right now. Initially, the company will provide some indication of their internal matrix, but over time with better relationships, the university will understand the company's needs. It is in the company's own interest to share information to find the right university partners. DuPont utilizes two different methods of science dating to find the right university partners. One approach utilizes published data and the second method utilizes the sharing of internal data between company and university. In the future, this could be accomplished utilizing big data analytics or machine learning on/of university/company published information. Third party companies could start offering potential matches between university and companies. As an output, the university and the company would gain a best fitting partner list based on published data. The university would find companies to engage based on potential fit. The same holds true for the companies. Universities that previously had never engaged with the company, could stand out on their best fitting partner list. Elsevier with their SciVal[c] tool has some capabilities to prepare such matches today. By using the right system, all recommendations would be seen in real time.

The more sophisticated method would be to use the internal matrix from the company and university in addition to the externally published data to find the best fit. The internal matrix provides deeper insights on where the

---

c. SciVal from Elsevier.

company and/or the university wants to go in the future. Priorities may be brought forth initially, but both sides could still find the best partner for future collaborations.

Science dating eventually would lead to a "science marriage" where the interests are already aligned and matched. Companies and universities would not waste time to chase down collaborations with very little potential fit.

As mentioned previously, DuPont's open innovation strategy focuses a great deal on collaborating with universities. In addition, there are other ways to accelerate into the open innovation. Government research and national labs, start-ups and ventures are all different entities which could be part of beneficial collaboration partners.

With this in mind, a program that can bring together all of these constituents has been put together: Dynamic Open Innovation Partnering and Engagement Place (DOIPEP). DOIPEP allows governments, universities, companies, start-ups, and ventures to work together to find comprehensive partners. Potentially, it could be useful for organizations to exchange information and to receive partnership portfolios. By using big data analytics or machine learning it would be an evergreen process. While Dynamic Open Innovation Partnering and Engagement Place will happen in the future, new models on how universities and companies should work together are needed today.

Since the landscape of research and open innovation is changing, the question is: Are traditional collaboration models between universities and companies still sufficient? The strategic decision making, based on online tools or website, shows its limits if the company stays in typical university industry relations. There are systematic challenges like IP and exploring common business opportunities, which necessitate a new collaboration model.

The primary goal of a university is to educate. The secondary goal of the university is to do research, and more recently universities have worked on commercialization through licensing and spin-outs. In contrast, the primary goal of a company is to commercialize new products, typically spending ∼5% of the revenue on R&D. As mentioned before, only 1%−2% of this research budget is used for university collaborations. From both, the perspective of the company as well as that of the university, collaborations such as these are only a small part of their overall activities. What actions from both parties, companies and universities, could increase successful and impactful collaborations?

From a company perspective, the industrial business model drives the engagement model with universities. The main goal of industry is to improve profits by the commercializing of products that customers want. When collaborations are initiated, the business impact is important for companies. DuPont has developed a new collaboration model with universities which has enabled a greater business impact. To gain business impact, the new model has to overcome the two major challenges, known as "Valley of Death" and "Most Start-ups Fail," see Fig. 2.4.

The traditional collaboration model is based on a classic research funding cycle: the government funds early-stage research at the university, while industry funds ideas that take the results of basic research and commercialize them into products and services that customers need. Consequently, industry funds precompetitive consortiums to watch what fundamental research is conducted and larger amounts as sponsored research projects in highly applied research, including the research necessary to translate the results into commercial products. The Valley of Death refers to the gap in funding between government-funded, early-stage research and industry-funded commercialization efforts (Fig. 2.5). Under a specific set of circumstances, venture capital, university start-up funds, foundation funding, and/or a limited number of government grants, focused on more applied research, can close this gap and support efforts to de-risk innovative ideas. However, the limited and sometimes sporadic nature of these resources perpetuates the Valley of Death. One approach to closing the funding gap is to spin out a university-developed technology into a start-up company, and for the start-up to use its seed funding to de-risk the technology enough to make it appealing to large corporations. Since the purpose of industry is to make and sell products, industry does not play a large role in funding basic science. However, industry has a vested interest in ensuring that innovative, new technologies successfully traverse the Valley of Death. It is well-known that a high percentage of start-ups fail for the lack of money, market knowledge, and scale-up capabilities. Venture

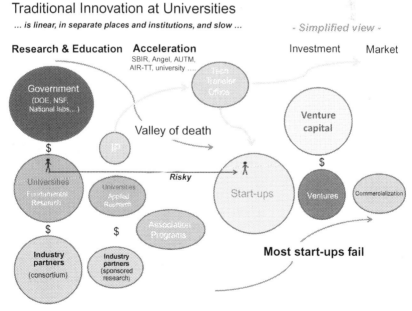

FIGURE 2.5 Linear innovation model starting with university research.

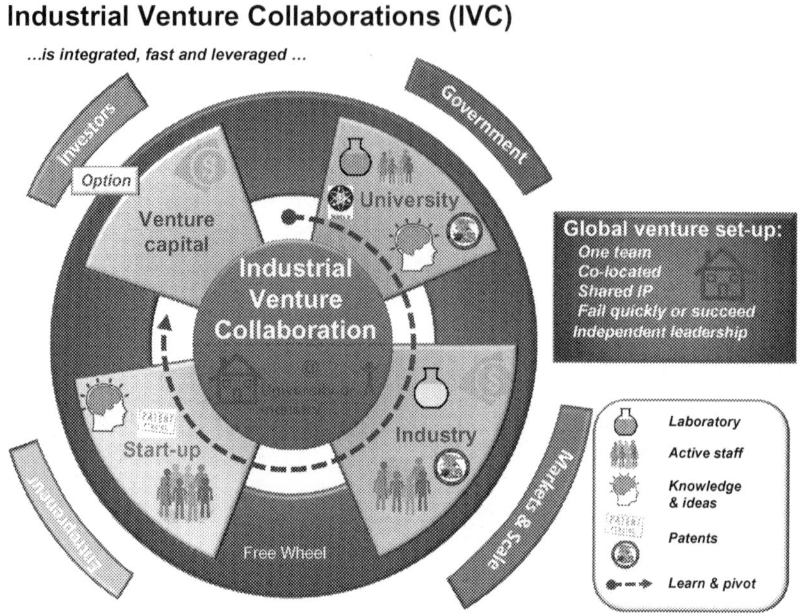

Industrial Venture Collaborations (IVC)

FIGURE 2.6   Integrated innovation model with university and industry.[d]

capital firms provide early investments; however, larger companies have greater insights into their markets, large-scale manufacturing knowledge, and the experience on how to commercialize. For these reasons, a new integrated collaboration model is needed to provide a means of assisting start-ups coming out from universities to succeed and as a way of enabling large companies to gain early access to promising technologies.

The new Collaboration Model is described in Fig. 2.6 and is called Industrial Venture Collaboration (IVC). It is a new way by which industry can collaborate with academia.

The new model presents a much higher business impact approach for both universities and companies. Industrial Venture Collaboration (IVC) is new way to collaborate, which brings several advantages together. This involves a company working closely with its university partners to identify and mentor promising start-ups. The idea is for the company and university to work together early to provide guidance, people, labs, and other resources to drive the technology to faster commercialization. While money is important in an IVC, knowledge and access to large-scale facilities and other resources found within companies are critical for a university-based start-up

---

d. DuPont's New Partnering Models, Karsten Keller, UIDP23 Meeting, Atlanta, October 5, 2016.

company's success. Instead of starting with venture capital, DuPont suggests universities evaluate partnering with large companies that can provide the money, guidance as to the marketplace, and other critical resources. Future possibilities include universities externalizing their research not only through licensing and startups, but also through potential start-ups coming out of these industry—academic collaborations.

2.5   CONCLUSIONS AND RECOMMENDATIONS

Many companies today struggle to quantify a real value of university relations, since it is a long-term investment, often without immediate tangible outcomes. The overarching goal is that companies are looking for a recipe to be more impactful with their university collaborations. Companies also have the challenge that they are not able to track what is actively going on with universities on a global scale. In addition, within companies, different activities (e.g., philanthropy, research collaborations, and recruiting activities) are executed by different functions. All these circumstances make the selection of universities for success very difficult. To overcome these challenges, DuPont is applying a systematic data driven approach that utilizes an internal website on university engagements.

Over the last 5 years DuPont has changed its collaboration mode from focusing on research & technology to a business impact model. It was important to structure and organize the university partners globally, based on their value for the company. To measure this, important activities are tracked now on an internal website. An underlying database is constantly evaluating and comparing the activities among all universities engagements in the company. DuPont measures success by tracking our university partners through a database based on an internal and external data matrix. The developed matrix provides guidance on what is important for the DuPont Company; however, this will differ from company to company. The criteria in the matrix are generally based on activities around talent, research & technology, and business perspective. DuPont prioritized the importance based on ever-changing business needs. The website provides guidance on how to rank and select universities to maximize business impact. By utilizing real data on universities, internal network teams in DuPont are actively driving university relations to the next level of success. It leads to smart science dating, but also offers new opportunities to optimize the collaboration model with universities, as proposed in the new Industrial Venture Collaboration (IVC) model.

The shown data analytics approach to track and rank university relations was built internally in DuPont due to a lack of a commercially available solution. The data analytics approach also helps to explore new research areas quickly and finds new university partners in key fields. To enable greater success from university—industry collaborations, having commercially available systems that connect academia and industry, would be valuable.

Our recommendations for every collaborating company are to:

- Create your own Matrix for what is important for the company.
- Measure the successes of all your university relations based on the chosen Matrix.
- Adjust your engagement with universities based on your assessments.
- Explore new collaborations through a science dating approach.

Chapter 3

Successful Pharmaceutical Innovation: How Novo Nordisk Matches Academic Collaboration Models to Business Objectives

Hans Ulrich Stilz and Søren Bregenholt
Novo Nordisk Research and Development, Bagsværd, Denmark

Novo Nordisk Facts and Figures (Fiscal Year 2016)

Company name:	Novo Nordisk A/S
Headquarters in:	Bagsværd in Denmark, affiliates and offices in 77 countries
Annual (total) revenue:	DKK111.8 billion
Number of employees:	~41,970 full-time employees worldwide of which 17,850 (43%) work in Denmark. Of these, 54% work in production, 29% in R&D, and the remaining 17% in other areas. Around 5900 employees work in R&D
R&D investment:	13% of Novo Nordisk's revenue was invested in R&D, equivalent to DKK14.6 billion
Industry:	Pharmaceutical
Product examples:	New-generation insulins, modern insulins, glucagon-like peptide–1, human insulins, diabetes devices and accessories, oral antidiabetic agents, obesity care compounds, biological medicines for Hemophilia, and pioneer in growth hormone therapy

Strategic Industry-University Partnerships. DOI: https://doi.org/10.1016/B978-0-12-810989-2.00003-5
39

3.1 INTRODUCTION

3.1.1 About the Chapter

Here we describe how different industry—academia collaboration models are used to accelerate pharmaceutical innovation. We describe a number of strategic objectives and we apply four different models to achieve these objectives. We then describe each model, its anchoring, operation, and governance garnered with specific examples. We tie it all together with specific learnings and recommendations at the end.

3.1.2 About Novo Nordisk

Since its inception in 1922 Novo Nordisk has been a dedicated diabetes care company focusing on refining and optimizing the treatment of both type 1 and type 2 diabetes. During the last decades Novo Nordisk has expanded into treatment of bleeding disorders, growth disorders, and lately obesity. Novo Nordisk has almost exclusively developed so-called biological drugs; therapeutic proteins and peptides administered by subcutaneous or intravenous injection. Furthermore, Novo Nordisk is developing a range of state-of-the- art injection devices.

This strong focus on a limited number of diseases and therapeutic modalities set Novo Nordisk apart from most of our peers, and has allowed the company to develop a very strong internal translational drug development engine. The focus and approach sets the direction for where and how Novo Nordisk engages with academia.

3.1.3 Drug Development—From Idea to Patient

The process of translating discoveries into innovation and eventual pharmaceutical products is the key competence of the pharmaceutical industry. Developing a new drug requires both cutting edge biological competence as well as access to a broad and state-of-the art technology base.

Developing pharmaceuticals for human diseases is a long, complex, and very expensive undertaking. It starts with years and resources invested in basic research at universities to lay the scientific and technological foundation, followed by approximately 10—15 years of research and development (R&D) in the pharmaceutical company, and finally it requires a massive economic investment of around US$1—1.5 billion before it actually can benefit the patients.

Over the last decades treatments for diseases like cancer, diabetes, cardiovascular, and autoimmune diseases have become increasingly effective and safe. This has primarily been driven by a deepened biological disease understanding, increasingly sophisticated technologies, and the advent of new treatment modalities beyond the classically orally available small molecule drugs.

The development of a new drug combines deep knowledge and expertise across a number of disciplines, such as basic disease understanding, the pathophysiology, and underlying molecular mechanism leading to the disease, which is primarily the outcome of academic research in university and hospitals. Equally important, understanding the molecular mechanisms and identifying potential targets for intervening in the pathology are prerequisites for being able to develop a drug. The identification of drug targets has historically been the result of academic research, although pharmaceutical and biotech companies have embarked on drug target identification.

Once a new potential drug target is discovered, the drug targets need to be validated with an investigation thereof; can the prototype molecule be designed in such way that it interferes with or corrects the pathophysiology in model systems that are relevant for the disease? Thus, even with a validated target, designing new drug candidates is not trivial; a number of parameters including pharmacology, efficacy, specificity, safety, and manufacturability must be considered and carefully designed into the molecule.

Over the last 20 years the pharmaceutical industry has struggled with productivity challenges; due to the increasing investments in R&D not resulting in proportional increases in new product launches. Increased competition, increased regulatory requirements, bigger and more expensive clinical trials, and the unwillingness from health care providers to pay for incremental innovation, amongst others, has made it challenging to develop new products. Therefore you will see different attempts to combat, such as mergers, pipelines swaps, codevelopment alliances, restructuring, increased in-licensing, and a lot more innovative collaboration with academia across the pharmaceutical innovation value chain.

As described earlier, drug discovery and development, requires both a deep biological insight and a exploratory mind-set, that typically are held by academic scientists, as well as access to disease models, resources, and knowledge of downstream requirements characterizing the industrial researcher. Leveraging the competencies in both academia and industry is the prerequisite to be successful.

3.2   BUSINESS ANCHORING AND ENGAGEMENT MODEL

To ensure the optimal return-on-investment when engaging in academic collaboration—as in any other business endeavor—it is important to have a clear business objective. And, that organizational anchoring, leadership, and governance are all designed and aligned towards supporting the objectives.

Novo Nordisk engages with academia to achieve four objectives:

- Leverage scientific and technological expertise and know-how to *address specific project challenges* or objectives, e.g., associated with a drug candidate.

① Research collaboration	② Fellowship program	③ Public private partnership	④ Alliance
What we seek Access to technology, Know-how, Capacity	Talents, Academic network, Know-how	Know-how, Capacity, Risk sharing	Novel compounds, Novel technologies, Novel IPR, Know-how
Novo Nordisk contribution Funding	Funding, Know how	Funding, Know how, Researchers	Funding, Know how, Resources

FIGURE 3.1 Collaboration models used by Novo Nordisk to address specific business objectives.

- Engage in shared research projects to *cocreate new opportunities and inventions* based on new technological or biological insights—to identify and develop new drug candidates.
- Get *access to intellectual property rights* (IPRs) on new technologies, drug targets, or compounds.
- Establish access *to science talents*, in order to build a broad network of future collaborators and potential employees.

These four objectives above align with the requirements of a sustainable pharmaceutical R&D organization and correspond with a range of company objectives, tactics around specific projects, strategic imperatives like progression of the R&D pipeline, and to corporate talent attraction. The four objectives cover considerable range in time lines, investments, resources, and leadership attention.

The model below describes the four approaches Novo Nordisk R&D use to address the objectives. An overview is provided in Fig. 3.1.

3.3 RESEARCH COLLABORATIONS

To address specific scientific and technological challenges Novo Nordisk has over the years established a diverse portfolio of bilateral research collaborations, including individual investigators and research groups from top-tier research institutions globally. These collaborations provide a flexible vehicle to access state-of-the-art technologies, specific scientific competencies and know-how, and as a way to leverage skilled resources outside the organization.

The research agreements we enter are generally medium-sized commitments supporting a few researchers and they are often driven by a specific research plan with clearly defined objectives and milestones. Budgets are often linked to specified activities supporting the specific objective of the collaboration.

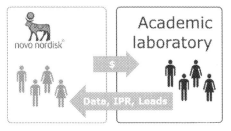

FIGURE 3.2   In research collaboration Novo Nordisk primarily provides financial support.

Collaborators are identified based on scientific excellence, the availability of specific assays, models, or technologies, and in some cases the need for geographical proximity. In most cases the research is conducted exclusively at the host research institution with Novo Nordisk supporting the research financially and, when required, with materials and know-how. Although the activities support research ongoing at Novo Nordisk, joint project groups are only seldom formed (Fig. 3.2).

As these collaborations are designed to directly complement ongoing internal R&D efforts, they are managed and funded in the line function or project team responsible for solving the given scientific or technological challenge. Only in rare cases are the resources allocated from central budgets.

Line management reviews and approves research collaborations for funding, and research scientists from the project manage the interactions with the academic researchers.

As these collaborations often are centered on specific inventions or even drug candidates, where Novo Nordisk has already filed for, or secured IPR, the company retain the full ownership of data, results, and IPR. Often the academic institutions are granted the right to IPR pertaining to new technology or methodology resulting from the collaborations and occasionally we agree to copublish the results of the work with the academic researcher.

The simplistic governance structure allows agile decision-making and reduces the resource need on the organizations, but can be a significant disadvantage if the collaboration gets off-track in terms of results or budget. Hence it is recommended to ensure anchoring at a higher organizational level, to have a dispute solving mechanism in the collaboration, although such anchoring is not always easy to secure at the academic institution.

3.4   FELLOWSHIP PROGRAMMES

Novo Nordisk has established a number of PhD and Postdoc programmes to attract and develop science talents. These programs allow us to explore new science at the periphery of our core research focus and often function as a vehicle in establishing collaborations with top-tier research institutions globally.

The first fellowship programmes were implemented in the late 1990s as a means to pursue basic research projects together with universities. Engagement with local and international universities was driven as a bottom-up process with no explicit strategic focus. As a result, a wide network of relationships and collaborations around the world was established. A significant learning from the first 15 years of running fellowship programmes is that operations of such a wide network are very complex and resource demanding, while not providing critical mass at the individual institution to create sufficient traction.

This has led to a strategic refocus on the fellowship programme on larger investments with fewer universities in selected locations in North America, Asia, and Europe. In addition, we have diversified the fellowship programmes into three main categories serving distinct business needs:

1. The Science Talent Attraction Retention (STAR), a PhD and Postdoc programme supporting both fellows working in Novo Nordisk laboratories and fellows working within a limited network of international research institutions. Priorities for funding are determined by a Novo Nordisk internal review process to align project allocations to business needs.
2. Dedicated regional programmes to train talent within specific scientific fields to support the recruitment needs of primarily the Danish Novo Nordisk R&D organization.
3. Institutional elite Postdoc programmes with University of Oxford (OU) and Karolinska Institute (KI) to support the next generation of scientific leaders.

3.4.1 The Science Talent Attraction Retention Programme

The STAR PhD and Postdoc programme was launched in 1999. Since its inception, this programme has supported more than 400 fellows with projects ranging from drug discovery to drug delivery. Over the years, approximately 40% of the program alumni have been recruited to permanent positions in Novo Nordisk. Currently 70 alumni are employed in Novo Nordisk.

The programme is built around three main components: a fellowship project addressing a relevant scientific issue, collaboration with an academic laboratory, and the fellow adding innovative capacity to the company (Fig. 3.3).

The programme is anchored by a bottom-up process within the R&D organization, allowing Novo Nordisk scientists to bring forward project proposals to be funded through the programme. Projects are eligible for funding through review by an internal leadership group and scored by a set of defined criteria including significance of training opportunity provided, innovation and novelty, as well as alignment with R&D business needs. This

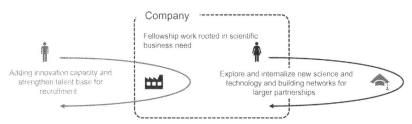

FIGURE 3.3   Flow and purpose of Novo Nordisk fellowships.

review process mitigates the risk that fellowship programmes are used to fill short-term resource gaps in, e.g., pipeline project. Once projects are approved for funding, implementation relies on two main approaches:

The first branch of the programme supports international Postdocs to work within Novo Nordisk research laboratories in Denmark. Here the objective is to test new technologies, concepts, or hypothesis, to train scientists in industrial R&D, and to attract international talent to the organization. As the focus of the programme is on talent development and attraction, Novo Nordisk enables early publications with, in most cases, limited emphasis on securing IPRs.

Within the second branch of the programme, Danish-based scientists are supported to work or study at international research institutes. This provides an opportunity to train local talent in new frontiers of science, in top laboratories anywhere in the world. At the same time, the fellows learn to navigate within the international science community and, often, to establish lifelong international networks that they can capitalize on later in their career.

The programme further serves as a mechanism for Novo Nordisk to nurture an international science network and to foster closer contacts to key international academic institutions. Often the placement of a single Postdoc has stimulated more extended research collaborations. As such, the programme serves as an early entry point to engage and explore potential broader collaboration with global top laboratories and universities.

The programme and the associated budget is anchored in a corporate R&D unit with overall responsibility for the strategic and operational aspects of the programme. In particular, this unit manages the internal bottom-up project proposal flow, the prioritization and the review processes across functional areas, the contract negotiations with international research institutions, and the recruitment and associated processes.

For each fellow, Novo Nordisk assigns an internal scientist as mentor and contact person to support and anchor the scientific collaboration in Novo Nordisk to ensure the fellow gets good guidance on how to navigate in the Novo Nordisk R&D organization.

3.4.2 Dedicated Programmes to Train Scientific Talent

Novo Nordisk works closely together with Danish universities to developed fellowship programs in selected scientific disciplines where Novo Nordisk has been challenged to recruit sufficient talent.

As an example, the LIFEPHARM PhD School in pharmacology was established together with the University of Copenhagen (UCPH) in 2010. The PhD School, including a professorship, is fully funded by Novo Nordisk. At the time of writing 10 PhDs have graduated from the programme—the majority are employed at Novo Nordisk. Presently, 20 fellows are pursuing their PhDs as part of the program.

Research projects are jointly defined by the UCPH and Novo Nordisk and reviewed by a joint Advisory Committee. The UCPH professor acts as director of the programme and is responsible for selecting and hiring candidates.

As for the STAR program, each fellow is assigned a Novo Nordisk scientist as a mentor. A dedicated partnership manager oversees the programmes and ensures processes, budgets, and constructive collaboration with the fellows and the UCPH.

We have established similar although smaller programs with the Technical University of Denmark (DTU) and Aarhus University (AU).

3.4.3 Institutional Postdoc Fellowship Programmes

In 2013, the OU and Novo Nordisk jointly established an international Postdoc fellowship programme with the aim to develop the next generation of science leaders in the fields of diabetes, metabolism, and endocrinology, and at the same time, promote excellent basic and clinical research within these fields (Box 3.1). The programme is fully funded by Novo Nordisk while the Postdocs are employed at OU.

The total program covers 32 individual 3-year fellowships. At the time of writing, 12 postdoctoral fellows have been enrolled. The first fellows are graduating from the programme, some of whom have already been recruited into permanent positions at Novo Nordisk.

The programme is orchestrated under a fixed annual schedule, starting with an annual request for research proposals from the OU faculty.

A joint steering committee (JSC) composed of senior OU and Novo Nordisk R&D leaders is charged to review and prioritize the incoming proposals. Priority is given to proposals that marry a focus on ground-breaking science with a strong academic learning environment. Hence, it is ensured that criteria typically used to assess industrial relevance are not prioritized; instead, research topics that are not currently addressed within Novo Nordisk R&D laboratories are prioritized.

Selected research proposals are posted internationally. Candidates are reviewed by a recruitment committee with the Principal Investigator at OU

BOX 3.1 Institutional Postdoctoral fellowship programme with OU.

press release

Novo Nordisk and Oxford University join forces to further enhance diabetes research

Bagsværd, Denmark, 5 November 2013 – Today, Oxford University and Novo Nordisk announced the establishment of an international fellowship programme that aims to support the career and scientific development of young, exceptional research talent within diabetes. The partnership will establish a number of postdoctoral fellowship opportunities that will be hosted by Oxford University and funded by Novo Nordisk.

"We are honoured to establish the International PostDoctoral Fellowship Programme with Oxford University, which has such valuable expertise in the study and treatment of diabetes. By combining our company's discovery and clinical development strengths with the research expertise and academic tradition of Oxford University, we can support the development of a new generation of exceptional diabetes researchers to eventually drive innovation further and improve the lives of the patients," said Mads Krogsgaard Thomsen, executive vice president and chief science officer at Novo Nordisk.

As part of the agreement, a total of 12 young leading researchers will be offered a 3-year grant to support their research within the fields of diabetes, metabolism and endocrinology. The goal of the new programme is to support the development of a new generation of research leaders while further developing scientific excellence within diabetes.

"This new programme will support the best young researchers doing novel work in the understanding of diabetes and its treatment. It is these early career researchers that will produce the new ideas, discoveries and advances that will improve diabetes treatment and care in the future. We're delighted to partner with Novo Nordisk to provide this level of funding and support which will be important in enabling both their research and their career development," said Professor Hugh Watkins of the Radcliffe Department of Medicine at Oxford University.

Novo Nordisk A/S Corporate Communications	Novo Allé 2880 Bagsværd Denmark	Telephone: +45 4444 8888	Internet: www.novonordisk.com CVR no: 24 25 67 90

making the final decision on which candidate to recruit for the individual research project.

The postdoctoral fellows are supervised by their Principal Investigators at OU. In addition, Novo Nordisk assigns an internal scientist as mentor and contact person to support and anchor the scientific collaboration in Novo Nordisk and to help the fellow to navigate in the Novo Nordisk R&D organization.

The fellows are encouraged to visit Novo Nordisk research groups to strengthen the interaction with their industrial mentors and to provide the opportunity for them to get more familiar with industrial R&D. Collaboration and relationship building is further facilitated by an annual symposium at OU bringing together all stakeholders, including fellows, OU Principal Investigators, Novo Nordisk mentors, and key scientists from both institutions.

A comparable but somewhat smaller programme has more recently been established at KI, in Stockholm, Sweden. This programme is focused on basic and clinical endocrinology and like the OU fellowship program, overseen by a JSC with senior leaders from both organizations. To ensure the best internal alignment, a number of Novo Nordisk representatives serve on the steering committees of both fellowship programs.

The interaction between the fellows, the universities, and Novo Nordisk supervisors is of critical importance to drive the project in the proper direction and ensuring industrial input to the project, and that Novo Nordisk accesses appropriate know-how and data. To ensure this, a partnership manager is allocated to each fellowship program, with the responsibility to facilitate the collaboration both at institutional and individual project level.

In unison the fellowship programmes constitute the Novo Nordisk R&D Fellow Community. On an annual basis, we bring together the global community of Novo Nordisk fellows at our global headquarters in Denmark. These meetings enable scientific exchange, tuition, formal training in, e.g., IPR or the pharmaceutical value chain, as well as opportunities for fellows to explore career opportunities within Novo Nordisk.

3.5   PUBLIC PRIVATE PARTNERSHIPS

Novo Nordisk has identified a number of objectives that are not easily addressed by any of the engagement models described so far. These include tools and capabilities to facilitate development of new therapies in areas with high unmet medical need or significant technological or scientific challenges. These challenges include development of experimental models, biomarkers, and diagnostics, tools for patient stratification, as well as specific insights to support sector-wide dialogue with regulators to, e.g., establish regulatory pathways for advanced therapies, e.g., cell and gene therapies.

These objectives are not easily achieved by Novo Nordisk or any single stakeholder alone. Instead, solutions to these challenges require the concerted engagement of several stakeholders across the sector, including academia, health care providers, regulators, and industry working closely together in public—private partnerships (PPP).

The largest existing PPP within life science is Innovative Medicine Initiative (IMI). The current and IMI-2 programme has a €3.3 billion budget for the period 2014—24. Of this, half the budget comes from Horizon 2020, the EU's framework programme for research and innovation. The other half is committed to the programme by the European Federation of Pharmaceutical Industries and Associations (EFPIA) member companies, which includes most large pharmaceutical companies including Novo Nordisk.

The first IMI programme (IMI-1) running from 2008 to 2014 and comprising a budget of €2 billion—also with a 50/50 share between the EU and EFPIA companies—had a portfolio of more than 50 projects. At its inception in 2008, IMI focused on the R&D processes to develop new tools and technologies at shared cost to improve the overall productivity within R&D by reducing attrition and time to market. Since then, IMI has evolved further to more broadly support the implementation of research, regulatory, and industry policy agendas. The framework is now driving initiatives to increase the uptake of innovation across Europe and to adapt the regulatory framework by aligning and collaborating with payers and regulators on health care priorities and adaptive developments based on real-world data and patient needs.

Novo Nordisk has been participating in IMI from its launch in 2008. Our initial focus was on research projects to develop new capabilities and tools to reduce attrition in the early part of the R&D value chain. This focus on research business needs has allowed Novo Nordisk to anchor projects within the global research governance.

To ensure alignment with the company's R&D strategy, the engagement in IMI is anchored with an independent corporate unit in R&D mandated to broker IMI project ideas within Novo Nordisk to explore interest across research areas. A central R&D budget is allocated towards the IMI engagement, thus providing a flexible framework to participate in selected projects. Final IMI project commitment is subject to R&D leadership endorsement.

This framework initially worked well to support opportunistic project engagement during the initial phase of IMI. However, limitations in internal governance became increasingly apparent along with a broadening of the scope of IMI. Hence, projects over time required engagement and resources across the various R&D functions which could not be effectively handled by a single unit.

After a IMI portfolio and strategy review, we have changed our IMI engagement from opportunistic engagement at the periphery of our business area to a more strategically driven engagement to support our core therapeutic areas and facilitate establishment of capabilities and know-how in new therapeutic and technology areas that the company is considering entering.

Coincidentally, the central governance of the IMI was restructured around so-called Strategic Governance Groups focusing on fewer disease areas and delegating more decision mandates to the engaged companies. Together, these changes called for a restructuring of our internal PPP governance setup.

As a consequence we have reengineered our internal processes and governance to reflect the breath and aspiration of IMI within Novo Nordisk (Fig. 3.4).

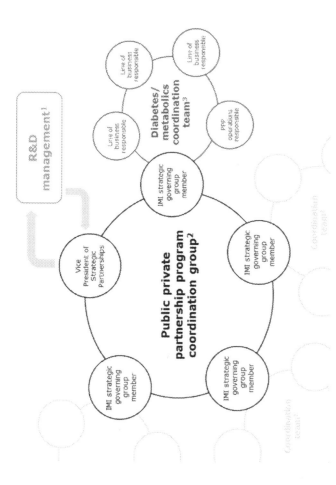

1 Responsibility:
- Decision body deciding to engage or not. Overall endorsement

2 Responsibility:
- Recommend prioritization of potential engagements within a PPP
- Owners of strategic framework for Novo Nordisk engagements in PPP
- Responsible for consolidated progress follow-up on program level
- Evaluate engagement in new PPPs

3 Responsibility:
- Evaluation of PPP proposed suggestions within own scope
- Follow-up on progression within own portfolio
- Ideation process
- Prioritization within own field
- Internalization of project outcomes

FIGURE 3.4 Novo Nordisk IMI governance structure.

For each of our key therapeutic areas—diabetes, obesity, and hemophilia and associated technology areas—we have created a cross-functional governance structure with representation from key functions across R&D, including research, clinical development, and regulatory affairs. Within this new internal governance structure, a dedicated team are charged to bring forward initiatives in support of our core business needs with the potential to be best addressed through IMI. At the same time the team continues to evaluate the relevance, potential business impact, and scientific standard of project proposals brought forward by our peers within EFPIA.

For these cross-functional teams, senior R&D leaders are responsible for ensuring internal progress and anchoring Novo Nordisk IMI activities within the external IMI governance framework.

A core team of the cross-functional group leaders coordinates the Novo Nordisk IMI effort across therapy areas, sets priorities, reviews progress, and secures R&D leadership endorsement and funding. In addition this group also ensures alignment with our engagement in other multistakeholder programs like TransCelerate, EIT Health, and NIH Critical Path program. As a result we have developed a portfolio of IMI projects supporting two strategic intents:

1. Directly support the achievement of our objectives within our core therapeutic areas like diabetes.
2. Establish know-how capabilities within new therapeutic and technology areas to support our future efforts in these.

As an example of IMI projects supporting our diabetes business area, Novo Nordisk is leading an effort with industry peers to address the science, burden, and implication of hypoglycemia for diabetes patients (Fig. 3.6).

This project is patient-centered and is intended to improve the understanding of the nature of hypoglycemia occurring in clinical trials and real life. It is a cross-functional effort anchored within Novo Nordisk across a wide range of functions to enable a coordinated effort bridging research, clinical development, device R&D, regulatory, and health economics. Project management and coordination between all internal and external stakeholders resides within a central R&D unit supporting the industry scientific project leader from Novo Nordisk (Fig. 3.5).

Within therapy areas adjacent to diabetes, Novo Nordisk participates in several IMI projects focusing on biomarker and noninvasive diagnostics development in areas of high unmet medical needs, e.g., liver diseases, with the aim to drive the maturation of the field as well as support the progression of the Novo Nordisk project pipeline (Fig. 3.6).

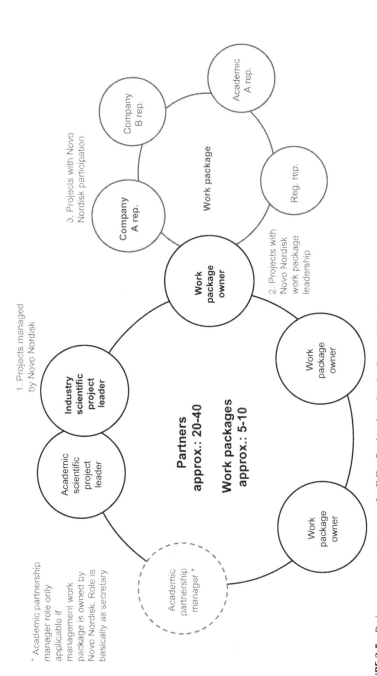

* Academic partnership manager role only applicable if management work package is owned by Novo Nordisk. Role is basically as secretary

1. Projects managed by Novo Nordisk

Academic scientific project leader

Industry scientific project leader

Academic partnership manager *

Partners approx.: 20-40

Work packages approx.: 5-10

Work package owner

Work package owner

Work package owner

2. Projects with Novo Nordisk work package leadership

3. Projects with Novo Nordisk participation

Company A rep.

Company B rep.

Academic A rep.

Reg. rep.

Work package

FIGURE 3.5 Project management structure for IMI reflecting three levels of potential project engagement.

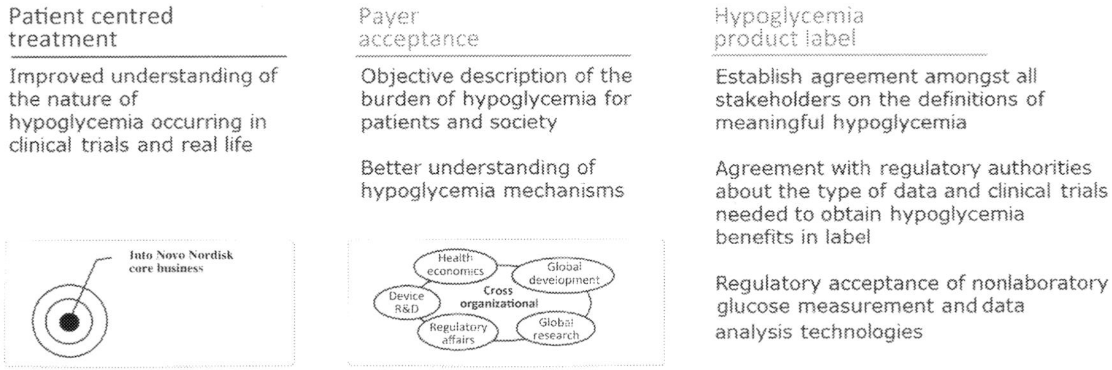

Patient centred treatment

Improved understanding of the nature of hypoglycemia occurring in clinical trials and real life

Into Novo Nordisk core business

Payer acceptance

Objective description of the burden of hypoglycemia for patients and society

Better understanding of hypoglycemia mechanisms

Global development

Health economics

Cross organizational

Global research

Device R&D

Regulatory affairs

Hypoglycemia product label

Establish agreement amongst all stakeholders on the definitions of meaningful hypoglycemia

Agreement with regulatory authorities about the type of data and clinical trials needed to obtain hypoglycemia benefits in label

Regulatory acceptance of nonlaboratory glucose measurement and data analysis technologies

FIGURE 3.6 Cross-functional project design within the hypoglycemia IMI project to address the core business need to establish an improved understanding of hypoglycemia events in clinical trials and real life.

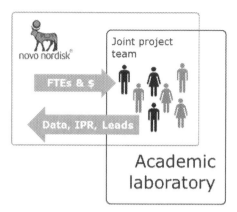

FIGURE 3.7   Strategic alliances are characterized by the close collaboration between the academic and industrial laboratories.

3.6   ACADEMIC ALLIANCE

To address open-ended exploratory science or innovation issues, such as exploring new disease biology and pathways, discovering new drug targets, or developing new technologies, the collaboration models described elsewhere in the chapter are not likely to be successful. Instead, closer collaboration, projects and complementary capabilities and expertise are required to succeed. Hence, Novo Nordisk engages with top academic groups, offering access to relevant technology, internal capacity, and know-how, as well as funding for staff and experimental work (Fig. 3.7). The projects are often multiyear with clearly defined milestones, stopping and extension criteria.

To be able to manage these multiyear collaborations it is crucial to upfront define the business objectives of parties as well as their scope, specific outcomes, and collaboration model to maximize the probability of success. In addition to business objectives, projects duration, and budgets, alliance contracts should include high-level research plans, with relevant milestones that may govern stop/go or extension options.

Although the objective of the collaboration might seem obvious and aligned, the academic and industrial researchers are rewarded by different outcomes, e.g., bringing a potential drug target forward in the company versus publishing a high-impact paper on that drug target. Likewise terms like "target validation" and "lead candidate" are likely to mean different things in the academic and the industrial lab. Clarifying, aligning, and agreeing on how to handle these differences in the collaboration at the beginning is a must to avoid trouble later on.

The key to a positive alliance outcome is to ensure alignment and agreement to a set of ground rules on how to collaborate—in a way where all parties can contribute the most. Such rules will allow the academic collaborator to engage in a way that leverages their expertise, technological edge, and exploratory approach to the fullest. This may run contrary to the often minimalistic and milestone and timeline-focused approach of industrial research. Hence it is important to address these differences at an early stage of the collaboration, and agree on basic objectives and rule of engagement. Further the agreement needs to strike a balance allowing for freedom of exploration on the academic side and at the same time allowing the industrial researcher to influence the collaboration by providing insight, guidance, and end goal focus to the project.

The duration, larger budgets, and the sometimes significant allocation of internal staff for this type of collaboration, call for more comprehensive governance than what is needed for other types of academic collaborations. In Novo Nordisk, strategic alliances are anchored at a relatively high level in the organization, at the level of relevant subportfolio ownership, and have specific budgets allocated for the term of the alliance commitment.

By anchoring the alliances with the subportfolio owner the best alignment between Novo Nordisk's overall portfolio and business objectives are ensured. In these alliances Novo Nordisk is looking for concrete, tangible outcomes including biological target identification and technology development. To further emphasize the strategic alliance, the subportfolio owner reports to the corporate governance system on equal terms as internal projects, ensuring transparency in resource allocation, progress, etc. Nevertheless, as strategic collaboration are based on legally and morally binding multiyear commitments they cannot be as easily up- or downprioritized or adjusted as internal projects.

The management of the alliance itself is structured to facilitate that decisions are made at the lowest appropriate level in order to ensure speed, agility, and proximity to the issue to be solved. Thus, day-to-day scientific dialogue is handled between researchers from the collaborating parties, whereas larger and more tactical decisions are handled by the dedicated project leaders from each side. Decisions involving the adjusting or reconfirming business objectives, scope, and budget are handled by a JSC comprised of appropriately empowered and mandated leaders from each party.

To support the JSC members and alliance owners Novo Nordisk allocates a Partnership Manager to each alliance. The role of the partnership manager is to facilitate the efficient executions of the collaboration: that decisions are made timely and within the scope and legal frame work, that budgets are adhered to and to serve as early dispute resolving mechanism.

As the outcome of this type of collaborations might have significant future value for both parties, e.g., new drug targets, a new drug lead or technology, access to resulting IP rights is important. Often, the resulting IP will be jointly owned or owned by the university with the industrial partner being granted a right to a license, or to negotiate a license. Most universities are reluctant to negotiate licensing terms at the onset of the collaboration as it is hard to assess the commercial value of an invention before it is made. Therefore, it is crucial to establish what constitutes the IP of the parties at the start of the alliance and how it can be used, or the principles and a process for establishing ownership of a resulting IP, or a process for negotiating IP licenses, and—if possible—agree upfront on terms for IP licensing.

As an example Novo Nordisk recently announced a multiyear collaboration with Massachusetts Institute of Technology (MIT) to develop "alternative drug delivery technology." Achieving the objective of the collaboration—developing new technologies to deliver biological drugs more conveniently, cheaper, and safer—depends on our ability to combine the specific technological and biological capabilities of the MIT team and the disease understanding, molecular engineering, and drug development capabilities of the Novo Nordisk team. The project is manned by researchers from MIT and Novo Nordisk and is jointly led by a project leader from each party. The project progress is overseen by a JSC.

3.7 BREAKING NEW GROUND, A COCREATION CENTER AT OXFORD UNIVERSITY

At the time of writing, Novo Nordisk and OU had announced the establishment of a first-of-its-kind research center at the university's Old Road campus. Fully implemented, the Novo Nordisk Research Centre Oxford will house more than 75 Novo Nordisk researchers with access to the university facilities as visiting fellows. The common vision of the two institutions is to leverage and combine world class basic research and technologies with world class industrial translational capabilities to create new innovative pharmaceutical within diabetes, obesity, and other metabolic diseases. The center is operated as an integrated part of Novo Nordisk global research organization. The alliance is overseen by a JSC primarily responsible for selecting and funding collaboration projects, in line with the specific IP provisions governing the collaboration.

Successfully implemented, this collaboration will serve all of the four objectives for academic collaboration in Novo Nordisk. Together with the existing fellowship program it will help establishing a pipeline of high-potential future scientific leaders, it will facilitate access to know-how and technologies at one of the world leading research institutions, and hopefully it will support the discovery and development of new innovative drugs to the benefit of patients suffering from serious chronic diseases.

3.8 CONCLUSION AND RECOMMENDATIONS

In this chapter we have introduced four business objectives addressed through collaborations with academic institutions. We have also described a number of approaches we use in Novo Nordisk to optimize success and return-on-investment from collaborating with academic institutions. Whether it regards talent development or development of new technologies or drug leads, it is crucial to have clear and agreed-on business objectives.

The key messages on how to ensure organizational anchoring, leadership, and governance are all designed and aligned towards supporting the objectives:

- Ensure the goal of the collaboration is aligned with your strategic objectives and business needs at an early stage of the project.
- Ensure the individual and mutual collaboration objectives are understood and agreed by all parties.
- Anchor the alliance as close as possible to the project or function responsible for achieving the business objective.
- Consider building a central "alliance management" resource to support your collaborations.

Chapter 4

Building Global Innovation Ecosystems though Public Private Partnerships: How IBM has Leveraged Academic Collaboration for 70+ Years

Chris Sciacca and Alessandro Curioni

IBM Research – Zurich, Zurich, Switzerland

IBM Facts & Figures (Fiscal Year 2016)

Company name:	International Business Machines Corporation (IBM)
Headquarters in:	Armonk, New York
Annual revenue:	US $79.1 billion
Number of research employees:	3000
R&D Budget:	US $5.7 billion
Product examples:	Watson, IBM Cloud, Blockchain, Security, Big Data Analytics, z Systems, System Storage

4.1 INTRODUCTION

This chapter will travel through time from the mid-1940s to today to provide a unique look at IBM Research's collaborations from the past to the present with various academic institutions in the United States to Switzerland to more recent collaborations in Africa.

Founded in 1914, IBM is a global cloud platform and cognitive solutions company headquartered in Armonk, New York. With operations in more than 170 countries, IBM attracts and retains some of the world's most

Strategic Industry-University Partnerships. DOI: https://doi.org/10.1016/B978-0-12-810989-2.00004-7

talented people to help solve problems and provide an edge for businesses, governments, and nonprofits.

Innovation is at the core of IBM's strategy. The company develops and sells software and systems hardware and a broad range of infrastructure, cloud, and consulting services.

IBMers are working with customers around the world to apply the company's business consulting, technology, and R&D expertise to build systems that enable dynamic and efficient organizations, better transportation, safer food, cleaner water, and healthier populations.

One of the underlying themes you will read throughout this chapter is IBM's ability to create and grow new technologies and markets, such as computer science and outsourcing services. The challenge of course is that when new markets are created, they typically lack the skills to support them. This new demand for skills is one of the key aspects of IBM's academia strategy. For example, the IBM mainframe was announced in the mid-1960s, and today it is responsible for billions of transactions a day from the second type in your credit card number to booking a flight. Incredibly, many of these mainframes are decades old and as they age, so does their skilled users. In 2010, according to Bloomberg, the average age for a mainframe professional is between[1] 55 and 60 years old. This alarming statistic didn't go unnoticed to IBM's hardware division, which triggered a number of activities including the development of IBM's zSystems Academic Initiative and a student competition called IBM master the mainframe contest. Today, 1400 colleges and universities participate much to the relief of some of the largest banks and airlines in the world.

As you look back and jump forward, you will be guided throughout this chapter by what IBM calls the "six pillars" or "six Rs" used to measure the vitality of its university programs: research, readiness through skills, recruiting, revenue, responsibilities, and regions.[2] Combined, these pillars enable IBM to *mix and match collaboration formats and strategies with the needs* of the company in any of the more than 170 countries where IBM conducts business.

The first "R," the research pillar, is about fostering collaboration, and this is driven by award programs, which you will read about later. In addition, IBM also employs a collaboratory model with universities around the world focused on knowledge creation using IT and its application on the grand challenges of the planet. For example, in 2015, IBM launched such a collaboratory with University College Dublin which is focused on applying cognitive computing technologies to augment human decision-making and

---

1. Tech Republic, July 20, 2015, Mary Shacklett, How IBM is answering CIOs' calls for workers with mainframe skills.
2. IBM's University Programs, IEEE Computer, 2010.

delivering the next level of advanced collaboration between people and computers.

The second pillar is readiness through skills. This pillar is the focus of the IBM Academic Initiative program, which helps educators worldwide to teach students market-ready skills. One such effort started this year at the University of Lugano in Switzerland. Working with IBM scientists in Zurich, the school will begin offering a new Master of Science Program on cyber-physical and embedded systems, in cooperation with the Politecnico di Milano (Milan, Italy) and ETH Zurich. The program aims at forming young engineers equipped with both theoretical knowledge and truly hands-on experience required to make an impact in the continuously growing fields of the Internet of Things. The team in charge of developing it believes that it's the first one in the world, as it integrates courses from different disciplines, such as microelectronics, telecommunications, physical modeling and control, computer science, machine learning, and mobile computing.

In another example, IBM is bringing its cloud technologies to universities around the world. The so-called Academic Initiative for Cloud is creating a cloud development curricula using IBM Cloud in over 200 universities, reaching more than 20,000 students in 36 countries. Additionally, a series of industry hackathons are regularly organized to create innovative hands-on experiences that propel radical ideas and innovation in cloud application development.

Faculty members will also receive 12 months of access to the IBM Cloud trial for themselves as well as up to 6 months access for students in their program. Both faculty and student accounts are renewable and do not require a credit card.

"Leaders in business and higher education must come together to foster a new generation of digital-savvy talent," said Kevin Werbach, a professor and expert on gamification at the Wharton School of the University of Pennsylvania. "It's great that IBM is so committed to connecting with top universities like ours, and to giving students and faculty exposure to the latest cloud technologies and business concepts. This experience will help prepare our students as they enter the marketplace."

The third pillar and the easiest to measure is recruiting. This effort is led by the human resources function and is focused on finding and placing the brightest talent worldwide at IBM. Within our research division, IBM has predoctoral and postdoctoral candidate positions and various internship programs which range in length from summer to up to 6 months. One of the more successful internship programs is called Great Minds.

Now in its tenth year the Great Minds initiative is a competition for 3–6-month internships at one of the IBM Research Labs in Africa, Zurich or Dublin for students from central and eastern Europe, the Middle East, and Africa. It provides students with the unique opportunity to work alongside IBM scientists on real projects.

To participate, students must have a faculty recommendation letter, which is followed by a 1–2-page position paper. The position paper is looking for the candidate to propose creative and innovative ideas that could be turned into concrete projects, based on IBM's research areas.

One of the previous winners, who also eventually accepted a position at IBM's Zurich lab, is Stanisław Woźniak, a PhD candidate from Poznan University of Technology in Poland.

"IBM Research − Zurich is a unique place where you can meet some of the smartest people from all over the world. I never suspected that I would work in such a multinational team. The atmosphere is truly great when you have a chance to meet all these experienced researchers and discuss both your assignments and personal views."

Another Great Mind's winner and PhD candidate Adela-Diana Almasi from Romania adds, "One thing that I particularly appreciate is the fact that here, as interns, we have the freedom to make design decisions on the project that we are part of. Our opinions and input are valued."

Revenue is the fourth pillar, which may be surprising, but after all, universities are run today like mid-size businesses and they have IT needs, so why not? One such client is Southern Connecticut State University which is using IBM cognitive analytics to zero in on the factors that truly influence students' performance, enabling more effective, data-driven decision-making on how and where to offer extra education support.

Responsibility, the fifth pillar is all about charitable donations, volunteerism, and corporate social-responsibility programs. One of the most visible efforts here is the World Community Grid. The World Community Grid was started 12 years ago, and it essentially borrows the compute resources of its 750,000 members to build a giant virtual supercomputer tasked with simulating and analyzing data to benefit society. Back in May it was used by scientists from Brazil, the Skaggs School of Pharmacy and Pharmaceutical Sciences at University of California San Diego, and Rutgers New Jersey Medical School to find drug candidates to treat Zika, the fast spreading virus which the World Health Organization has declared a global public health emergency. Taping the resources of the virtual supercomputer, the university scientists can run virtual experiments on chemical compounds that could form the basis of antiviral drugs to treat the virus.

According to IBM computer scientist Jim Spohrer, who developed the six pillars with colleagues, the sixth "R" has recently been added to include regions, which targets start-ups and regional economic development. Driving this pillar is the IBM Global Entrepreneur Program for Cloud Startups which is intended to help start-up businesses around IBM's key initiatives by providing resources, global reach and in-depth knowledge and experience with the world's largest enterprise customers. Participants in the Program will be eligible for IBM Cloud usage credits of up to either US$ 1000 or 10,000 per month for 12 months, depending on the details of their participation.

If this book chapter is updated in a few years, a seventh "R" may be added for reputation, which includes the challenging task of reaching millennials with IBM messages. Why? Well IBM is a B2B company with very minimal direct contact with consumers, and a generation accustomed to using apps and devices everyday, none of which have the IBM logo on them, makes it even more challenging, yet just as important.

Now, buckle your seatbelt and prepare to travel to New York City c. 1940.

Six pillars (six Rs) to measure the vitality of university programs

Research	The creation of SSME which focuses on theories and methods from a variety of disciplines to address problems specific to the services sector, such at the $25 billion business process outsourcing market
Readiness through skills	Working with IBM scientists the University of Lugano is now offering a new Master of Science Program on cyber-physical and embedded systems
Recruiting	IBM established its first lab with Columbia University in New York. 20 years later, it chose a professor from the Swiss university ETH Zurich to be its first lab director and more recently, its two labs in Africa are on the campuses of universities
Revenue	Southern Connecticut State University is using IBM cognitive analytics to zero in on the factors that truly influence students' performance, enabling more effective, data-driven decision-making on how and where to offer extra education support
Responsibility	Skaggs School of Pharmacy and Pharmaceutical Sciences at University of California San Diego, and Rutgers New Jersey Medical School used the charitable IBM run World Community Grid to find drug candidates to treat Zika
Regions	IBM's Kenya lab offers a Resident Scientist Program, an international recruitment program to reach pre- and postdoctoral researchers from Kenya and other parts of Africa, with a 1-year tenure with options extension

SSME, service science, management, and engineering.

4.2   THEN AND NOW: MORE THAN 70 YEARS OF INDUSTRY–ACADEMIA COLLABORATION AT IBM

Sandwiched between two large apartment complexes, the unassuming building located at 612 West 116th Street holds a secret. Unbeknownst to the New Yorkers who live in this Morningside Heights neighborhood of upper Manhattan, without this building, we may be living in a world without hard disks, online travel reservations, or LASIK eye surgery.

It was here in 1945 (Brennan, 1971), where IBM Research was born, not only fostering a new era of science and innovation but also laying some of the early ground work of academic–industry collaborations.

4.3   STARTING FROM SCRATCH

While most of the local newspapers were busy reporting on the Yalta Conference and Europe's post—World War II reorganization, on 6 February, the presidents of International Business Machines Corporation (IBM) and Columbia University jointly announced the Watson Scientific Computing Laboratory.

Located on the university's campus and outfitted with the latest IBM computing hardware, the new lab was promoted as "a world center for the treatment of problems in various fields of science whose solutions depends on the effective use of applied mathematics and mechanical calculations."

> *Best Practice Tip: Interesting to note that IBM chose to be on the campus of a university. Management followed a similar strategy 60 years later with the opening of two new labs in Africa.*

It was reported that IBM and Columbia had various connections spanning over 15 years, but the new formal arrangement was a win—win for both. For IBM, the company would gain stronger access to fresh talent, while also benefiting from new application ideas for its calculating computers. As for the Columbia professors and their students, they would have the latest computing at their fingertips and could potentially shape the future of this emerging industry. Staff members were also encouraged to teach classes, a tradition which carries on today across several of IBM's academic collaborations.

Seven years later in 1952, the collaboration was showing signs of success with a string of promising calculator projects for astronomy and defense, and management was ready to expand. The IBM lab director, Wallace J. Eckert, spoke with Columbia about establishing a solid state physics department, which would include another innovative concept in academic—industry relations: the employment of graduate students from the university to do their thesis research at IBM. Today, more than 50 students at IBM's Zurich lab are working on their thesis, while being employed by IBM.

Only 1 year later, the new department was full staffed and in looking back at these few years Eckert explained "Our agreements with the university were exceedingly informal. The best way to describe it is that we were invited to the campus to operate a laboratory with the understanding that if we didn't like being here or they didn't like us to be here the situation could be terminated. We never had detailed agreements about who would provide what or who was to do what."[3] While this may be less practical in today's litigious business environment, some aspects are possible with the right partner.

4.4 THE WORLD IS OUR LAB

By the mid-1950s, IBM formally set-up an independent research division with significant expansion in the United States with plans to go abroad.

With the Watson Scientific Computing Laboratory at Columbia already overcrowded and several senior scientists sharing desks, IBM decided to build a new campus approximately one hour north in Yorktown Heights, NY. By the end of the decade, all of the basic research established at 116th street was gradually transferred, and an agreement between IBM and Columbia was reached to close the site by the fall of 1970, but IBM's CEO, Thomas Watson Jr., wasn't quite done just yet.

Best Practice Tip: Distance from the stress of HQ can be important for innovative thinking.

At the time, IBM's profits were healthy with gross annual sales of $500 million and 50,000 employees worldwide, and Watson Jr. knew that to continue this success, innovation had to remain a top priority, which meant investing in research and development.

In addition to the new Yorktown Heights lab, around the same time, IBM looked beyond New York and built a second lab in San Jose, California. Management felt that a lab with significant distance from the day to day pressures of headquarters would improve creative thinking. After several years, it was deemed an outstanding success, which gave management the confidence to look abroad toward Europe.

While much of the computing industry can be traced to the United States, IBM knew that connecting with the established European scientific community would be beneficial, not to mention this would also open up access to the talented graduates.

---

3. IBM Oral History of Computer Technology, Interview TC-1, Part II, with W.J. Eckert, July 20, 1967.

In January 1955, the idea of a European lab gained traction (Speiser, 1998). Watson Jr. trusted the task to IBM brilliant engineer Arthur Samuel, who was asked to secure a location, achieve government support, and choose a lab director. He focused his initial efforts on three countries: England, Switzerland, and the Netherlands, in this order.

As with IBM's newest labs in Australia (2011), Kenya (2013), and South Africa (2015), Samuel chose these locations for their accessibility to talent and skills via local top universities.

In 1955, England had a high level of activity in computing, particularly thanks to Alan Turing and his Digital Electronic Universal Computing Engine,[4] but after spending a month in the country, he came across several significant challenges.

First, they didn't want the IBM lab to be located near a university, but near a new economic development area called "New Towns" which Samuel described as "the most dismal places that I have ever seen (Speiser, 1998)." The other hurdle was foreign visas. Officials wanted to maintain the historic unemployment levels of 1% and required IBM to give preferential treatment to British nationals for jobs. These requests pretty much closed the door on Britain, particularly since it was only 2 years earlier when Watson Jr. published his equal opportunity hiring policies stating, "It is the policy of this organization to hire people who have the personality, talent and background necessary to fill a given job, regardless of race, color or creed."[5]

After closing one door, Samuel opened another one in Zurich, Switzerland, where he received a completely different reception. Switzerland was attractive for one key reason, the Swiss Federal Institute of Technology or ETH Zurich. ETH was founded by the Swiss government in 1854 with the mandate to educate excellence in science and technology and to be a community hub for innovation between academic and industry, certainly a mission statement which didn't go unnoticed by Samuel.

Samuel met with the equivalent of a U.S. senator who said foreign nationals are welcome. Coincidentally, the senator was the father of an associate professor of computer engineering at the ETH Zurich named Ambros Speiser, who Samuel already had his eye on for the lab director position.

Samuel never made it to the Netherlands. After getting the approval from IBM management, he then set his eyes on Speiser, eventually arranging a flight to New York for him to meet with none other than Watson Jr. himself.

Best Practice Tip: While obvious now, accessibility to mass transit to connect the lab with an academic partner is critical for the long-term stability of the relationship.

---

4. Timeline of Computer History, Computer History Museum.
5. Building an Equal Opportunity Workforce, IBM Icons of Progress.

By the summer of 1955, Speiser became the first lab director of IBM Research—Zurich. But more importantly he laid the foundation for what would become an exemplary public private partnership in science, but it wasn't always so easy.

4.5   OVERCOMING BIAS

By 1955, no template existed for establishing an international research lab, Speiser truly was a pioneer and at 33 years of age, he had no idea what he was in for.

He knew that before he could begin recruiting, he needed a location and his instincts told him to be near Zurich. Recognizing the need to be accessible via public transport, he eventually settled on a wing of the Pelican building in Adliswil, Switzerland, approximately 20 minutes from the city.

Speiser had traveled across Europe and hired 50 scientists by the time the lab officially opened in October 1956. But as the lab grew and gained more attention, the Swiss became concerned that the American laboratory would inflate salaries and strain the Swiss job market. In addition, many of the leading professors at ETH Zurich turned a cold shoulder at the lab puzzling and frustrating the young lab director.

At one point, Speiser hired a young talented engineer from Brown Boveri, a Swiss engineering firm known today as ABB, which resulted in a tense call from an executive at the firm who used the situation to cement his frustration with the new lab. Speiser was urged by the executive and others in the business community to not to hire Swiss graduates, a major set-back since he knew he needed to recruit the best talent to build a solid reputation. Adding salt to the wound, he was also told not to hire foreign nationals.

Nobel Laureate and IBM scientist Georg Bednorz, who works at IBM's Zurich Lab to this day, reflected on these early challenges at the ground-breaking ceremony for a new nanotechnology center being built on IBM's campus in June 2009.

This corporate lab was met with certain reservations when it opened from both from the public and the scientific community at large. The latter did not really regard this newcomer as part of the country's scientific scenery, causing many difficulties in hiring talented local graduates or sometimes even foreign candidates.[6]

6. Speech by Georg Bednorz on June 2, 2009 in Rueschlikon, Switzerland.

Speiser confirmed as much in his memoirs. After meeting with one of ETH's leading physics professors and sharing the news that the lab was hiring, Speiser received only one candidate for the job, who was apparently a student with less than average grades.

This troubling opinion had also spread to ETH's applied mathematics department. When Speiser began interviewing a group of mostly German mathematicians, ETH professors had essentially sabotaged his attempts at hiring them.

"Only one of these candidates was honest enough to tell me what had happened: He had been told that as an employee of the IBM laboratory, he would not be considered a member of the Zurich community of mathematicians. He would have trouble funding scientific contacts and he would not be a welcome guest at ETH" (Speiser, 1998).

Eventually, Speiser turned to the press to address what was turning into an increasingly ugly situation, and he penned an op-ed in the leading regional newspaper the *Neue Zurich Zeitung (New Zurich Newspaper)* in the summer of 1958. He addressed everything from salaries to saving Swiss jobs from brain drain to the United States, and it seemed to cool the flames.

It would take several more years for IBM and ETH to form the public—private partnership which they both benefit from today. Part of this was initiated by William Prager, a professor from Brown University who joined the IBM lab on a sabbatical assignment. Prager, a world-class mathematician in his own right had instant success in building a small department, which eventually established itself as a high caliber team.

Arguably any remaining ice had completely thawed in the late 1970s which eventually resulted in the second Nobel Prize for the lab. Bednorz told the following story during the ground-breaking ceremony:

"The first steps towards a closer interaction between ETH and the IBM Lab were made in 1977 with an individual initiative by K. Alex Mueller at IBM and Heini Graenicher from ETH. In a joint study agreement they decided to place a solid state physics PhD student at IBM to work on problems closely related to actual research topics critical to the strategy of the IBM Zurich lab. I [Bednorz] happened to be this student."[7]

Today, IBM has more than two dozen ETH students at the Zurich lab working on projects ranging from nanotechnology to microfluidics to cancer-imaging analysis, but Bednorz was the first—talk about big shoes to fill.

4.6   A PUBLIC–PRIVATE PARTNERSHIP IN NANOTECHNOLOGY IS BORN

By the mid-1980s, the IBM lab was well on its way to making a name for itself in the annuls of science led by back-to-back Nobel Prizes in Physics.

In 1986, Heinrich Rohrer, who joined IBM in 1963 after graduating from ETH Zurich, and German student Gerd Binnig received the Prize for the invention of the scanning tunneling microscope—a tool which opened the nanoworld to mankind and can be found in most scientific universities and labs today.

As stated earlier, ETH students, Bednorz and Müller, who were also remarkably hired in 1963 achieved high temperature superconductivity in early 1986, reaching 35 K for the first time. A little more than a year later in 1987—the shortest time between the discovery and the Nobel Prize—they followed in the footsteps of their colleagues and made the famous trip to Oslo.

There is no doubt that without the IBM–ETH groundwork laid by Speier, Prager, Mueller, Graenicher, and others, these two accomplishments may never have happened.

Best Practice Tip: Start small with academic collaborations leveraging internships and joint projects and then build up over time.

The leadership that these determined individuals put in place continues to this day 60 years later, and at its pinnacle is perhaps the most unique public private partnership in science, the Binnig and Rohrer Nanotechnology Center (BRNC).

---

7. Speech by Georg Bednorz on June 2, 2009 in Rueschlikon, Switzerland.

As told by Matthias Kaiserswerth, the retired director of IBM Research—Zurich, the BRNC was a result of perfect timing and scientific ambition.

By the mid to late 2000s, Kaiserswerth was under intense pressure from the lab's physics department to modernize its cleanroom facilities and equipment, which dated back some 20 years. Around 2007, he requested funding to John Kelly III, senior vice president, IBM Research, who responded with a surprising answer.

"I went to John with our proposal and he came back and said, 'great idea, just make it bigger and find a partner.' I couldn't believe it."

Kaiserswerth went back to Switzerland and it was immediately clear who he had in mind for such a partnership, ETH Zurich. After meeting with ETH president Peter Chen at an industry conference, the deals were worked out over dinner, and a new cutting-edge nanotechnology center in Switzerland was born at a cost of $90 million.

On 25 June 2008, the two partners issued a press release with Kelly III quoted stating "We see this type of collaboration as an emerging model for future industry—academic partnerships." The model would include several unique provisions.

First, it would be located on the Swiss campus of a publicly traded, US-headquartered $80 billion company in IBM. Typically, such a lab would be hosted at the site of a university, never the opposite.

Referring back to the staggering $90 million investment, the cost of the building was $60 million, which IBM would cover, but the remaining $30 million for the tooling and equipment would be split between both IBM and ETH. In addition, ETH would pay rent for access to office and lab space and to the new cleanroom for a total of 10 years.

This meant that ETH students and professors would essentially be colocated with IBM scientists. While this sounds are simple enough in practice, the legal ramifications required the lawyers at IBM and ETH to develop some innovative solutions of their own.

IBM patent attorney Peter Klett was involved in these contracts from the beginning. All of the following quotes are attributed to Klett.

"For the preparation of the contractual setup, our goal was to provide a legal framework for the scientists to collaborate under, which was as innovative and flexible as the scientific tools they were using for their research. Perhaps the most novel concept we developed was a pre-agreed modularly structured template for the various types of projects we envisioned to be useable today but also 20 years from now."

"In the end we had three basic templates within the framework. A standard joint research agreement, a sponsored research agreement and an agreement for collaborations with third parties, including under the European Union's FP7 and Horizon 2020 programs or national programs of Switzerland's Commission for Technology and Innovation (KTI).

In addition, we procured a 'Safety Net', which was a catch-all contract to cover both parties' interests for general every day work."

We deemed the "Safety Net" template to be particularly useful from a practical standpoint, because we understand that researcher's activities sometimes go beyond their original goals. Their creativity does not necessarily stop where the agreement stops.

Furthermore, when it comes to intellectual property (IP), every detail matters, including the equipment you are using and how you are using it.

Best Practice Tip: Anticipate for tomorrow: the lawyers not only planned for today but also for the future by developing flexible "catch-all" contracts.

"Let's say a scientist is using a tool and makes various adjustments to the tool for his/her experiment. Those adjustments are a form of IP, but can we really expect the scientists to reset the equipment back to its OEM settings each time after they've used it? Probably, not. So the "Safety Net" also covers how the equipment is used as part of the IP. Thereby we ensure freedom of action for all scientists who share such equipment."

Another potential sensitive topic the "Safety Net" is supposed to catch relates to third party collaborations. For example, what if ETH wanted to collaborate with one of IBM's biggest competitors?

"The contract stipulates that in principle any third party brought into the lab for a collaboration can be vetoed. But I am happy to say, in the seven years since the Center has been opened we haven't used this clause even once. Again, freedom of action is key to research activities, and we want to maintain this principle to the maximum possible, for ourselves and our partners. While we can control exchange of sensitive information with such third parties, the real challenge with a third party is again the use of the equipment and hence, the IP. We added a simple clause called 'Ease of Operation' stating that if an ETH partner used the equipment, the terms applicable to ETH would transfer to the partner."

The "ease of operation" also covers confidentiality for the operations of the lab. For example, IBM employees are responsible for the day-to-day operations from procuring equipment to maintenance. This exposes them to knowledge about what ETH is developing. Therefore, the clause also covers this knowledge.

One final legal best practice is referred to as "freedom of action," which provides joint ownership to IP which was developed by both ETH and IBM.

"Inventions covered under 'Freedom of Action' can be used by both parties and if IBM can license it, they can keep 100 percent of the revenue, same for ETH. You don't even have to tell the other party."

The rationale is simple. IBM has a large IP sales organization, as does ETH with ETH Transfer. These teams are responsible for licensing and bringing innovations to market. Eventually, licensing is not a self-propelling money machine. It is a costly and risky business to generate licensing income from IP. Therefore, if a team spends the resources to successfully license something, they should be able to reap the rewards. Clearly, the only obstacle is that the patents cannot be licensed to any one party exclusively.

4.7 IBM AND ETH TODAY

On your average day at IBM's Swiss lab, you'll find several ETH professors and dozens of students intertwined with hundreds of IBM scientists—the lines of this public private partnership have blurred in the past 60 years and the result is real-world scientific innovation.

Just recently, thanks to the unique Noise Free Labs in the basement of the BRNC, former IBM predoc and ETH student Fabian Menges and IBM scientist Dr. Bernd Gotsmann invented a breakthrough technique to measure the temperature of nano- and macrosized objects. The scientists hope the invention will eventually become a standard tool for scientists around the world as they explore the nanoworld, following in the footsteps of IBM pioneers Binnig and Rohrer.

4.8 BRINGING PUBLIC–PRIVATE PARTNERSHIPS TO AFRICA

Prior to 2009, when Dr. Kelly III presented a map of IBM's global labs, he would often reach out his hand on the map and draw an imaginary line for the equator emphasizing the point that IBM Research needed to expand into the Southern Hemisphere.

This goal was reached in full force by the time the second decade of 2000 began with new IBM labs opening in Brazil (2010), Australia (2011),

Kenya (2013), and South Africa (2016) and in all but one, Brazil, the labs were established with academic partnerships in place from the start, to the point where they are colocated with local universities, such as the two in Africa.

IBM's strategy was simple, to work on Africa's grand challenges it needed to be embedded with them and live them every day including energy, water, transportation, agriculture, healthcare, financial inclusion, and public safety.

The lab in Nairobi is located at the Catholic University of Eastern Africa giving IBM direct access to local talent. One of the unique aspects of the lab is the Resident Scientist Program, an international recruitment program to reach pre- and postdoctoral researchers from Kenya and other parts of Africa offering a 1-year tenure with options extension.

Resident scientists are fully integrated into the IBM Research—Africa lab as well as IBM's global network of labs and each recipient receives hands-on, practical training and will be assigned to work on significant national projects under the focused mentorship of an IBM researcher.

Further South in Johannesburg, IBM has partnered with the University of the Witwatersrand (Wits), which was recently ranked amongst the top 10 in emerging economies by the Times Higher Education World University Rankings—once again, direct access to local talent.

Dr. Solomon Assefa, a native Ethiopian, who was educated at MIT and worked at IBM's lab in New York, is now running both Africa labs. At the opening of the Johannesburg lab on August 25, 2016 he said "Inside the lab, the entire research team put meticulous thought into every corner and turn to encourage collaboration internally and with our university and client partners. Our agile work spaces provide a collaborative environment for IBM scientists to train and mentor Wits students and local start-ups, including a dedicated maker space, which provides a lab to tinker and build things – for example, radio frequency tags for tracking tuberculosis and a 3-D printer for prototyping designs."

While only a few months young, the South Africa lab already is overwhelmed with requests for internships and collaboration projects. Assefa adds "We have created a monster and I love it."

4.9   DEVELOPING ACADEMIC CURRICULA

While only a year old by the end of 1945, the collaboration between Columbia University and IBM was already gaining a strong reputation, particularly as it succinctly combined academics with corporate research under the same roof—but the innovation didn't stop there.

The following year, the lab also laid the foundation for what would become the world's first computer science curriculum, with Columbia offering the first academic-credit courses in computing[8] with others following suit including Harvard in 1947 and Cambridge University in 1953. IBM's involvement included setting up labs and providing hardware for teachers to train on, such as an astronomy lab at Columbia. IBM also gave employees paid time off to teach at the schools, which often resulted in internships and new recruits.

Today, more than 190 universities offer computer science degrees and the US Bureau of Labor statistics projects that technical occupations are one of the fastest growing during the 2014−24 projections decade.[9]

While computer science as a career took a nose dive in the mid-2000s, due to the outsourcing trend to low-cost regions of the world, another scientific discipline began to emerge for the same reason.

In 1973, *The Coming of Post-Industrial Society*, by sociologist Daniel Bell, predicted that in several decades knowledge-based services would surpass manufacturing for economic growth, including employment. His prediction came to term nearly 35 years later when in 2007, the International Labour Organisation reported that people in services worldwide overtook manufacturing and agriculture for the first time.[10] This was mimicked at IBM where services represented 37% of income, while hardware dropped to 23%.

---

8. IBM Icons of Progress: The Origins of Computer Science.
9. Employment Projections: 2014−24 Summary—Press Release.
10. The emergence of Service Science: toward systematic service innovations to accelerate cocreation of value, Jim Spohrer and Paul Maglio.

Best Practice Tip: When innovating into new business models, it's important to think about the long-term education and training needed to keep the model thriving.

As IBMs services revenue increased, so did the need for research and just as importantly, talent.

The challenge was clear enough. Calculating a complex 10-year, multi-million dollar or billion dollar contract, involving outsourcing of equipment and labor, with 99% reliability and a healthy profit margin was extremely difficult. And then to find scientists who could develop innovations to improve this process was at the time impossible. Why? Well according to an internal survey, conducted by IBM at the time, the necessary skills to draft such a contract span across technology, business, and social science degrees.

While a daunting challenge, it didn't stop IBM computer scientist Jim Spohrer from accepting the job to build-up IBM's newly formed Services Research department. After seeing firsthand how difficult it would be to find the right candidates, he rang up his friend Henry Chesbrough, a professor of business and innovation at the University of California at Berkeley, who eventually told him, "IBM started computer science. You should start service science."

Just as the invention of computers drove the need for a computer science discipline, this shift to services triggered another new discipline: service science, management, and engineering (SSME).

SSME focuses on theories and methods from a variety of disciplines to address problems specific to the services sector, such at the $25 billion business process outsourcing market, [11]which relies on new concepts to improve client satisfaction, or as Spohrer writes

"After all, service innovation—our ultimate goal—creates changes to a service system, which is made up of clients and providers co-creating value, and which has direct impact on the evolution of the system."[12]

To begin to shift academia into SSME, which today comprises 450 universities in 54 nations and even its own association, the International Society of Service Innovation Professionals, Spohrer and his colleagues advocated the shape of the ideal information worker, which looked like a "T" and was eventually given the name "T"-shaped professionals—the opposite of the more common "I" shaped person, which has great technical depth in one particular field.

The T-shaped professionals should have "breath of knowledge," the horizontal top of the "T" and vertically, "depth of expertise." T-shaped professionals have a special empathy that motivates them to understand their

---

11. Total contract value of the outsourcing market in the Americas from 2000 to 2015 (in billion U.S. dollars), Statista.
12. Spohrer, Maglio, Bailey, and Gruhl, 2007.

teammates, and they are more adaptive innovators, highly socially networked, lifelong learners, and potentially excellent entrepreneurs. It was believed that this combination makes these individuals ideal candidates for services science.

To drive the regional development of T-shaped professionals, IBM created Collaborative Innovation Centers (CICs) to work with local government, academia, and industry on this model. The basic goal was to keep local jobs by developing in-demand skills which would eventually drive regional economic development. Today, CICs can be found in Singapore, Italy, the Netherlands, Canada, and US at renowned universities including Delft, UMass, and Ben Gurion University.

The CIC also advises academic institutions and governments on the importance of building up policies to encourage university spin-offs and start-ups, critical for economic success. For instance, it has been shown that university spin-offs are more innovative than comparable firms due to their openness to frequently collaborate and focus on IP development. ETH Transfer, the spin-off arm of the aforementioned Swiss university, has reported that they are responsible for founding 315 spin-offs since 1973. Of these, where they found data, 122 of the spin-offs created nearly 2500 jobs and revenues of 585 million CHF in 2013, alone. They also have a 40% better chance of surviving than other start-ups in the country.[13]

4.10 BUILDING AN ECOSYSTEM FOR THE FUTURE OF COMPUTING

Whether it's SSME or quantum computing, IBM offers academia several collaboration models ranging from long-term partnerships to financial and technology grants and expertise.

After beating two humans at the Jeopardy!, Trivia game back in 2011. IBM quickly understood the value of building an ecosystem around its Watson cognitive technology to have the greatest impact on society. This led to the establishment of the IBM Watson University program, which provides full semester courses, online classes, access to application interfaces and competitions.

In 2016s students at the University of Texas at Austin won the first Watson University competition, which included $100,000 USD in seed funding to help launch a business based on their winning app named CallScout providing Texas residents with fast and easy access to information about social services in their area.

In addition to cognitive computing, two other emerging computing fields are being studied to address the challenges of both power density and

---

13. Overview and analysis of the performance of Spin-offs at the Swiss federal Institute of Technology Zurich and their effect on the Swiss Economy, January 2015.

efficiency. The first is neuromorphic computing, which takes inspiration from the incredible efficiency of human brain and applies it to computing. One such project is a public–private partnership known as SyNAPSE, which is a collaboration between IBM, DARPA, and several universities including Stanford, Cornell, and Columbia.

Part of the success of SyNAPSE can be attributed to a 3-week long boot camp IBM hosted in 2015 with more than 20 universities in attendance. The boot camp walked attendees through the processes of building applications for the neuromorphic chip, step by step or in the words of IBM Fellow Dharmendra S. Modha, "We're giving them the Lego building blocks, and now I'm looking forward to seeing what they create."

The other red hot field is quantum computing. It was in 1981, at a conference coorganized by MIT and IBM, where the famously brilliant physicist and Nobel Laureate Richard Feynman urged the world to build a quantum computer, and today scientists around the world are beginning to finally deliver.[14]

In May 2016, IBM did its part by placing five quantum bits or qubits in the cloud, calling it the Quantum Experience, to help launch an ecosystem from students to start-ups.

This caught the attention of the president of the European Physical Society who wanted to get the technology in front of the top Swiss students, and eventually IBM's Zurich lab hosted nearly two dozen physics students from ETH Zurich, Paul Scherrer Institute, EPFL, University of Bern and the University of Basel for a minihackathon.[15]

Nikolaj Moll, one of the IBM scientists hosting the event expressed why he wanted to be involved in the effort, "If we want to reach 50 qubits in the next few years we don't have a second to spare, but clearly without building up a quantum ecosystem in advance we won't have any users for such a system. So both research and community building need to be done in parallel, it's not either/or, it's both."

Following the event, in 2017 Swiss-based EPFL is now using the Quantum Experience in their classroom lectures.

4.11   ACADEMIC GRANTS AND AWARDS

Perhaps less innovative, but just as impactful are grants. IBM University Awards support basic research, curriculum innovation, and educational assistance in areas which are strategic to IBM including cybersecurity, Internet of Things, cloud, and cognitive computing.

---

14. The Dawn of Quantum Computing is Upon Us, Dario Gil.
15. Students Live the Quantum Experience at IBM's Swiss Lab, December 14, 2016, https://www.ibm.com/blogs/research/2016/12/students-live-the-quantum-experience-at-ibms-swiss-lab/.

The awards are broken up into four programs which span from offering stipends for 1-year fellowships to shared research grants to faculty awards for up to $40,000 USD per year.

4.12 GOING BACK TO THE BEGINNING

Nearly 50 years before Henry Chesbrough published his now required reading book *Open Innovation: The New Imperative for Creating And Profiting from Technology*, Thomas J Watson Jr. spoke about this concept a the opening the IBM Zurich Lab in 1956.

"Teamwork, not only within the borders of a country, but also among countries, has become an imperative necessity of our jet-age era. Advances in the fields of human endeavors are due to a large extent to the cooperation of the best brains and talent available everywhere. Team-work on an international level has made possible the tremendous strides made in the development of radar and in the universal fight against disease, just to mention two well-known examples."

With this in mind, we recommend:

- Make sure your academic collaborations are lined up with your research and business needs, and if they aren't, look at it as an opportunity. Universities need to attract students and businesses alike, and chances are if your firm recognizes an emerging technology, i.e., mainframe, cloud, quantum, chances are the universities will want to get in early on offering a certified curriculum. This is a true first to market differentiator.
- T-shaped graduates with deep technical skills and industry expertise will be in high demand. Leverage your employees and offer mentorships while these students are still at university to built bridges for eventual recruitment. In addition, T-shaped talent needs to be comfortably working as part of a large team, therefore encouraging them and even offer team-based challenge projects.
- The importance of creating and building global ecosystems should not be taken lightly. Thousands of developers are being trained in programming languages and are accessing application programming interfaces (APIs) in the cloud in the development of web services and mobile applications. The tools of choice for these individuals could be "make or break" moments for the largest enterprises and the smallest start-ups. Engaging with these developers at the university level using hackathons, freemium business models and internships will need to become business as usual.
- University relations is a marathon, not a sprint. Start with a handful of academic partners and branch out from there. In Europe, the Horizon

2020 program is an excellent starting point because it facilities collaboration between industry and academia for both start-ups and enterprises, it's structured around basic research for multiple years, and it offers matched funding models.

REFERENCES

Brennan, J.F., 1971. The IBM Watson Laboratory at Columbia University: A History. IBM, Armonk NY.
Speiser, Ambros P., 1998. The early years. IEEE Ann. Hist. Comput. 20 (1).

Chapter 5

Rolls-Royce University Technology Centres: Relationships Matter

Mark Jefferies and Kate Barnard
University Research Liaison, Rolls-Royce Plc, United Kingdom

Siemens Facts & Figures (Fiscal Year 2017)

Company name:	Rolls-Royce Group
Headquarters in:	London, United Kingdom
Annual revenue:	£15.1 billion
Number of (engineering) employees:	50,000 (18,245)
R&D budget:	£1.4 billion
Industry Branches:	Aerospace, Power Systems, Marine, Nuclear
Product examples:	Aero engines, reciprocating engines for power generation, distributed energy solutions, propulsion and handling solutions for ships

The Rolls-Royce University Technology Centre (UTC) network spans the globe and embraces a broad diversity of engineering and technology disciplines—most of which apply to all Rolls-Royce products and customer business areas.

This chapter concentrates on the vital nature of people and relationships when building sustainable collaborative partnerships and why they shouldn't be underestimated. It explores the views of some of those involved—including both industry and academic perspectives—and discusses not just the benefits but also some of the risks, encouraging the reader to think about what may work for their organization, and discussing some helpful tools and

Strategic Industry-University Partnerships. DOI: https://doi.org/10.1016/B978-0-12-810989-2.00005-9

metrics. We suggest seven key areas that support a relational perspective to university partnerships.

5.1   BUILDING ON A CENTURY OF ENGINEERING EXCELLENCE

Rolls-Royce in the 21st century is market leader in high-performance power systems serving the civil and defense aerospace sectors, the marine industry, nuclear, and power generation markets. Its global customer base spans 120 countries, comprising 400 airlines including numerous nations' flag carriers, 160 armed forces, 4000 marine customers including 70 navies and more than 5000 operators in the power and nuclear industry.

Technical excellence has been at the heart of Rolls-Royce since the company's earliest beginnings under the watchful eye of innovators and founding fathers, Sir Henry Royce and The Honourable Charles Rolls. To produce the world's best motor cars was their single-minded goal in the early years of the 20th century, and their attention to the finest technical detail was legendary.

The company has come a long way since then, selling off its by-then niche car business in the 1970s and focusing on its core gas turbine and power systems product base, expanding its market reach enormously. Yet throughout that century or more Rolls-Royce never lost sight of Sir Henry's original vision, and today's company continues to invest heavily in engineering capabilities, to develop its technical skills, and to recruit exceptional talent in order to secure its place in the top rank of engineering companies with world-class products and services.

In 2017, of the company's $\sim 50,000$ employees in 50 countries, over 18,000 are engineers, firmly underlining its commitment to innovation and technical prowess. In recent years, Rolls-Royce has invested more than £1.2 billion per annum—around 10% of its annual revenue—in research and development. This includes support for its multinational network of 31 University Technology Centres (UTCs) that are pushing back the boundaries in a wide variety of scientific and engineering disciplines.[1]

---

1. In addition to the UTCs, an international network of Advanced Manufacturing Research Centres (AxRCs) has been created to transform production capability by accelerating the development and deployment of step-change manufacturing technologies. These AxRCs engage companies, multiple industrial sectors, and universities in a collaborative quest to bring about step change improvements across a wide range of manufacturing techniques and accelerate them into early use on the shop floor. Forerunner of this highly capable network was the original AxRC, near Sheffield, which was established in 2008 by the local university and aerospace giant Boeing. Founding members of the AMRC include Rolls-Royce, which established the associated Factory of the Future, but its 60 industrial members today comprise a broad multisectoral representation. Additionally, Rolls-Royce has of course other university relationships for specific research projects, but here we concentrate on those that are regarded as "strategic."

Additionally, Rolls-Royce has always recognized and utilized the strength and depth of engineering and technology expertise within the academic community, nurturing potential engineers of the future from an early age, through Science, Technology, Engineering, and Mathematics outreach within schools, through to the well-established Rolls-Royce Science Prize and sponsoring other academic prizes including, for example, one for the best PhD paper from the over 500 doctorates in its' academic network.

"Vision," as well as being something Rolls-Royce has consistently demonstrated in the wake of Sir Henry, is also the name adopted for its research and development strategy today. The three-phase Vision program underpins its approach to innovation and technology acquisition by creating a clear view of market trends and customer demands, identifying the technologies required for future products, and embedding an inherent resilience to changing market opportunities.

The first chronological horizon, "Vision 5," encompasses "off-the-shelf" technologies that are effectively available today for new product developments expected to be required by customers within the next 5 years. "Vision 10" technologies are those currently in the validation stage with a likely timescale for application in new products in a 5—10-year time span. Beyond that, "Vision 20" targets a more distant horizon, evaluating emerging or as yet unproven technologies to assess their likely effectiveness for new products or markets required in a 20 + year timeframe.

Rolls-Royce also broadly classifies its Research and Technology (R&T) programs as strategic or applied, reflecting Technology Readiness Level (TRL),[2] which undergo regular reviews and pass through formal assessment "gates" as they mature. Our University partners typically support a broad range of TRL from 1 to 4 and often taking concepts through to TRL 4 at which point they can be transferred back to the company for validation, advancing it toward TRL 6 by which time it can be actively considered as a feature or concept for new product design, or for example, a tool to be used in the design process. Universities also act as "horizon scanners" for the much longer range, promising though unproven technologies, pre-TRL 3—which are also scrutinized and analyzed for potential by the company's own in-house Future Technologies Group and its network of senior Engineering Fellows (Fig. 5.1).

5.1.1 Developing the University Technology Centres—From an Ad Hoc to a Strategic Approach

By the mid-1980s, despite being a much smaller company than it is today, Rolls-Royce was pursuing around 80 or more separate university relationships in the United Kingdom alone. These largely came about through

---

2. https://www.nasa.gov/topics/aeronautics/features/trl_508.html.

Robust capability acquisition

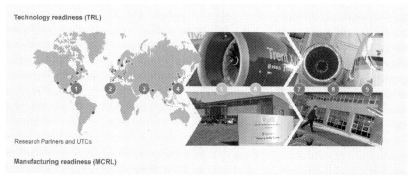

FIGURE 5.1 Pulling capability through from concept, to demonstration, to market.

personal contacts rather than any strategic goals, with the involvement of multiple departments and research teams risking duplication, and few programs demonstrated real critical mass in terms of either human or financial capital.

Facilities and infrastructure supporting the projects was understandably limited, and the lack of focus watered down any arguments for priority investment. Furthermore, for a company with an increasingly global footprint, there was little external research activity outside the United Kingdom.

A strategic decision was taken by the senior Engineering and Technology executives of the day that involved both a cultural as well as organizational transformation in the way the company conducted its research. A coordinated high-level view of research requirements looked to utilize and focus upon proven, world-class research groups, while dismantling competing internal research. As a result, since 1985, Rolls-Royce has been creating and building a network of "centers of excellence" called "UTCs." The development of the UTCs thus illustrates well that commitment to change within an organization involves a shift in culture as much as structure.

UTCs were to be long-term, stably funded arrangements, with the company and the university each agreeing to ensure adequate staffing and infrastructure as well as financial support.

Initially most centers were established in the United Kingdom, where the company is headquartered, but today there are UTCs in Europe, North America and Asia. The first two UTCs were formally established in 1990 at London's Imperial College, focusing on "Vibration," and Oxford University, researching "Solid Mechanics." Whilst the technology and capability may have changed, both of these are still busy tackling scientific challenges in partnership with Rolls-Royce today, more than a quarter of a century on.

Such continuity depends on the quality of individuals, cohesive and committed teams and forging increasingly strong bonds along the way.

Current and former students, staff, and colleagues at the Oxford University Technology Centre 25th anniversary.

The most recent universities signing UTC agreements—both in the United States, the University of Virginia and Virginia Tech—have increased to the global total of Rolls-Royce UTCs to 31 (Fig. 5.2).

One our newer UTCs at The University of Virginia—celebrating the opening of a new lab.

Study topics in the UTCs currently range from noise, performance, aerodynamics, combustion, materials and composites, to hydrodynamics, electrical power systems, thermal management and nuclear engineering. As new technologies emerge and gather momentum, such as opportunities in digital, internet of things or hybrid propulsion, Rolls-Royce will partner with other

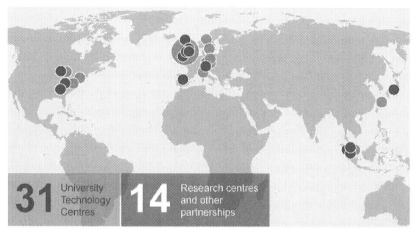

FIGURE 5.2   The current strategic network of UTCs and other research partnerships. *UTC*, University Technology Centre.

specialist university teams as it shapes and molds its future university network to match business needs.

The UTCs produce hundreds of technical papers or other publications each year—either independently or in conjunction with Rolls-Royce engineers—and the company averages over 700 patent applications annually, with up to 10% of these resulting from interactions with the UTC network.

UTC Director Prof. Graeme Burt of Strathclyde University along with author Kate Barnard celebrating the contribution of the university inventors.

Though there is no guarantee that a UTC will continue indefinitely (and agreements are reviewed and renewed at regular intervals), the formula under which they operate does engender trust, collaboration and a longer term approach—and some of the individual UTCs have already been in existence for more than 25 years. There are UTCs that have been closed, for example, because the technical topic no longer required such a strong focus and hence a critical mass within a university or for other mutually agreed reasons. However, Rolls-Royce has a policy of not ending someone's study and will, for example, continue to support a PhD to its conclusion. Relationships with individual academics often continue.

Such is the company's confidence in the effectiveness of the UTC model around 85% of its fundamental research is now conducted within universities rather than in-house.

Longevity and integrated working inevitably strengthens relationships both collectively and individually. Trust grows and, with it, an understanding that risks as well as benefits must be managed as part of such close cooperation.

5.1.2   The Value of the Strategic Approach

UTCs clearly offer a number of improvements over the prior ad hoc approach to university collaboration. Fundamentally, the typically 5-year rolling contracts see an end to piecemeal short-termism, giving those within the UTC time and confidence to think more deeply about the challenges in front of them, and the opportunity to mold and build capability by recruiting and training skilled personnel.

Public cofunding provides a significant benefit which should not be underestimated in enabling critical mass through stronger infrastructures, specialized equipment, longer term planning, the recruitment and development of talent and program continuity—all crucial ingredients for a truly mutually beneficial innovative environment.

These two-way benefits strike an important balance. While the high-quality technology that emerges satisfies the needs of the business and its customers, the leading-edge technical objectives set by Rolls-Royce provide real-world industrial challenges that attract highly-capable academics and students. This, in turn, benefits the universities through quality of research, subject matter for high quality papers, real life examples for teaching, and over time, an upward curve of reputation for research that makes an impact.

The specific research activity often opens a two-way door on the talent pool, as university staff and students can also take on specific short-term tasks within the company, and Rolls-Royce employees can work and complete higher degrees within a UTC.

Over 1000 people, not directly employed by Rolls-Royce, are involved in the Company's UTC network. Among them are more than 500 doctorate students, plus academics, technicians and support staff representing around 40 different nationalities. Access to this large and diverse pool of talent offers a further potential employment benefit as around a quarter of the students emerging with higher degrees and doctorates—having already been stimulated by the exacting technical ambitions of the company—ultimately secure jobs with Rolls-Royce. Others join companies within the Rolls-Royce supply chain or related organizations, and yet more remain within the academic community supporting the company's goals.

5.1.3   The Organization and Working-Model of UTCs

Each UTC is led by a senior academic holding a world-class reputation in their field and is under joint governance of Rolls-Royce and the University. The day-to-day activities of the UTC are supported by a team of academics, research fellows, research assistants, technicians and a number of students undertaking doctorates or similar higher degrees. Each relationship is unique and has guiding principles rather than a strict method of operation; it has to be able to adapt to the different cultures not just in the different countries but also the universities themselves. There is no "one size fits all."

The relationships are managed by having close cooperation between Rolls-Royce and the university at all levels, including senior engineering leaders who shape and manage the overall balance of investment for technical challenges, in collaboration with the university, along with senior business leaders who work with the university executive to agree strategic priorities. Each university partnership has a management and governance structure to support the near and long term activities, driven by a "Coordinator" from Rolls-Royce who ensures frequent contact between the teams (cf. also Chapter 6: Siemens' Centers of Knowledge Interchange—Managing Strategic Partnerships via Intermediaries).

Appropriate funding is made available, from the corresponding business unit, to each UTC covering research activities spanning typically 1–5 years. This allows each center to take a long-term view of how to achieve those program targets agreed with Rolls-Royce. Progress against measured goals is reviewed periodically and, assuming achievement of agreed success factors, funding is renewed for a further extended period of study. Further funding in support of fundamental and collaborative studies may also be competitively won from complementary sources such as the EU or national research institutions such as A-Star in Singapore or, in the United Kingdom, bodies such as Innovate UK and the Engineering and Physical Sciences Research Council (EPSRC).

As the Rolls-Royce collaboration model has matured, it has often been cited as a positive template for others to follow, and many features of it have been acknowledged in independent reviews of best-practice collaboration between universities and industry.[3] However to avoid complacency it requires external benchmarking at regular intervals.

5.2   RELATIONSHIPS MATTER

We will in the following section take a more in-depth look at the relational factor in the UTCs, with a particular focus on seven different ways in which Rolls Royce supports strong relationships[4]:

1. Share your knowledge and goals
2. Extend trust
3. Value diversity
4. Share your network
5. Celebrate wins—big and small
6. Continuously evaluate the health of your relationship
7. Have dedicated people

5.2.1   Share Your Knowledge and Goals

Once an exhaustive selection process has settled upon those universities best equipped to handle research programs, which Rolls-Royce has processes for assessing research excellence of potential partners, not covered here, but experience of other companies is covered elsewhere in this book. The company accepts that it must share its strategic goals and welcome deeper levels of knowledge sharing in order to not just engage but excite academic teams in a quest for technologies that will result in real commercial and societal impact.

---

3. Examples include: "Ingenious Britain: Making the UK the leading high tech exporter in Europe" A report by James Dyson for the Conservative Party, March 2010, p. 38 Models for new research centres of excellence; "The Wilson Review of Business–University Collaboration," Feb 2012, Sir Tim Wilson, commissioned in response to the UK Government's White Paper White Paper: Putting Students at the heart of higher education, p 52; "The Lambert Review of Business–University Collaboration," Dec 2003, pp. 38–39.
4. Fostering strong and trusting relationships was one of the key recommendations from 2015's *The Dowling Review of Business-University Research Collaborations* (http://www.raeng.org.uk/policy/dowling-review/the-dowling-review-of-business-university-research). Author of the report, as President of the Royal Academy of Engineering, is Professor Dame Ann Dowling. Much decorated, and formerly Head of the Department of Engineering at Cambridge University, Professor Dowling has first-hand knowledge of the UTC concept as lead academic and Director for many years of Cambridge's University Gas Turbine Partnership with Rolls-Royce. Critically the report concluded that people are central to successful collaborations, echoing many of the specific benefits experienced by Rolls-Royce and its academic partners during the past quarter of a century.

Rolls-Royce has also come to understand that this sharing of knowledge and goals, and the ensuing collaborative research, has become closely linked to a willingness by both organizations (i.e., the company and the university) to invest in research infrastructure that supports truly collaborative working. This may include dedicated research facilities that allow the researchers to work together or investing in tools and methods that support collaboration such as video conferencing or web-portals, or simply providing opportunities for people to get together.

At Oxford, for example, the Osney Thermofluids Laboratory is one of the most capable of its type in the world. It has proved to be the scene of numerous breakthroughs in aeropropulsion and power generation systems technology and continues to conduct research ranging from turbine cooling to hypersonic flow. Similarly, the Whittle Laboratory at Cambridge—a world-leading center for research in fluid dynamics and thermodynamics, derives a sizeable proportion of its project work from the Rolls-Royce partnership with the Engineering department.

Two of the most recent investments, announced in 2015–16 at the universities of Nottingham and Loughborough, attracted coinvestment funding from both industry and the UK government's national and regional agencies. A leading-edge facility, costing £5.6 million and including highly capable test rigs, is to be housed at Nottingham University to support next generation aero gas turbines and transmission system development. At Loughborough, the new National Centre for Combustion and Aerothermal Technology (NCCAT) is being established also with support from Rolls-Royce and the Government. The confidence gained through the existing UTC at Loughborough has resulted in Rolls-Royce being the lead industry partner. The center will be a training ground for future engineers in this critical skill area as well as accelerating new combustion technologies into being, aligned with national strategies.

Construction begins; ground-breaking ceremony for the Loughborough-based hub for aerospace engineering and technology.

5.2.2   Extend Trust

We don't always get to choose with whom we're collaborating. Sometimes it's with people we don't know, or people of whom we're unsure. Give everyone the benefit of the doubt and extend your trust first, and assume positive intent. It's amazing how the simple gesture of extending your trust can break down barriers and foster life-long relationships. Remember we don't know the challenges everybody else has got going on in the background.

Oxford University is home to one of the very first Rolls-Royce UTCs which is still thriving more than a quarter of a century later. Trust and confidence are things that underpin all organizational and individual relationships between Rolls-Royce and its UTC academics. We trust them to deliver excellent results, and they trust Rolls-Royce to engage the academics and students on significant research challenges that will result in true impact to the outside world.

Peter Ireland, who is Donald Schultz Professor of Turbomachinery at Oxford's Department of Engineering Science, points to trust as a key success factor in this lasting relationship. This trust is expressed through the confidence UTCs are given by Rolls-Royce to deliver results without a backup plan:

"Very early on in our relationship," recalls Prof. Ireland, "a Rolls-Royce director of technology told me 'there is no Plan B', which meant our success came only after a rigorous selection process and that, from now on, both parties must take the relationship very seriously indeed. We knew then, and still know today, that under-performing is simply not an option."

"By the same token, the company has made a strong commitment to our development," assures Prof. Ireland. "It has supported multimillion-pound funding in our laboratory; it's down to us to consistently prove our track record and deliver research of significant economic impact." Another sign of trust from Rolls-Royce is that Oxford is fully committed to this partnership. Oxford was recently adjudged by the UK's joint higher education councils as the very best of 62 national universities subjected to a detailed technical assessment under the Research Excellence Framework, with four of its 10 impact case studies being associated with Rolls-Royce.

Rolls-Royce avoids duplicating its research, commits fully to its selected Universities, and relies on those partnerships. This trust is rewarded by the academics and their universities in the levels they go to, in support of the Company, sometimes even at the expense of delaying publication to maintain competitive advantage.

The benefit of extending trust first is that it creates a bedrock for you to build knowledge and continuity of staff, establishing long-term relationships.

5.2.3   Value Diversity

Wherever they are in the world, the top universities and research establishments will deliver a deep talent pool of often world-leading academics and the very best research students. But disconnects can take a number of forms and can be potential barriers to effective collaboration. Language can be a barrier, of course, as can failure to understand and abide by local customs, though taking the trouble to learn these should be a prerequisite for a meaningful relationship. Established systems, procedures, and organizational structures are not always so easily overcome. So, be prepared to adapt your approach but do not let go of your fundamental principles. When you value diverse input, meaningful partnerships blossom; these are bolstered further by strong individual relationships that have helped mold resourceful research teams.

The global network of UTCs demonstrates that while location may well be a factor, geography is no barrier to collaboration in itself as long as both partners accept and embrace the different cultures, both between corporate and university and even between continents. Success comes from a team of different, but complimentary thinkers, each contributing their individual experiences and capabilities.

One example is the transatlantic trilateral bond that has been created between Virginia Tech in the United States, Rolls-Royce and Nottingham University in the United Kingdom.

This arrangement allows an additional opportunity to support international studentships through the US-based National Science Foundation. The Industry/University International Research Experience for Students (IRES) program, which began in 2014, enables students to undertake research projects in partnership with Rolls-Royce at Nottingham University and encourages an exchange of knowledge between trusted partners while providing an excellent international learning experience for the students.

Dr. Jack Lesko, Associate Dean of Research and Graduate Studies for the College of Engineering at Virginia Tech, looks back at the challenges faced in setting up this arrangement: "Negotiating the research agreement was difficult at times as we had to align respective motivations, perspectives, and value propositions, but what made the difference, and brought the agreement to fruition, has been everyone's strong commitment — people being prepared to work outside their normal work scope and dig into the detail. That's proved vital."

Dr. Lesko continues: "One particularly crucial factor was how the students' focus has helped to strengthen the IRES scheme. They spend three weeks back in the US planning, scoping and refining their research project, then seven weeks at the University of Nottingham undertaking the research before coming back to write up their project. We've had several very successful outcomes and expect multiple papers to result from 2016's IRES projects."

Cultural differences could have proved problematic, but the "human approach" and strength of the growing relationships—not to mention the commitment of the students undertaking the projects—has overcome these potential hurdles. One research task undertaken by a pair of Virginia Tech students that was proven to provide a significant quantifiable business benefit to Rolls-Royce is described *in the case study below*

Case Study—Global project success

Strong collaborative ties between Nottingham University, in the UK and Virginia Tech in the United States have resulted in research projects undertaken by students for industry "clients" under the IRES (Industry/University International Research Experience for Students) scheme.

One such project involved Virginia Tech students Vy Nguyen and Ryan Hehir. Operating under the guidance of academics including Professor Hervé Morvan, Director of the Institute of Aerospace Technology and academic lead for the Gas Turbine Transmission Systems UTC at Nottingham, Vy and Ryan set about investigating the effectiveness of a particular Rolls-Royce engine component.

They explored design features such as shape and dimensions and analyzed video simulations which concluded the current hardware would benefit from a redesign or alternative material. The evidence of this research was then offered for consideration by Rolls-Royce and its supply chain.

The stimulation of this project work and the inspiration drawn from realizing they have made a difference in the real world of engineering prompted a second major outcome—as both Vy and Ryan have since reconsidered their futures and decided to move onto a higher level of academic achievement.

5.2.4   Share Your Network

Our University relationships are not about "outsourcing" advanced research; rather they're about helping each party fulfill their potential for mutual benefit.

Dr. Rune Garen, R&T Director for Rolls-Royce Marine, draws motivation from regular contact with his academic counterparts. "Innovation is actually about interaction and the UTC arena gives me an opportunity to expand and take advantage of my academic network," he says. "It means I can pick up the phone or visit the UTC and talk to people who can provide me with important information or data … they are my extended team that I can tap into for inspiration and insight."

However sharing information and technical expertise within a single UTC environment is one thing, but bridging several individual networks is a further step in brokering knowledge across organizational boundaries and broadening the scope for innovation.

Rolls-Royce has done this, for example, with its materials development program, assembling a strong academic network initially involving three leading university departments, and established in 2009, cofunded by Rolls-Royce, the universities, and the UK EPSRC.

Each university involved has a well-earned research reputation, in its own right, but is happy to work collectively in tackling the broader research challenges in the materials field. Working with these and other materials specialists, Rolls-Royce is able to win not just funding but also leverage a huge vault of ingenuity within the academic research base. And this extended network—courtesy of its long-term, well-funded approach—was recognized for its contribution to the aerospace industry and its supply chain, by winning the Transportation category in *The Engineer* magazine's 2016 "Collaborate to Innovate" awards.[5]

Once you have established a trusted network, you can develop technology collaborations on an even grander scale, where multiyear, multilateral research programs are launched at the regional or even global level. One such program, the European NEWAC,[6] project investigating novel aeroengine concepts witnessed Rolls-Royce working in partnership with direct competitors on fundamental technologies, while technology subgroups often involved several of its UTCs. By listening, helping, and working together across multiple teams the NEWAC project was a success. Below is a further case study looking at how multiple UTCs contributed to the development of a key technology for Rolls-Royce.

> **Case Study—Six UTCs in concert for Trent fan blade**
>
> *Bridging boundaries is an important way of maximizing shared expertise and collective knowledge of novel technologies and latest methods. The development of the fan blade for the Trent 900 and subsequent variants benefited from key contributions by at least six separate Rolls-Royce UTCs.*
>
> *The Materials UTC at Birmingham University investigated fracture mechanics, while the Solid Mechanics UTC at Oxford studied the effects of foreign object damage (such as bird strike) on this ultralarge fan blade. Imperial College tackled complementary blade integrity research, working on vibration issues, aeroelasticity, and unsteady flow modeling.*
>
> *Meanwhile, the Whittle Laboratory at Cambridge University validated a range of fan flow models that were based on complex 3D flow calculations, enabling the design of a strong yet efficient blade design. The Noise UTC at Southampton studied the flow effects of fan noise and introduced an acoustic liner to eliminate the fan tones that generate "buzz-saw" noise, while Nottingham's Manufacturing UTC delivered tooling concepts for a more efficient process of blade production.*

Being at the forefront of innovation offers the UTC teams—and the individuals working within them—constant opportunities to taste some of the world's most exciting engineering challenges.

Two senior academics involved in Rolls-Royce UTCs, Dr. Jack Lesko and Prof. Hervé Morvan, both relish their collaborative roles and feel very much part of the Rolls-Royce family.

"I like the human approach Rolls-Royce takes with us. They recognise that taking the time, and doing things together so we get to know each other better, will pay dividends and bring real long-term value to the relationship," believes Jack.

5. *The Engineer Magazine, Collaborate to Innovate Awards 2016, Transport Category*, https://www.theengineer.co.uk/collaborate-to-innovate-winners-annnounced/.
6. NEWAC (new aeroengine core concepts), an Integrated Project co-funded by the European Commission within the Sixth Framework Programme.

Hervé Morvan, Director of the Institute for Aerospace Technology, APVC Innovation, Business Engagement & Impact, and Professor of Applied Fluid Mechanics, Faculty of Engineering, feels fully integrated into the UTC team: "When I push back it is understood why and our opinions are respected. When a new engine component or architecture is designed, Rolls-Royce engineers often visit Nottingham for our views. Like any relationship, it's not without the odd disagreement, but I feel it's getting stronger all the time."

By listening, understanding, and helping each other, it is possible to build partnerships that would not otherwise be possible. Successful partnerships come about because of the tacit unwritten rules, it isn't just a checklist of tasks, and a relationship has to be built.

Nicole Key is Professor of Mechanical Engineering at Purdue University in Indianapolis and tells how she became a part of the UTC network:

"I was doing research outside the UTC framework for about nine years and, as that programme grew, Rolls-Royce recognised I could be an important part of the family," explains Nicole. "I was invited to several UTC Directors' meetings and was encouraged to interact with other universities in the network. I learned a lot about the company's technology development and, as my understanding grew, I think that was instrumental in getting to the next level."

High Speed Compressors Lab with Professor Nicole Key and Students—Purdue University.

However, you can read and follow all the UTC guidelines and processes yet still be unsuccessful: Sometimes you have to "feel" it. This is an incredibly important aspect when Rolls-Royce brings a new UTC on board. Professor Key earlier described the UTCs as a "family," and to be part of that means getting on with all the "relatives." As leaders of the university network, the authors of this chapter personally introduced Nicole to a few pertinent UTCs that she could exchange experience with. As one of our senior engineers used to say, "this is a contact sport"—and for Nicole the Loughborough UTC was the perfect starting point.

The Loughborough UTC has grown over 25 years, starting in a similar place to Nicole's compressors lab and transitioned from "start-up" (researcher and a few students plus rigs) to a multimillion-pound annual turnover enterprise with around 50 people and now attracting external funding from key stakeholders to build national facilities.

Prof. Jon Carrotte has been part of the Loughborough UTC since its inception and is now its director and holder of a Royal Academy of Engineering Professorial Chair. He was able to offer advice to Nicole from his experience of the journey of learning when and how to adapt roles and processes to ensure growth whilst maintaining leading edge research, and in return gain fresh ideas and different perspectives from Nicole.

The ethos of human capital is recognized at all levels in Rolls-Royce. Chief Executive Officer Warren East explains the key to success is in taking it seriously, "there is a subtle clarity about what goes on at Rolls-Royce." The company must put enough people into making the university thing happen. "You put 10 people in and you get 100 people's worth of activity out. The danger where perhaps people fail is that they think they are going to get a hundred people out for putting two people in."[7]

By sharing the knowledge within the UTC network, keeping an open mind, working with people who are openly curious and generous, you are creating the potential to rise above the individual technical projects to address wider company, and even societal, challenges.

5.2.5 Celebrate Wins—Big and Small

Teamwork is a vital constituent of any cohesive partnership but so is recognizing specific contributions and behaviors within the team. Rolls-Royce has a number of ways of rewarding individuals within a UTC environment and is always open to new ideas and suggestions.

The company includes its worldwide academic partners in its Patents Award scheme, which additionally assures eligibility in the company's annual flagship Sir Henry Royce Awards designed to recognize the very best innovation and engineering excellence.

An annual prize for the best Doctorate students is competed for by those working on a project supported by Rolls-Royce through its global UTC network. Similarly many of the sponsored research groups compete for recognition within their own organizations or for national and international recognition. This also provides an additional check that you are not being complacent—benchmarking you and your teams against others.

---

7. *Ingenia—"Taking engineering to industry," Michael Kenward, issue 69, December 2016,* http://www.ingenia.org.uk/Ingenia/Articles/1062.

The Loughborough—Rolls-Royce team, author Mark Jefferies far left; proud recipients of a Loughborough University Enterprise Award.

Rolls-Royce facilitates celebrating success and sharing knowledge across organizational or disciplinary boundaries through regular seminars and conferences. The annual UTC Directors' Seminar includes the leaders of all UTCs, other leading academics, senior Rolls-Royce managers, funding stakeholders, and government agencies. Similar events are staged annually in Germany by the engineering community at Rolls-Royce Deutschland, for example, involving stakeholders focused on that region. The events are set up to include a sharing of the Rolls-Royce strategy and the direction of future research, some activities to aid collaboration and presentations on particular highlights from the Company and the UTCs, sharing best practice and celebrating success.

Guests gathered at the annual UTC Directors' Seminar, bringing together the leaders of our research network from around the world.

There are also themed forums: one on materials, held biennially, involves over 100 PhD students, research associates, and academic staff from the UTCs linked by a Materials Partnership, and the Rolls-Royce Composites, Aerothermal, and Mechanical UTCs are among those staging similar events each year.

5.2.6 Continuously Evaluate the Health of Your Relationship

A study in 2012—*A Review of Business–University Collaboration* by Prof. Tim Wilson[8]—stressed the importance of aligning key elements of any such collaboration, from the respective missions and visions to timescales, capacities, and capabilities. Inadequate funding, burdensome bureaucracy, a mismatch of objectives, and an inability to agree intellectual property (IP) issues were all cited as reasons why business–university collaborations sometimes fail to get beyond initial contact.

The Rolls-Royce model has been successful in part because the failure mechanisms of others have been understood. Metrics and success measures are taken into account during the earliest stages of collaboration and are used to continually assess the health and vitality of the network.

All organizations need to think about what is important to them and write them down. Sounds obvious really, but it's surprisingly difficult to do while ensuring everyone is aligned, especially if you are working with partners and collaborators spread around the globe and in different types of organization to your own.

Make it part of the routine management that these items are discussed with each of your partners and be open to feedback on how the other party sees your own organization. Use it as part of your operating model, but remember to revisit it periodically such that you continuously refine and evolve how you work. By involving a range of people in an assessment, all of whom are positively committed to making the relationship better and open to two-way dialog, both sides can find ways of continually improving the collaboration. Encourage people to be curious about what can be done, and remain open to new ideas and exploring what is important to others.

Committing to a long-term partnership is not without risk, so be sure to consider and understand these risks and build them into your operating

---

8. *The Wilson Review of Business–University Collaboration, Feb 2012, Sir Tim Wilson, commissioned in response to the UK Government's White Paper White Paper: Putting Students at the heart of higher education: A Review of Business–University Collaboration*, https://www.gov.uk/government/publications/business-university-collaboration-the-wilson-review.

model. Much is written on the positive aspects of collaboration, but it's also important to keep an eye on what can go wrong and have a process in place to deal with it before it becomes a major issue.

With the inherent uncertainty of specific outcomes and likely success factors from the outset of research programs, it is especially important to monitor and measure project inputs, outcomes, and impact as they progress. The metrics need to be quantitative and qualitative, and both retrospective and prospective.

Rolls-Royce was acutely aware of this from the earliest days of its UTCs and has in the succeeding quarter of a century developed a "scorecard" spotlighting specific measures grouped into four main categories—strategy, leadership, resources, and output. Each is assessed via a number of criteria and methods that are agreed as critical to our particular business. The number of patents, recruitment levels, the sources, level and leverage factor of funding, extra skill levels achieved through training, and specific outcomes achieved by centers are all objective measures that are applied, while subjective appraisals are made through such means as peer assessments and annual reviews.

Universities also have public measures on their performance, which have typically been publications, citations, and performance league tables but, in the United Kingdom at least, are now broadening to include the impact of that research on the economy. Whilst not perfectly aligned, with careful management a balance can be struck, evidenced, for example, by many of the collaborative papers written going on to win international recognition—such as ASME's International Gas Turbine Institute best paper awards. Benefit can also often be seen in the local region, with strong research collaborations going on to have impact beyond the initial partnership.

Case Study—Dresden UTC's broader economic benefits

Lighter aircraft translate to reduced fuel consumption, lower costs, and better environmental performance, so when Rolls-Royce decided to establish a Lightweight Structures and Materials UTC it turned to Germany's TU Dresden, with which it had already collaborated for more than a decade.

Four departments within the university—Turbomachinery and Flight Propulsion, Thermal Power Machinery and Plants, Materials Engineering, and Machine Elements—plus Dresden's Institute of Lightweight Structures and Polymer Technology are involved in the research, bringing not just academic expertise but a wealth of development, production, analysis, and testing capabilities and facilities. In such an environment, working cohesively with Rolls-Royce research, engineering and production staff has necessitated strong interrelationships—and yielded excellent results.

(Continued)

(Continued)

Inaugurated in 2006, the Dresden UTC has also proved a great economic engine for the Saxony region as well as garnering key innovations for Rolls-Royce, many of which were then utilized by one or other of four spin-off companies created to manage the manufacture of resulting hardware.

The UTC has worked on 150 joint research projects to date, involving up to 100 scientists and technicians. Over 60 TU Dresden graduates and postgraduates have been taken on directly by Rolls-Royce, its supply chain or research partners and, together with the spin-off start-ups, 80 new jobs have been created. TU Dresden also collaborates with researchers and scientists at Imperial College and the universities of Oxford and Bristol in the United Kingdom, which has so far opened the door for 150 exchange students to study and conduct research at these partner institutions.

Dr. James Lander is an aerospace graduate who now works as a Composites Manufacturing Engineer at Rolls-Royce. He has a dual perspective having also previously spent 3 years in Bristol University's Rolls-Royce Composites UTC. In both posts, he's also liaised closely with the Bristol-based National Composites Centre.

He believes that sometimes the sharp focus of targeted academic research—together with IP concerns of wanting to maintain competitive advantage and therefore prevent publishing—can blinker university teams to the genuine commercial opportunities presented by licensing core technologies or new manufacturing methods to industries entirely outside Rolls-Royce's core business areas.

The lesson in all this is to think about what is important to you and put metrics in place to enable mutual success. Remember that this success can come in many forms, and so include both quantitative and qualitative metrics, take into account the timescale of your business, and don't forget to acknowledge those things or people that lay the groundwork for the future.

5.2.7 Have Dedicated People

In practice, and in addition to the pure specialists, each relationship requires a number of key individuals—sometimes called "boundary spanners"—that are not (just) technical experts in their field but are also able to navigate the political, strategic, and wider aspects of the business. This can be a rare combination and sometimes not recognized by traditional measures of performance in an organization, so buy-in from senior leadership is essential.

These people should, of course, also have an eye to the future, how far depends on the timescales or technology cycle of your business, but typically when working with universities this would be of the order of 5 years especially if your model is to engage doctoral students. Even if not particularly senior, these boundary spanners should be good communicators and comfortable dealing with students, academics, industry peers, and senior management, both of their own and of partner organizations.

As the network grows, in addition to the people focusing on each relationship, some overall coordination is required to ensure each one fits with the broader and longer term aspirations of the company (beyond that of those focusing on each university). This need not be a large group of people but does need to be individuals who are connected to the strategic direction of the company and are able to set overall policy and governance "groundrules."

Rolls-Royce colleague Professor Dave Rugg agrees: "Those interfacing with the university have to think very carefully about defining questions that are both clear and tractable, thereby giving the academics a broad scope for technical creativity and freedom."

They should also, ideally, be able to influence what is often known as the "innovation landscape"—in other words be connected to the outside world via those agencies and organizations that are important to the company such as Government, research funders, education and training organizations, professional bodies, and, of course, their own and University executive management. All of these represent a form of stakeholder management.

The same is true for a small proportion of the university leadership, reflected by Prof. Hervé Morvan of Nottingham University suggesting that working in the sometimes pressured environment of a UTC requires "a certain type of academic − one who is a team player and capable of compromise, which is not always the case."

A paper from MIT Sloan management review in 2010 also pinpointed the need to choose effective and adaptable leaders, who demonstrate good communication skills and the vision to look beyond their own jobs, and who instinctively share acquired knowledge across their appropriate networks:

"They help translate academic results into corporate impact by disseminating research findings beyond just the R&T community and across a broader audience inside the company including those managing production and manufacturing issues. Just as importantly, information about how the technology is being applied needs to flow back to the university researchers in order to ensure the research remains aligned with the company's needs."[9]

---

9. *MIT Sloan Review, October 2010, Best Practices for Industry−University Collaboration, June 2010, Julio A. Pertuze, Edward S. Calder, Edward M. Greitzer, and William A. Lucas,* http://sloanreview.mit.edu/article/best-practices-for-industry-university-collaboration/.

Boundary spanners need to be carefully selected individuals who become the cornerstone of your relationships. Select people with the characteristics you wish to promote in the team.

5.3 CONCLUSION

This chapter considered the vital nature of people and relationships in building sustainable collaborative research partnerships and explained some of the factors that are important in forging strong teams and lasting bonds.

By exploring the views of those involved—from both industry and the academic community—it has examined the need for a cultural shift toward collaborative working, longevity, and the acceptance of reward over risk to bring about the trust and confidence essential for effective partnerships with true two-way benefits.

Even set against the insistent modern world, there's evidence that taking time to get to know each other pays distinct dividends. Embracing diversity and exchanging ideas and staff help to build the team ethos, and it's always worthwhile recognizing individual contributions and rewarding the quality of individuals.

- **Share your knowledge and goals**. Work with partners who share your ambition, and look for ways that the partnership might result in success for everyone—not just you.
- **Extend trust**. Once you have decided who you are going to work with, invest time and resource into those people and let them know you rely on them. Don't forget that it works both ways—you have to earn trust too.
- **Value diversity.** Seek out and value different ideas, welcome the perspectives of others especially where you are working across organizations, cultures, or borders.
- **Share your network**. As you build a network of connections, help those in it to find new opportunities; expect that they do the same for you.
- **Celebrate wins—big and small.** Recognize the successes of your colleagues, reinforce the behaviors and achievements that are important to your organization(s), be it individual, team, or at organizational level.
- **Continuously evaluate the health of your relationship**. Use of a mixture of metrics and views from a variety of people. Determine what is important to your organizations and ask questions that remind people of what you consider to be the important factors.
- **Have dedicated people.** You of course need technically strong people, but you also need people who are highly skilled in crossing the boundaries between organizations and cultures, and who are aware of the broader context of the research. Remember these can be different skill sets; don't assume everyone can do everything, pay attention to the mix in your teams.

These factors, together with establishing long-term arrangements and introducing technical challenges with care and at the right pace, build a solid foundation on which innovation and creativity can grow and thrive.

ACKNOWLEDGMENTS

The authors are grateful for the contribution from their colleagues, including Professor Nicole Key, Professor Peter Ireland, Professor Dave Rugg, Dr. Jack Lesko, Dr. James Lander, Dr. Rune Garen, Professor Hervé Morvan, Professor Jon Carrotte, and Mr. Gary Atkins.

Chapter 6

Siemens' Centers of Knowledge Interchange: Managing Strategic Partnerships via Intermediaries

Natacha Eckert[1], Lars Frølund[2,3] and Max F. Riedel[1]
[1]*Siemens AG, Munich, Germany,* [2]*Aarhus University, Aarhus, Denmark,* [3]*Massachusetts Institute of Technology, Cambridge, MA, United States*

Siemens Facts & Figures (Fiscal Year 2017)

Company name:	Siemens AG
Headquarters in:	Berlin & Munich, Germany
Annual revenue:	EUR 83.0 billion
Number of (R&D) employees:	372,000 (37,800)
R&D budget:	EUR 5.2 billion
Average number of University R&D collaborations p.a.:	>1000
Industry branches:	Power generation and management, industry and building automation, mobility, healthcare
Product examples:	Gas turbines, wind turbines, power plants, energy transmission equipment, automation sensors & controllers, drives, PLM software, building management systems, trains, traffic control systems, medical imaging devices, lab diagnostics automation

---

Bringing two large organizations, such as a big industrial company and a top university, closer together in a strategic way is challenging. There usually are many individual ties between the two and even more stakeholders, e.g., cooperating researchers, company employees who still have strong ties to their alma mater, or the HR department and the universities' career service. And there are at least as many expectations toward the partnership as

Strategic Industry-University Partnerships. DOI: https://doi.org/10.1016/B978-0-12-810989-2.00006-0

there are stakeholders. Building a strong partnership on an organizational level, which is more than sum of the individual ties, requires a community of intermediaries who manage all those different expectations and understandings of university collaboration. This chapter focuses on the success factor "Dedicated people, processes and organization," i.e., on how to create an organization of dedicated people to foster partnerships.

The chapter is structured in the following way: we begin by introducing Siemens AG and give some facts about university collaboration and R&D at Siemens. We then move on to introducing the Centers of Knowledge Interchange (CKI) program, Siemens' strategic program for university collaboration with a focus on the reasons for developing a strategic program, the selection criteria for becoming a part of the CKI program, and the governance and management of the program. In the following section, using real-life examples, we describe the value of the bridge builders in the CKI program. In the fourth section, we connect the value of the bridge builders to three key skill areas. Finally, we conclude and give recommendations.

6.1 SIEMENS AG—A BRIEF INTRODUCTION

Siemens was founded in 1847 by Werner von Siemens as a start-up for communication technology and is today Europe's largest industrial conglomerate. It is one of the world's largest producers of energy-efficient, resource-saving technologies and a leading supplier of systems for power generation and transmission as well as medical diagnosis. In infrastructure and industry solutions, the company plays a pioneering role. As of September 30, 2017, Siemens had around 372,000 employees in more than 200 countries. In the fiscal year 2017, they generated revenues of €83.0 billion. Siemens R&D expenditure in the fiscal year 2017 was €5.2 billion (6%), the company had 37,800 R&D employees, and held approximately 63,000 granted patents worldwide.

Siemens' product and solutions portfolio is very broad; it is structured in 10 divisions: Power and Gas, Wind Power and Renewables, Power Generation Services, Energy Management, Building Technologies, Mobility, Digital Factory, Process Industries and Drives, Healthcare, and Financial Services. It is also constantly changing as new companies are bought and merged while other businesses are carved out. Synergies between its more than 70 Business Units, for example, in technology or customer base, vary.

Corporate Technology is the central crossdivisional research unit with 7800 employees, comprising 5300 software developers and 1600 researchers. It acts as a service provider for Business Units, a technology and process consultant, and a governance unit. About one-half of the Siemens' contract research volume for universities is commissioned by Corporate Technology and about half of the public funding money that Siemens receives is acquired by Corporate Technology.

6.2   THE STRATEGIC PROGRAM—CENTERS OF KNOWLEDGE INTERCHANGE

In 2001, Siemens launched its strategic program for university collaboration called CKI. This was a major shift in Siemens' way of collaborating with universities. Before 2001, university research collaborations were predominantly established by individual Siemens engineers, focusing on specific aspects of their research needs. This also meant that research partners were predominantly chosen based on personal experience, network, and vicinity, often a very important factor besides academic excellence. For example, a university research partner might be chosen because the Siemens project leader completed his PhD thesis there or was hosted by the professor as a guest lecturer. This personal contact and familiarity made initiating, steering and solving problems within the collaboration effective. All in all, the rationale for university partner selection was about familiarity, and the collaboration partner was an individual researcher or lab leader and not the university as a whole.

Another essential feature of Siemens' university relations before 2001 was that collaborations were often an "extended work bench," which meant that a project often had a quite narrow scope in order to help solve a concrete problem in a current research agenda for which the Siemens engineer either did not have the capacity or the competence. These collaborations usually had small volume and a short time-scale in order to be flexible.

The challenge of this ad hoc and piece-meal approach was that Siemens collaborated with a large number of universities with no synergy and that each collaboration contract had to be negotiated individually, which put a high workload on legal departments and almost always lead to delays in the project start. These challenges of the ad hoc approach are also recognized in the research (see Perkmann and Salter, 2012).

It was therefore evident that Siemens could benefit from a strategic approach to university collaboration. In 2000, a team close to the senior management began to outline a strategic program that should create synergies between research projects and move collaborations from "Extended Workbench" to "Grand Challenge". The use of Siemens-wide master research agreements (MRAs) should create transparency on collaboration activities with universities, enhance Siemens' negotiation position, and enable projects to start faster.

The result was the CKI program with three goals:

- *Increase university research collaborations in general.* In times of shortening innovation cycles and increasing distribution of competences, it is inevitable to cooperate. Universities are powerhouses of research and also provide an innovation ecosystem, which is essential to tap.
- *Concentrate Siemens research collaborations at the CKI universities.* This will reduce effort for contract negotiations and create good

conditions in our MRAs and have both the research network and the management's attention to launch large, long-term projects with strategic impact for the company.

- *Align research, talent acquisition, and employer branding activities* at these universities to become more effective and efficient in promoting Siemens as the employer of choice.

The CKI program consists of two core elements: (1) a set of strategic partner universities—the so-called CKI Universities and (2) a central university relations unit (UR unit) at Siemens Corporate Technology with reference to the Chief Technology Officer (CTO). The UR unit is part of a global community of Siemens-internal and -external intermediaries who do not conduct research but act as bridge builders between Siemens and the universities, similar to key account managers for the most important customers and suppliers (Fig. 6.1).

To understand the core elements of the CKI program, we describe below the selection criteria for the CKI Universities and the governance of the

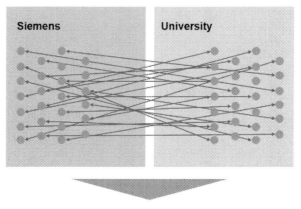

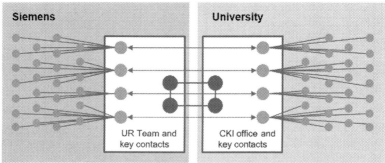

FIGURE 6.1 Siemens–university relation before and after introduction of the CKI program. The four central interconnected dots represent the team of bridge builders in the UR unit that we later will describe in detail. *CKI*, Centers of Knowledge Interchange; *UR*, university relations.

program. We then describe in detail the unique organization of dedicated people that is an important success factor for the CKI program.

6.2.1   Selection of the CKI Universities

CKI Universities are the tier-one strategic partners of Siemens for both research collaboration and talent acquisition. Currently there are eight CKI Universities worldwide: four of them in Germany (RWTH Aachen, Friedrich-Alexander-University Erlangen-Nürnberg, Technical University of Berlin, and Technical University of Munich), two in the USA (Georgia Tech, UC Berkeley), and one each in Austria (Technical University of Graz) and China (Tsinghua University) (Fig. 6.2).

There are several criteria a university has to fulfill to become a CKI University (see Box 6.1). Most important is an existing good relationship based on a strong history of joint research as well as a pipeline of planned projects with at least two Siemens Divisions.

A university can be suggested by a Siemens board member, a Division CEO or CTO, or by the head of Corporate HR Talent Sourcing. Note that it is on purpose, that some of the nomination criteria to become a CKI University are formulated in a soft manner. In the end, the overall picture counts and careful alignment among all internal stakeholders are most important.

When a university is nominated as a CKI University, a contract with the university is signed in which the partnership is confirmed, responsibilities of both Siemens and the university are defined, and financing by Siemens is regulated. Note that this contract for a CKI University does not cover any terms for contract research. This is regulated in a separate Master Research Agreement.

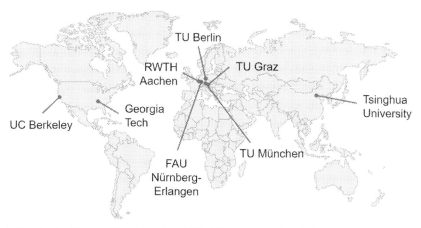

FIGURE 6.2   Siemens CKI Universities 2017. *CKI*, Centers of Knowledge Interchange.

BOX 6.1 CKI University selection criteria.

Research quality and frame conditions
- Internationally leading quality of Siemens-relevant research and education, international top ranking in relevant disciplines
- Quality of infrastructure and labs (especially in identified R&D focus topics)
- Favorable R&D framework conditions (intellectual property rights, costs)
- Broad access to public funding opportunities
- Transparency on ongoing and planned R&D and HR activities over at least 5 years (usually previous 3 years and upcoming 2−3 years)

Previous relation with Siemens and strategic fit
- Good relationship and completed joint projects (timeframes, budgets, results)
- A minimum budget spent for contract research by Siemens in the previous 3 years
- A minimum amount of publicly funded projects in cooperation with the university in the previous 3 years
- Proximity to Siemens location; proximity to customers/markets
- Fit in existing network of universities considering growth potential, global/political aspects, and strategic focus of the company
- Engagement of at least two major Siemens stakeholders (e.g., Divisions, Corporate Technology)

Talent acquisition
- Relevant number of new hires in last 3 years or "anticipated" number of hires for new strategic partnership

---

6.2.2   Governance and Management of the CKI Program

The CKI program is managed by a central UR unit, which is a part of Siemens Corporate Technology and has a direct reporting line to the CTO. The team-members of the UR unit are all key account managers (so-called UR Managers R&D, which we will describe later in detail) for at least one university and take care of several cross-university activities, like contract-support, open innovation activities, collaboration partner consulting, coordination of publicly funded projects, or maintaining the university relations database. The majority of the team (currently 10 members) is located in Germany with some additional members in the United States, United Kingdom, and China. The UR unit concentrates on research-related activities and is in close alignment with the "Talent Sourcing" and "Employer Branding" units at corporate Human Resources and the regional Human Resources teams. The UR unit is led by the head of university relations.

The program has two governance pillars:

- A **"Global University Relations Steering Committee,"** which meets twice per year. This is the main tool for setting the overall directions for the CKI program. The Global UR Steering Committee reviews the overall results of the CKI program and decides about Siemens-wide UR related initiatives. Examples of such initiatives are the introduction of a Siemens-wide database for university collaboration, a fund for cofinancing research with selected CKI universities, or a global student talent pool. Another important task of the Global UR Steering Committee is to review the Siemens university partner landscape and (de)nominate CKI universities. In preparation of such a decision, the past and future activities between a university and Siemens are first analyzed by the UR unit. The suggestion to nominate a university for the CKI program is aligned with Divisions who have significant research activities with the university and with the local and corporate HR departments. The UR unit and especially its head play an important role in mediating internally any possible conflicts during this process. We will have a closer look at this important process in the next section.

- A "**CKI Steering Committee**" for each CKI University with representatives from both Siemens and the university, which meets once per year. This serves as the main tool for setting the overall directions for each of the CKI universities in the program. The meetings are often held as a closed-door workshop as part of a public annual CKI conference, which aims to bring Siemens and university researchers together and attract students to Siemens as an employer of choice. The CKI steering committee reviews the CKI partnership, plans activities to foster further collaboration, and addresses open or controversial issues in the collaboration, be it on the legal or cultural side (Fig. 6.3).

6.3 THE SUCCESS FACTOR—AN ORGANIZATION OF INTERMEDIARIES

Expectations toward the CKI program from the different stakeholders in Siemens and the universities are manifold. The head of an R&D group at Siemens Energy Management, for example, puts his requirements on research collaboration this way: "I can usually not plan my R&D budget well beyond the next fiscal year, so I need a certain flexibility in project execution. Also, clear protection of sensitive results is a must—I cannot risk any unexpected patent litigation—especially not with a competitor who might be working with the same university chair." Some Siemens' researchers look more for an extended workbench; others look for a long-term strategic collaboration with the right experts and facilities. They all expect to be supported in legal contract negotiations and other administrative tasks and, ideally, to be cofunded for their research. Also, support in placing talented students within the Siemens organization is appreciated.

Dr. Norbert Gaus, head of the Corporate Technology research on digitalization and automation, supports the program whole-heartedly and comments:

Siemens-internal intermediation   *Each CKI University:*
                                           External intermediation

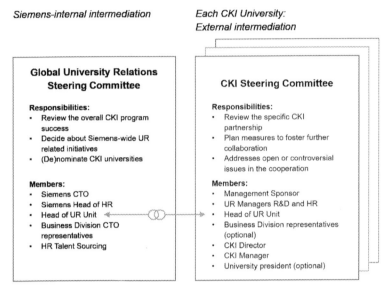

FIGURE 6.3   Governance of the CKI program through two types of Steering Committees. *CKI*, Centers of Knowledge Interchange.

"The CKI program should 'make' our R&D departments work mainly with strategic partner universities. For this it needs to create the right incentives and to come up with opportunities for strategic projects. I also expect transparency on all collaborations with strategic partners and on collaboration with other universities to see the difference the program makes."

There are other managers who have close ties with a specific university, which is not yet a strategic partner, and try to push the nomination of "their" university to become a part of the CKI program.

On the other hand, the academic partner needs challenging research questions, a dedicated budget for a set timeframe (typically the duration of a PhD thesis), the possibility to publish and teach the results afterwards, and more and more the opportunity to commercialize the results by himself or together with another industrial partner in case of a missing interest of Siemens.

So, running the CKI program successfully is all about managing the many understandings and expectations of the program.

Two things are important:

- First, the UR unit drives the internal processes to make sure that personal interests do not dominate selection and interaction with the strategic partner universities. This is the internal intermediation in the CKI program.
- Second, the different expectations and understandings between Siemens and the CKI universities are managed through four intermediary positions. This is the external intermediation in the CKI program.

6.3.1 Internal Intermediaries—The Value of a Central UR Unit

The CKI program establishes strategic partnerships on an organizational level, i.e., a partnership between *all of* Siemens and *the whole* university. However, each stakeholder at Siemens primarily has the interests of his department in mind. It is therefore crucial that the central UR unit (1) has transparency on all collaborations and can thus act as an internal knowledge-broker and a neutral advisor to decision-makers when reviewing the partnership, (2) mediates between all internal stakeholders in case of conflict, (3) ensures top-management buy-in, and (4) promotes Siemens−university cooperation in the public. The head of the UR unit is indeed the only person who is a member of both the internal Global UR Steering Committee and all CKI Steering Committees. As an example of the value of the UR unit let us look at the internal review of a CKI partnership.

Example 1: Review of a CKI University

Normally, the CKI status of a university is recommended for a review if some of the selection criteria (see above) are no longer fulfilled or at least are at risk to be no longer fulfilled. This is caused very often by decreasing project volume with the partner over a longer period or some serious issues that question a trustful and sustainable partnership in the long run. In this specific case, both of the above-mentioned reasons led to the decision to review the CKI partnership; a weak bilateral project volume over the last years (oscillating around the minimum required project volume to become CKI) had been noticed for a while by the UR unit in their regular collaboration analysis. This was possible because all university collaborations are collected in a central database, hosted by the UR unit. When, additionally, various contractual issues questioned the reliability and commitment of the university as a strategic university partner, a review was proposed by the head of the UR unit and confirmed by the Global UR Steering Committee.

The review was conducted by a dedicated Siemens team consisting of people from the UR unit and Technology & Innovation representatives from all partnering Business Units. Based on manifold interviews with the Siemens principal investigators involved in projects with the CKI University, colleagues from talent acquisition, and other involved stakeholders, the project team assessed the current CKI status and concluded: keep CKI status, impose clear conditions, and re-evaluate by the end of next calendar year.

One challenge for the review team was to find the right balance between a fact-based evaluation and the political importance of the CKI University respective of the negative impact of a potential removal from the program could have. Especially for the Siemens stakeholders in the region, the CKI

University was of high importance thanks to its close ties with the city and its infrastructure projects—even if the Siemens stakeholders were not directly involved in research projects with the university, but more in opinion-leading initiatives jointly with the city and the university.

Another challenge was to impose clear conditions on the CKI University in order to keep the status in the future. As communication was very sensitive, the UR unit involved the Siemens Management Sponsor for the CKI University (see later for a detailed description of this position) to first internally discuss the issue and then inform the university management accordingly. An action plan was elaborated by the team and confirmed by the Management Sponsor. The Management Sponsor tasked both parties to come up with a strategic roadmap of common research topics for the upcoming years. At that time, a huge digitalization initiative was started in the university, which offered excellent opportunities for Siemens businesses and researchers to jump onto it. The UR unit contacted the CEO of the digitalization initiative, and thus got access to the topics and activities at a very early stage. University—industry tandems were formed and discussed dedicated fields of collaboration.

At the same time, the contractual issues that were one of the triggering points for the review were handled on the university's top-management level. Creative solutions were designed and discussed with the UR unit, and the principal investigators were asked to follow the new process. The university's top management became personally involved in the discussions and workshops. Step by step the partnership went back to normal. So, the review and its follow-up actions, orchestrated, and mediated by the UR unit, have shown the strong commitment on both sides to trustfully and openly work together—even in a more challenging phase.

From this example, we can learn how the UR unit acted to orchestrate the review:

- Even a critical review does not need to result in a negative outcome, but can give new impulses to a partnership. The UR unit took the initiative to start the review when it deemed such impulses necessary.
- Even if a review is a formal process driven by objectivity, it needs empathy to conduct it in a smooth way. The UR unit acted as an intermediary that set the right tone, steered communication in an appropriate way, and balanced different expectations.
- Management commitment from both parties is key. The UR unit had the necessary connections and trust on both sides to ensure this commitment and steer it into constructive action.

6.3.2   Intermediation Through Four Positions

Siemens has established a unique organization for the CKI program consisting of four positions that all work as intermediaries between Siemens and the CKI universities: (1) a Management Sponsor for each university. The Management Sponsor is usually a Siemens board member or a country CEO. He is supported by a team consisting of (2) a University Relationship Manager for research and development (UR Manager R&D) and a University Relationship Manager for Human Resources with a focus on employer branding and recruitment (UR Manager HR). On the university side, these positions are mirrored by a CKI office, headed by a (3) CKI Director, who is usually a university vice president or dean. The CKI Director is supported by a (4) CKI Manager. Siemens finances the CKI offices and pays a part of the CKI Managers' salary.

The four positions can be depicted in a matrix, as in Fig. 6.4. The figure shows how intermediary organization is designed to bridge the gap between Siemens and the strategic partner universities and the gap between the executive level and the "working level." The UR Managers R&D/HR work closely with the CKI Managers. Together they support requests from the executive level, but they also drive many initiatives on their own. As we will show later, it is an important lesson from the CKI Program that the working-level intermediaries are not "only" coordinators, but also an active driver of e.g., new projects and collaboration formats.

As a result, we have an intermediary organization consisting of four intermediary positions that we will describe briefly in the following. See Box 6.2 for a brief description of their responsibilities.

	University	Siemens
Executive level	CKI director	Management sponsor
Working level	CKI manager	UR manager (R&D / HR)

FIGURE 6.4 The Four Intermediary Positions in the CKI Program. *CKI*, Centers of Knowledge Interchange.

BOX 6.2 Roles and Responsibilities.

UR Manager R&D/HR
- Central point of contact for R&D- and HR-related requests and activities regarding the CKI Universities.
- Develops briefings on current R&D projects and HR-related activities with the CKI Universities.
- Plans and coordinates events for collaboration and actively enhances network-building with the CKI Universities.

CKI Manager:
- "One-stop shop" for all Siemens requests toward the CKI universities and supports contract management.
- Proactively promotes collaboration with Siemens through, e.g., expert workshops, conferences, and recruiting events.
- Prepares CKI Steering Committee Meetings and the annual report about CKI University.

Management Sponsor:
- Executive contact to the senior management of the CKI University with regard to R&D projects, educational policies and student activities, and chairperson for bilateral steering committee meetings.
- Promotes and supports collaboration projects throughout Siemens for R&D and HR.
- Annually reviews the partnership and future roadmaps.

CKI Director:
- Executive contact to the Siemens Management Sponsor and Siemens management with regard to common R&D projects, educational policies, and student activities, in close alignment with the university president.
- Promotes and supports collaboration projects throughout the university for R&D and HR.
- Annually reviews the partnership and future roadmaps.

Working-Level Intermediaries

UR Managers R&D & HR: The UR Managers R&D are members of the UR unit (see above) and spend about 20% of their capacity on this task per university. Usually, each of the UR Managers R&D are in charge of only one CKI University of which, ideally, they are an alumnus or have other personal ties to. In this way, they can concentrate on building a network with a unique focus on the university, and they also have the role of Siemens' "spokesperson" for the university when CKI universities are compared to each other. Since all UR Managers R&D are part of the UR unit, knowledge exchange across universities is easy. UR Managers HR are part of the human resource organization in a specific country and are usually human resource specialists in talent management and employer branding. They spend about 10% of their capacity per university. In countries with more than one strategic partner university, they take care of several universities. Both UR Managers are closely aligned and in regular interaction. In some cases, they are also supported by a local UR Manager from a Siemens location close to the university.

CKI Manager: The location and employment of the CKI Manager varies. Some universities have dedicated Industry Liaison Offices and the CKI Manager is then usually one of the liaison officers. In the CKI program, this is the case for Tsinghua University, UC Berkeley, and Georgia Tech. In Europe, Industry Liaison Offices are still developing to become a mature part of the University landscape. That is why we see a large diversity in where the CKI Managers are located. They are usually affiliated with a department of the university that has close connections to industry, e.g., TUM International at the Technical University of Munich, International Academy at RWTH Aachen, or simply at the university chair of the CKI Director (e.g., Friedrich-Alexander-University Erlangen-Nurnberg, TU Berlin). In these cases, the CKI Manager often has an additional position in her/his job profile and spends between 50% and 80% of her/his capacity as a CKI Manager.

Executive-Level Intermediaries

Management Sponsor: The Management Sponsor is a senior executive who acts as Siemens' representative for the bilateral relationship with the strategic partner university. This includes discussing new formats of collaboration with the university's senior management. Acting as Management Sponsor covers a variety of different roles: chairperson, executive contact, promoter of the collaboration (financially as well as mentally), and trouble-shooter, challenging contract negotiations. The Management Sponsors in the CKI program are either from the management board of Siemens or a country CEO.

CKI Director: The CKI Director is the counterpart for the Management Sponsor on the university side and work in close alignment with the university president. CKI Directors are chosen on three criteria: (1) close relationship with Siemens, (2) close relationship to the senior management of the university, and (3) a strong network within the university. As a result, the CKI Directors are often either a provost, vice president, or dean.

6.3.2.1 The Value of the Working-Level Intermediaries

The working-level intermediaries deliver value to the CKI program through their position as the central point of contact and as coordinators of several activities such as bilateral expert meetings and recruiting events. But it is also notable from the CKI program that their value is not limited to the role of the central point of contact and the coordinator. The UR Managers and

CKI Managers are also valuable when it comes to (1) creating unexpected connections between people and different domains of knowledge and (2) creating a common understanding and aligning expectation in the collaboration. We will in the following describe this value of the working-level intermediaries in more detail through two cases taken from typical situations in the collaboration.

Example 2: The Global University Challenge—Brokering People and Knowledge

In 2016, Siemens launched an ambitious idea competition for students of eight different universities in four different countries: The Global University Challenge (GUC) on "Enabling the digital twin." A key aspect in future industry is the availability of a digital representation of machines, components, or manufacturing processes. That is the so-called digital twin. Measurements and data acquisition methods are the key to gather information for the digital twin and ensure product quality. In the GUC, the students were asked for new ideas on both the technical aspect (how to design the measurement and data acquisition methods to seamlessly enable the digital twin) as well as the business aspect (how to build business drivers around the digital twin).

Among the eight participating universities, there were four CKI universities and four universities outside of the CKI Program. The universities outside of the CKI program were invited due to their strong expertise in the subject area. In the preparation, execution, and even the results of the competition, the differences between CKI universities and non-CKI universities became obvious. For example, the engagement of students from the four CKI universities was about twice as high as the engagement from the four non-CKI universities (22 vs 12 ideas submitted; 62 vs 36 active users with 307 vs 143 comments at the online portal). One of the reasons was that the UR Manager and the CKI Manager used their extensive knowledge about the CKI universities to put unexpected research areas and people together. This was only possible because the UR Managers and CKI Managers were known and respected at the universities, and because they knew the specific culture of the universities and Siemens, they could act as bridge-builders to create a common understanding and align expectations. Ilaria Carrara-Cagni, the UR Manager responsible for GUC puts it in this way:

> The CKI Managers know the Siemens business, our way of working and thinking and which students we are looking for. They also knew exactly the different people in research areas they wanted to work together — and importantly who to contact at the university to make it happen. In contrast, at some of the non-CKI universities, it took us weeks just to get in contact with the people at the university, and when we finally were in contact they could not help us in forming some interesting cross-disciplinary teams.

In the example of the GUC we can draw the learnings that

- the UR Manager and the CKI Manager created value when they went beyond the passive and neutral role of the coordinator to the active role of the broker of people and domains of knowledge and
- the shift from passive coordinator to active broker, was only possible because the UR Manager and CKI Manager were known and respected at the universities and knowledgeable about the specific culture of the universities and Siemens.

6.3.2.2 The Value of the Executive-level Intermediaries

It is essential for a strategic partnership that goes beyond individual bottom-up collaboration to be on eye's level with the senior management on both sides, and have an engaged Management Sponsor and CKI Director. Large, strategic projects need high-level, powerful spokespersons to be realized. The Management Sponsor can initiate actions within Siemens across organizational boundaries and lead a well-balanced dialog with university management, including the possibility to take the short-cut in case of contract negotiations being in a deadlock. The CKI Director, on the other hand, can make use of his university management contacts and his peer network of professors to promote strategic projects.

Example 3: "Think Big" — Establishing a New Collaboration Format

A good example of how the Management Sponsor and the CKI Director can leverage their position within both organizations to create a new form of cooperation are the so-called Siemens Forschungsbereiche (S-FB, Siemens Research Center) at RWTH Aachen.

The first S-FB "Rare Earths—Green Mining and Separation" was established in 2011 when prices for rare earth elements were dramatically increasing. Rare earth elements are important raw materials in key technologies and high-tech products, especially in high-power magnets. Siemens uses rare earth elements for a number of its products, for example industrial drives, generators in wind turbines, or modern medical engineering technology.

The idea for it was born at a CKI steering committee meeting by the CKI Director, Dr. Günther Schuh, the Management Sponsor, Dr. Siegfried Russwurm, and the head of the central research department of the Siemens Industry Sector, Dr. Dieter Wegener. Although there was a long list of ongoing joint research projects, the steering committee felt that this was too fragmented and that the partnership should be lifted to a new level. A brainstorming session on existing collaboration formats soon revealed that the German Research Foundation support instrument "Sonderforschungsbereich"

(SFB, Collaborative Research Center) could serve as a model for the new "Siemens Research Center."

> *Dr. Wegener remembers: "We were thinking about how to set up a collaboration which would involve several institutes conducting research on multiple aspects of a strategic problem. We suddenly realized that the 'Sonderforschungsbereiche' are doing exactly this. Because Dr. Russwurm was at the same time my boss, there was no question if we would have funding and resources for this project. Both him and Prof. Schuh were excited by the idea to create a novel cooperation format with a dimension that was unprecedented at Siemens and even at industry-adapted RWTH."*

The first S-FB was established for four years, involving six professors and 10 PhD theses, with a total of 6 million Euro funding from Siemens. A second S-FB on an electrical powertrain for e-cars was established soon after, also with Siemens Industry as the industrial partner.

The construct was well received by the university and the involved Siemens researchers and managers. Siegfried Russwurm, former Siemens CTO, was in fact so convinced about the format that he did not become tired of promoting it among Siemens top-management. As a result, a third S-FB "Future Train," funded by the Siemens Mobility Division, was announced in 2016.

This example gives us insight into how the Management Sponsor and CKI Director add value to the cooperation:

- The executive-level intermediaries are able to "think big" and back their ideas with decision power and budget. No project manager would have suggested such a large-scale, strategic cooperation because the S-FBs by default go beyond the scope of a single research unit.
- The Management Sponsor used his influence in the company to promote the cooperation format beyond the Business Divisions he was responsible for. This way, one top-down strategic approach became the precursor for another one.

6.4   THE SKILLS OF THE INTERMEDIARY

In the following, we will have another look at the value creation of the internal and external intermediaries in the CKI program. This time we focus on the skills they have to create the value—like the necessary skills for the UR Manager and CKI Manager who actively create new and unexpected relations between different domains of knowledge or the Management Sponsor who by his or her decision develops a new and ambitious collaboration format. In other words, we connect the value creation with skill sets. This enables us to provide a fuller picture of the success factor of having an organization of intermediaries in the CKI program.

6.4.1   The Three Expert Skills Areas

To understand the skills of the intermediaries in the CKI program, we need to separate between general skills and expert skills. The dominant general skills cover technical fields of interest to Siemens (many of the UR Managers, CKI Managers, CKI Directors, and Management Sponsors have a background in natural science or engineering), legal knowledge, national government funding schemes, and collaboration formats.

The lesson from the CKI Program is that these general skills are necessary, but they are not sufficient to be a successful intermediary and are therefore supplemented by what we define as three expert skill areas:

- *People skills*—related to words and descriptions like "listening," "trust," "empathy," "patience," and "diplomat."
- *Organizational skills*—related to words and descriptions like "power," "positioning," "networking," and "knowing the right people."
- *Creativity skills*—related to words and descriptions like "curiosity," "persistence," "imagination," and "courage."

People skills: As already stated, university—industry collaboration is a people business. It is therefore not surprising that when we asked the UR Managers and CKI Managers at a global meeting of all intermediaries in the CKI program to name important expert skills areas, they immediately mentioned listening to other people's viewpoints and finding compromises that will satisfy both Siemens and the CKI universities. We saw this clearly in the way the UR Manager and CKI Manager were able to connect unexpected domains of knowledge and people. This was only possible because they were able to listen carefully and empathetically understood the different viewpoints on both sides. This was also the case in the example of the review process of the CKI University where the people in the UR unit fused the review process with empathy and the right tone in the delicate communication between Siemens and the CKI University. Our message is that the competent use of people skills is a prerequisite for all the intermediaries in the CKI Program, but they are especially important for the working level intermediaries (CKI Managers and UR Managers) since they often find themselves in situations where they do not have the power to make any decisions and instead must rely on their people skills to manage the different expectations and understandings.

Organizational skills: Siemens, like any other large organization, is a network of relations with formal power structures in the form of a hierarchy, but also informal power structures related to, e.g., the position in the organization and closeness (or remoteness) to the executive management. The organizational skills are about the ability to navigate in and out of these formal and informal power structures and are important for both the working-level and executive-level intermediaries. In the example of the GUC, we saw how the CKI Manager and the UR Manager used their network position to establish the connection between people. In the example of the S-FB, the Management Sponsor and CKI Director did not only use their formal executive power to realize a new ambitious collaboration format, they also used their knowledge about the "right people" in both organizations to make sure the idea about the new collaboration format was implemented.

Creativity skills: The third skill area is about being creative, which in this case means the ability of the intermediaries to imagine new research project ideas or simply create unexpected connections between people and domains. This ability demands not only good knowledge about organizations and the constant shifting power plays (organizational skills) or the ability to deeply understand "both sides of the fence" (people skills), but also the ability to facilitate ideas that transcend existing dogmas. It is not an easy task and takes courage to suggest a collaboration between people and domains of knowledge that goes against the standard way of doing things But the creativity skills are an essential way to constantly invigorate long-term collaborations, which have a tendency to become conservative. We saw this clearly in the example of the GUC. In this example, the strong collaboration between the UR Manager and the CKI Manager led to unexpected crossdisciplinary teams that won the challenge. To do this, they had to move beyond the passive and more neutral position of the coordinator, to the active position of the broker that uses his/her courage and imagination to connect people and the knowledge they have in news ways. The ability to imagine ideas that transcend existing dogmas was also seen in the example of S-FB. In this example, the Management Sponsor and CKI Director used their imagination to translate the SFB (originally developed by the German Research Foundation) into a Siemens context where it then became S-FB (Fig. 6.5).

Within the CKI Program, it is important to note that in many situations the intermediaries do not depend on a single expert skill area. Instead, they will

Level in the organization	Working level intermediaries (UR Manager and CKI Manager)	Executive level intermediaries (CKI Director and Management Sponsor)
Value creation	• Create a common understanding and alignment of expectations • Create unexpected connections between people and domains of knowledge	• "Think big"—ensure that the collaboration goes beyond the individual bottom-up approach • "Think across"—ensure that the collaboration enables collaboration between different business units
Expert skill areas	• *People skills*—related to words and descriptions like "listening," "trust," "empathy," "patience," and "diplomat" • *Organizational skills*—related to words and descriptions like "power," "positioning," networking, "knowing the right people" • *Creativity skills*—related to words and descriptions like "curiosity," "persistence," "imagination," "and "courage"	

FIGURE 6.5 the value creation and the key skill areas of the intermediaries.

have to use different expert skill areas depending on what is needed in the situation. This underlines that a competent intermediary does not naively use a specific skill in all situations, but adapt different expert skills areas *consciously* and *strategically* at the right moment (timing) to achieve a specific goal.

6.5 CONCLUSION

When moving from a collection of ad-hoc relationships on the individual level to a strategic partnership on an organizational level, we expect an increase in mutual awareness and interest, easier exploitation of synergies and eventually more larger and more successful cooperations in terms of research results and talent acquisition. But all this does not happen by itself and intermediaries play a vital role in this process.

We have presented the CKI program, the Siemens approach to strategic university partnerships, and its organization of intermediaries, consisting of both Siemens and university employees. On the one hand, they internally steer the program and the individual university partnerships by managing the expectations of many different stakeholders. On the other hand, they act as bridge builders between the two organizations.

The executive-level intermediaries have the influence to start and promote collaboration but also to critically question a partnership and thus potentially move it toward the better. Management commitment is key to a successful strategic partnership, but to work effectively, the team also needs to include working-level intermediaries who act as a central point of contact and as coordinators of various activities. Thus, they create wide awareness of the partnership and strengthen commitment from all parties involved. They bring additional value to the partnership by creating unexpected connections between people and different domains of knowledge and by creating a common understanding and aligning expectations in the collaboration.

Three expert skills are crucial to be a successful intermediary. People skills are required to gain trust, build a personal network and find diplomatic solutions in case of conflict. Organizational skills are especially useful to give impulses to start something new or to revitalize a stalling partnership. Finally, creativity skills might be the hardest to master, but also the most rewarding. Only when combining people and/or organizational skills with creativity, an intermediary can add real value to a strategic cooperation.

Against this back ground we recommend:

- Create a community of intermediaries tasked with the continuous management of the different internal and external expectations in a strategic partnership.
- Choose people for the community of intermediaries that come from both the working-level and from the executive-level and represent both the university and the company.

- Take special care in choosing the intermediaries as they will influence the quality of the partnership to a large degree and for a long time.
  - Choose people with a strong, long-term commitment, ideally routed in a personal experience.
  - Choose people with proven expert skills in "people," "organization," and most importantly "creativity."

REFERENCE

Perkmann, M., Salter, A., 2012. How to create productive partnerships with universities. Mit. Sloan Manage. Rev. 53 (4), 79–88.

Chapter 7

The New Criteria for Measuring the Success of Industry–University Relations: Insights from Schlumberger

Najib Abusalbi

Corporate University Relations, Schlumberger Limited (Retired), Houston, TX, United States

Schlumberger Facts and Figures (Fiscal Year 2016)

Company name:	Schlumberger
Headquarters in:	Paris, Houston, London, The Hague
Annual revenue:	US$27.8 billion
Number of (R&D) employees:	100,000 including Research, Engineering and Manufacturing (R, E&M). Number of R, E&M centers reached 95 in 18 countries
R&D budget:	US$1.0 billion
Average number of University R&D collaborations p.a.:	100–200 (2012–16)
Industry branches:	Upstream Exploration, Production, and Management of Oil & Gas resources
Product examples:	Seismic, drilling, characterization, completions, subsea production, production, processing and separation, well intervention, well testing

7.1 INTRODUCTION

In the 1920s, Conrad and Marcel Schlumberger, supported with seed funding from their father, built a company around their discovery of a method to simultaneously detect metal ores underneath the earth's surface and reveal details of subsurface formations. This single innovation enabled the brothers to grow their family business into the world's first well logging company. Since then, the

Strategic Industry-University Partnerships. DOI: https://doi.org/10.1016/B978-0-12-810989-2.00007-2

company has maintained its focus on the science of measurement. Today, the three values that were passed down by Conrad and Marcel Schlumberger still stand as the foundation of the company's culture.

- Our people thrive on the challenge to excel in any environment.
- Our commitment to technology and quality is the basis of our competitive advantage.
- Our determination to produce superior profits is the cornerstone of our future independence of action and growth.

Historically, Schlumberger recognized the critical nature of its relationships with universities and formally allocated the role of managing these relationships to the Schlumberger Foundation, which invested in higher education by establishing professorships as early as 1954. For decades, university relations activities revolved around support for higher education, basic and applied scientific research, and developing relationships with professors and students that would lead to brand recognition and enable access to the most talented science and engineering graduates who would consider the company as a prime choice for pursuit of their careers.

In 2011, University Relations within Schlumberger became a corporate function at the same level as Government Relations and Investor Relations. This made University Relations an integral component of our business and corporate identity, and was thus more in line with the company's focus on developing and accessing top talent from the world's leading academic institutions and collaborating and investing in the development of novel science and technology.

Our university relations activities include several hundred universities around the globe, with about one hundred regarded as strategic to our business and/or technology development. Our activities within the academic sector continue to position us as a leading global employer of choice for the science, technology, engineering, and mathematics (STEM) fields of study.

Strategic programs under our University Relations function are categorized into one of five rubrics: Education, Research, Technology Watch and Commercialization, Outreach, and Recruiting.

Under the rubric of Education, we participate in developing local talent in emerging economies in line with our business development plans. This includes placing our experts at the top institutions and providing internship opportunities for the most talented students as well as education grants. Schlumberger also donates software, data, laboratories, and equipment to facilitate energy-related disciplines of education. The education engagements also extend to developing our workforce through continuing education opportunities or specific training programs. For example, we have actively worked with universities regarded as the world's leading institutions in order to provide specific project management training to our technology experts.

In the area of Research, we sponsor research relevant to our products and services, typically under favorable intellectual property guidelines, and support industry—academia collaborative research that is often funded by multiple sources, including government agencies and industrial partners.

In relation to the Technology Watch and Commercialization rubric, we promote and support disruptive innovation and identify investment opportunities that will accelerate the release of research results to the market and the commercialization of differentiating energy-related technologies. Universities have various levels of maturity when it comes to commercializing technology and interacting with corporate investors. Those that directly foster entrepreneurship and innovation at their faculty and students' levels are typically better at attracting investors such as Schlumberger. In fact, our technology watch extends beyond the energy sector to include many other industries, such as health, pharma, automotive, and aviation.

When it comes to Outreach activities, we sponsor education initiatives at all levels, from primary to secondary (AKA K-12) and higher education, with a focus on STEM fields as well as health, safety, and environment. We also provide direct support to the Schlumberger Foundation flagship program, namely the Faculty for the Future program, which grants doctoral and post-doctoral research fellowships to women in countries with a low human development index and/or high gender inequality index (please see World Bank Development Indicators).

Finally, yet importantly, Recruiting is the function that harvests the activities and engagements across all the other programs. Each year we target a selection of universities where we engage in activities focused on raising awareness of our brand among the graduates whose disciplines and profiles could have a potential impact on our future leadership.

To monitor and measure the success within each rubric, we have identified specific indicators and implemented methods and measurements that track the impact of the collective set of activities undertaken by our functional groups, such as operations and product development. The selected metrics are inspired by and align with our values. In this chapter, we will present the methodology, governance model, organizational model, programs and activities within the academic sector, and rationale behind selecting a set of metrics to monitor and measure the success of all the activities within each rubric. The use of results-based metrics is presented along with recommendations regarding the set of performance indicators that not only measure efficiency of the organization conducting certain activities, but also the impact of these activities on the development and performance of the corporation. We have implemented metrics consistent with our values of employing highly talented people, developing high-quality technology, and delivering excellent competitive results and profits.

7.2 METHODOLOGY

We have developed our methodology upon the fundamental principles of Engagement, Development, Governance, and Sustenance.

With engagement, we become directly involved in various university events and activities, establishing our presence and strengthening our brand.

In terms of development, we strive to enhance energy-related curricula through direct involvement of our STEM experts who mentor, coach, train, and supervise young professors and students at various levels in all the key disciplines in order to provide them with industry experience.

We also provide governance of the relationship with our top-tier universities by establishing a team of business and technology leaders. An Ambassador who acts as an account director tasked with representing the mutual interests of Schlumberger and the university leads this team. In addition, one or more Champions—who are responsible for developing closer connections with the faculty members and students in various disciplines of interest—typically support the Ambassador.

To sustain and grow the relationship for years to come, the university relations leaders, the Ambassadors, and the Champions, develop and execute a strategic plan with clear goals and objectives governing all engagements.

7.3   GOVERNANCE

Supporting University Relations engagements is a strong governance team, as shown in Fig. 7.1, which includes executive sponsorship and direction as well as strong support and direct involvement by the business and technical leaders throughout our operating units and technology centers.

Executive sponsors include:

- Executive Vice President (VP) of Corporate Development, who provides overall oversight;

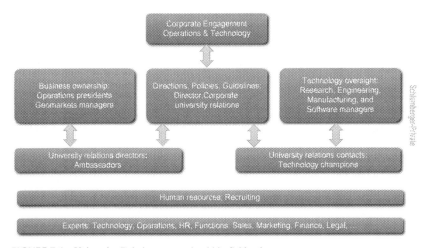

FIGURE 7.1   University Relations network within Schlumberger.

- Executive VP of Operations, who provides oversight of the programs related to operational units across the globe;
- Executive VP of Technology, who provides oversight of the programs related to research and technology transfer from leading science and engineering universities and currently includes activities across more than 100 Schlumberger centers for research, engineering, and manufacturing.

The Director of Corporate University Relations provides global oversight for all university related programs, setting policies and guidelines.

Supporting activities at various organizational and functional levels is a team of business and technical leaders, including the presidents of operations who act as business owners of the programs in their areas. The team's primary focus is attracting, developing, and retaining talent to support area operations. We typically select Ambassadors from among the leaders in each operational area, or they are technical experts, and act as account directors for their assigned university. Likewise, we select Technology Champions from the technical leaders across the company's product and service lines and act as primary contacts for our technology groups, namely, the research, engineering, manufacturing, or software groups. The Corporate University Relations Director coordinates activities across all the operating units and technology centers, including activities by the Ambassadors and the Technology Champions.

University Relations managers for each business unit are tasked with overseeing recruiting and related activities in their respective geographic regions. Technical Communities support activities in the universities connected to recruiting, education, and research where our science and technology experts take the lead.

Human resources (HRs) representatives work closely with each of these support groups to ensure access to graduates with the profiles who we believe will be able to help lead the company into the future.

This network also includes other key organizations, such as the Schlumberger Foundation with the Faculty for the Future program and the Schlumberger endowments; the Global Stewardship program (see the Schlumberger Global Stewardship Report), and the Corporate Ventures group that evaluates and invests in commercialization of mature research and university start-ups.

Members of this network often serve on university boards at all administrative and scientific levels within the university organization structure. The upper management team, including our executives, are members of Industry Advisory Boards that are established by university presidents, faculty/college deans, departments, or special purpose institutes across business, science, and engineering disciplines. Likewise, our research scientists and technical leaders are members of scientific committees that vary from undergraduate research projects (also known as senior design or capstone projects), graduate masters or doctoral research programs, and research consortia or industry-academic affiliate programs.

In addition to being members of academic educational or research-related industry advisory boards, many have also chosen to be members of the advisory boards of several universities' commercialization or technology transfer groups. These board seats help the universities with external networking, particularly about strategic, corporate investors because we often syndicate deals that open up new areas and partners for collaboration at the faculty level as well.

7.4 ORGANIZATIONAL MODEL

Overall, we have modeled the university relations function in Schlumberger after the principles of account management with an executive oversight, a corporate direction, and a very broad base of engaged employees across all functions. Just like account management, alignment with corporate goals and values is critical in driving success. Nonetheless, based on our experience and published case studies, we would like to assert that here is no single model that will fit every corporation. There are likely several methodologies, each with a set of related policies and guidelines, that a corporation may adopt and adapt to its goals and values in selecting the most appropriate academic partners in order to achieve an acceptable measure of program success. A corporation that has designed and implemented a successful university relations program can provide guidance for other corporations to create a model that best aligns with their own goals and values.

Recent market research from organizations such as the Corporate Leadership Council, Forrester Research, and the American Productivity and Quality Center (APQC) has shown a shift in the criteria used for evaluating the success of a bidirectional relationship between corporations and universities. Better metrics simply provide for better opportunities; the decisions based on metric analysis help steer leaders toward better opportunities, they make different choices as a result. Utilizing results-based metrics to track the success of talent programs and R&D collaborations enables one to make informed choices about which activities truly meet key performance goals for a company's university relations function. For example, corporations can assess results that compare the impact versus the number of students hired.

Recent research has identified changing trends among the corporations that have a university relations function. For instance, some companies are using HR analytics to improve the productivity of their talent identification, acquisition, and development programs. These HR analytics enable them to determine mineable and reportable metrics of value as well as define best practices. By using output-based success metrics—both as input to university selection criteria and as proof of successful university performance criteria—these corporations have had greater success in accessing the most talented graduates. In addition, their use has had a greater impact on the corporation through collaborations that produced innovative, game-changing or disruptive outcomes that achieved market differentiation and leadership.

With these goals in mind, Schlumberger evaluates its university selection criteria and program success criteria on a regular basis to account for emerging talent and technology trends. We analyze our HR and R&D projects data along with data from other collaborative projects in order to refine the set of key performance indictors (KPIs) that we use to monitor and valuate our university relationships. Thus, every year we are better able to quantify the performance of the entire set of programs and their impact on corporate performance.

The National Association of Colleges and Employers (NACE) recommends that a corporation develops a campus recruitment program targeting campuses "that best fit into its corporate culture and the number of students it needs to achieve its hiring goals" (NACE Recruitment Survey, 2006) and helps build the organization's brand within academic communities, especially among students and graduates. In addition, for firms that engage heavily in formal, research-focused alliances with universities, there is a need for a consistently applied performance measurement system that qualitatively and quantitatively gauges the success or outcomes of industry–university alliances, as recommended by organizations such as the Engineering and Physical Sciences Research Council (ESPRC).

When setting joint research goals with university partners, we continue to challenge the research teams within Schlumberger and at the universities to develop game-changing techniques or disruptive technologies that have the potential to revolutionize the industry in the years to come. Additionally, to support such an innovative and disruptive mindset within the academic sector, corporations must be prepared to invest in education-focused programs that serve two key goals:

- Developing talent that better fits future industry needs; and
- Fostering innovation in both technology and business.

7.5   PROGRAMS AND ACTIVITIES

Under the methodology and organization presented earlier, we continue to support several programs that we believe directly or indirectly contribute to corporate performance. Table 7.1 shows the key talent-oriented and research-oriented programs, as well as programs aimed at boosting business innovation.

For each of these activities, we evaluate one measure annually to ensure that the activity continues to deliver value to our corporation and academic partners. The measures are typically set against corporate goals that seek to

TABLE 7.1 University Relations Programs and Activities by Category

Activity	Category	Description	Geographical scope
Talent development	Education	• Helps develop energy-related science and engineering programs at local academic institutions • Based on socioeconomic need in the places where we work • Aligned with our global stewardship efforts (Schlumberger Global Stewardship Reports) • Examples: donating fully functional computational or analytical labs	Sub-Saharan Africa, Latin America, South East Asia-Pacific
Talent exchange	Education, research	• Places our experts as petro-technical professionals at key universities • Governed by a customized framework • Professors and research scientists fill short- or long-term positions at Schlumberger	Global (focused on locations with a high-level of operational activity or a high-concentration Schlumberger expertise)
Curriculum development	Education	• Provide input on development or evolution of curricula • Plays a key role in strengthening our relationship with these universities • Graduates are better prepared for industrial careers as a result	Global (focused on locations with a high level of operational activity or a high concentration Schlumberger expertise)
Visiting scholars	Research	• Schlumberger research scientists supervise and/or participate in research programs of interest to us • These scientists also supervise students and lecture, sharing their practical industry experience	Global (focused on locations with high level of Schlumberger research scientists and leading research universities or institutions)

Post-doctoral positions	Research	• Host doctoral research scientists for a 1- to 2-year our lab appointment • Schlumberger employees interested in post-doctoral research work with researchers focused on topics relevant to our technology portfolio for 1 year or longer if agreed	Global, United States (locations with research centers)
Grants and endowments	Education, research	• Schlumberger Foundation endowments support chairs and/or professorships in sciences and engineering • Approximately a dozen endowments globally • University grants support energy-related programs in return for branding rights	Primarily in the United States and a few global locations
Student internships and sponsorships	Education, research	• Several hundred internships per year at operational facilities and technology centers (300 in 2016) • Duration ranges from a few weeks to a few months • Cosponsor students typically pursuing STEM or business fields of study • Extends to Schlumberger employees who want to develop their careers via university residential programs or to blend these with a digital program	Global (where we work or develop technologies)
Future of STEM education	Education, outreach	• Engagement with global organizations concerned about the future of STEM education in general and in the energy sector; such as the Society of Petroleum Engineers (SPE), and World Energy Forum (WEF) • Helps to define how petroleum engineering and geosciences curricula should evolve to accommodate industry changes	Global

(Continued)

TABLE 7.1 (Continued)

Activity	Category	Description	Geographical scope
Professional societies and organizations	Education, outreach	• Support programs with a strong university engagement component, such as the Geoscientists without Borders (GWB) under the Society of Exploration Geophysicists Foundation. GWB has won awards for the use of geoscience technology toward humanitarian projects, such as evaluating underground water pollution, tsunamis, earthquakes, and health and safety hazards	Global
Professional societies student chapters	Education, outreach	• Engagement with chapters connected to professional organizations • Examples: Association of Petroleum Geologists (AAPG), SPE, Society of Exploration Geoscientists (SEG) • Includes sponsoring participation in regional and global competitions (i.e., AAPG's Imperial Barrel Awards, SPE's Petro-Bowl) • Often this is direct funding toward participation in regional or global events or competitions • Can also be in-kind support through coaching, training, and providing tools	Global
Software donations	Education, research	• Donates cost-free software licenses to over 700 universities, colleges, high schools, and other nonprofit research institutions • Trains the faculty members, research scientists, instructors, and students how to use the software	Global (where we work, typically at universities with earth sciences and engineering disciplines)

Graduate committees	Research	• Committee participation for doctoral and master level theses • Undergraduate research committee participation (senior design projects)	Global (where we have technology centers)
Joint publications	Research	• Actively encourages Schlumberger experts and research scientists to publish papers in collaboration with university professors, research scientists, and students	Global (where we work or have technology centers)
Technology commercialization	Research, technology transfer	• Supports the transfer of technology from universities to the energy sector, including our product groups • Commercializing emerging technology through investment in university start-ups, accelerating research to market, and licensing intellectual property from academia to the industry	Global (where we have technology centers)

sustain or develop our attractiveness as a global employer or as a leading innovator.

For example, we track our presence and impact on university programs, including the following measures:

- Level of engagement of our Ambassadors and Champions with academic institutions, including campus visits per year, lectures, info sessions, ongoing projects, and referrals;
- Scope and breadth of our representation on academic advisory boards and its influence on curricula and educational programs pertinent to our sector;
- Number of our experts serving on research advisory committees, including the number of professors and students they are reaching out to; and
- Number of applicants from these programs interested in pursuing Schlumberger careers.

7.6 BENEFITS

Allow me to point out that the literature is definitive when it states that deep engagement with universities results in benefits beyond the narrow objectives of specific projects or alliances. The higher education sector that universities represent is indeed a source of new techniques and instruments that enable industry to develop new, differentiating technologies.

Equally importantly, university alliances provide opportunities to screen potential recruits for positions in the industry. Working with universities also acts as a reputational device that increases the attractiveness of firms as employers and partners in barter-governed networks for the exchange of scientific and technical knowledge. Alliances with universities have long enabled firms to participate in networks focused on specific technical or scientific subject areas that, due to the openness of academic networks, extend far beyond the specific universities with which they have formal alliances. They may lead to new opportunities for engaging academics as collaborators or consultants.

According to research published in 2010 by the American Institute of Management (AIM) (Perkmann et al., 2010) titled, "How should firms evaluate success in university-industry alliances?" sourcing of knowledge from universities is being transformed from decentralized, informal, untracked, ad-hoc cooperation to larger-scale, multiannual alliances. As a result, many corporations are finding they have to adopt a more formal, systematic evaluation and measurement to assess initiatives a posteriori and monitor ongoing initiatives to enable adjustment and improvement for their university selections and investments.

In this context, corporations can also engage universities in larger-scale programs that scan multiple industrial partners and can address longer-term issues than can perhaps be addressed by simple engagement at the faculty level. One example is the Global Climate and Energy Project (GCEP) at Stanford University (Global Climate & Energy Project (GCEP)), which seeks new solutions to the challenge of supplying energy to meet the changing needs of a growing world population in a way that better accounts for current and future environmental concerns and regulations. GCEP's mission is to conduct fundamental research on technologies that will permit the development of global energy systems with significantly lower greenhouse gas emissions. This project develops and manages a portfolio of innovative energy research programs that could lead to technologies that are efficient, environmentally benign, and cost-effective when deployed on a large scale. There is currently an increasing number of breakthrough research projects taking place across disciplines throughout university campuses due to corporations pursuing extensive collaborations with leading institutions around the world.

Again, measuring such benefits is at the heart of our strategic engagements with universities. For example, we have seen additional (measurable) impact when a specific engagement is the outcome of a strategic plan established with the academic institution and contrasted to the outcome achieved through direct connections typically established between our research scientists or engineers and professors. We do however continue to encourage such grass roots connections given the benefits realized from strengthening relationships, increasing brand awareness, and exposure to talented students.

7.7 METRICS-DRIVEN SUCCESS CRITERIA

Case studies published over the past decade, such as the one by Dr. J. Sullivan on "Best Recruiting Practices..." (Sullivan, 2005), show companies moving toward a talent pipeline process modeled on a supply chain approach. An approach based on metrics, such as quality of hire and internal sourcing channel effectiveness, is typically complemented with scorecards showing impact on talent acquisition and retention success, along with an intranet dashboard for ad hoc analysis by company strategists. Similarly, a balanced scorecard approach for measuring industry—university collaboration efforts versus outcomes has also emerged as a strategic tool for measuring performance. All this is in keeping with several relatively recent trends in the valuation of efforts in talent management and novel science and technology practices. For example:

Forrester stated that HR has typically focused on tactical objectives such as responding to requisitions and hence finding the employees the business requested, negotiating the hires, bringing new employees on board, providing company training, setting up an evaluation schedule with individual goal expectations, and helping employees with career development. This mostly tactical role remains necessary, but it is no longer sufficient to retain viable candidates for leadership positions in a corporation. HR management has since taken steps to elevate its role to a strategic business partner by working with business leaders to create a talent strategy closely tied to business goals and results (Evelson and Schooley, 2011).

AIM research has also determined that, as with recruiting, corporations should assess the success of industry–university relationships, including formal collaborations, based on a set of performance objectives and indicators or outcomes.

APQC found that HR should look at easily mineable output or outcome measures as both input to and demonstration or proof of successful university ranking and selection criteria; namely, what recently recruited university graduates have achieved since joining the corporation. "To date, none of the major companies that rank colleges consider what The Chronicle of Higher Education calls the outcome measures, making the guidance provided by a few private education consultants or advisers—based on years of experience that includes following the success of students with whom they have worked—more important than ever before" (Mayer, 2011).

Additionally, APQC (2012) has produced useful, high-level, industry-neutral taxonomies for process improvements that enable organizations to see processes like university relations activities (and costs) in relationship to other industries. To do this, these models rely on consistent, explicit definitions of human capital activities and key measures for these activities.

Several resources enumerate a number of known output-based metrics currently in use by corporations to track the outcomes of recruiting programs and the success of industry–university collaborations (Corporate Leadership Council; APQC, 2012; Berlin Principles on Ranking of Higher Education Institutions, 2006; Holder, 2012; Al-Ashaab, 2011).

To be effective at using such output quality measures, corporations should evaluate the measures based on their effective use elsewhere in the industry. Select measures that are automatically mineable from available corporate data sources and fit into a scoring system that would directly contribute to ranking these institutions based on these measures.

Corporations may segment these measures along multiple dimensions for the purposes of analysis and internal comparisons by year, employee category, job domain or track, as well as for external comparison by published ranking systems such as the Shanghai World Rankings (Academic Ranking of World Universities). The measures may be aggregated automatically into easy-to-read reports with access through an intranet portal or mobile app.

The tables presented in this section are for corporations to consider what is pertinent to their goals and values and then refine the selected criteria to the few that have the most impact on performance. Below are tables from three categories related to the overall performance of university relations programs, the performance of talent acquisition, and the performance of collaborative programs.

TABLE 7.2 Criteria for Ranking Universities

Metric	Formula
Reach	Number of students and faculty members reached per year
Presence	Number of employees engaged in campus activities per year
Support	Number of fellowships or sponsorships offered per year
Globalization	National diversity per key programs and profiles

Table 7.2 reflects a collation of results-based criteria for ranking universities gathered from multiple resources or publications. The purpose is not to advocate using them as a recipe, but as guidelines that can be refined into a corporate performance scorecard for university relations. In general, the scorecard would highlight the performance of these relations and, in particular, the impact of its HR component related to access of the top student profiles, and its technology component related to access to novel sciences, engineering, and manufacturing know-how.

Quality of university relations: Schlumberger identified several metrics (Holder, 2012) that corporations can use to measure the overall effectiveness of their interactions with universities. The most common is the number of individuals "touched by" or "reached" due to one or more activities involving employees and university individuals. Others measure the corporate presence on university campus, the extent of support corporations may offer, and the referral rate. For global corporations we recommend measuring the national talent diversity of the university and engagement in global education.

Recruiting efficiency: Corporations have historically measured and focused on optimizing the efficiency and cost of their recruiting efforts. We selected several metrics to measure the acceptance rate of offers made to students, the cost per recruit, the elapsed time between a job requisition or posting and the acceptance of a job offer, the elapsed time from offer acceptance to actual start date, and the number of referrals from recent hires. Some corporations might want to consider adding a qualitative recruiter rating based on their individual ability to engage and close open requisitions (Table 7.3).

Recruiting quality: Though HR continues to seek efficiency improvements, it has proven more effective to include metrics that measure the quality of the recruiting processes as a function of the quality and caliber of the acquired talent. Such metrics include flagging recent hires as high-value contributing employees, noting job performance ratings plus any awards or recognitions received, ability to sustainably progress over the first few years of employment, professional visibility, and the rate of retention year-on-year. Table 7.4 describes these in more detail.

TABLE 7.3 Measures of Recruiting Efficiency

Metric	Formula
Offer acceptance	Percentage of offers accepted per total number of offers
Cost per recruit	Annual recruiting cost per number of closed requisitions
Offer acceptance time	Cycle time (days) from approval of job requisition to job offer acceptance
Job start time	Cycle time (days) from job acceptance to start date of new hire
New employee referrals	Percentage of successful referrals per new hire
Recruiter rating	A qualitative rating assigned to a recruiter based on engagement

TABLE 7.4 Measures of Recruiting Quality

Metric	Formula
High potential	Percentage of high-potential or highly contributing recent hires
Job performance	Average job performance rating of recent hires
Professional visibility	Number of patents or publications, internal and external, per number of hires
Recognition	Number of awards or recognitions received per number of hires
Leadership	Internal or external leadership positions held per number of hires
Promotion	Number of promotions achieved by recent hires
Retention	Number of recent hires retained over the first 12 months (or induction period) and sustained over the first few years of employment

Collaboration efficiency: Corporations often measure their collaboration activities through a set of numbers that represent their cash or in-kind investments in university projects, as well as their ability to recruit students involved in such activities, directly or indirectly. Table 7.5 shows the metrics we propose to measure such efficiencies.

Collaboration quality: It is imperative for corporations and universities to focus on the outcome of their collaborative engagements. For this, Schlumberger adopted a set of measures that emphasize results, such as the annual number of joint publications or patents; the exchange of expertise between the university and the company; the impact on our products,

TABLE 7.5 Measures of Collaboration Efficiency

Metric	Formula
Cash investments	Annual budget invested per year that supports collaborative projects
Joint projects	Number of joint projects initiated per year in research, education or otherwise
Engagement rate	Number of university faculty members and students involved and the number of company employees involved

TABLE 7.6 Measures of Collaboration Quality

Metric	Formula
Joint outcome	Number of joint publications, reports, patents per year
Expertise exchange	Number of university personnel or students engaged with the company and vice versa
Business impact	Number of products, services, or processes directly or indirectly impacted by the collaboration per year
	Number of investments in innovative startup companies that directly or indirectly impact our products and services
Talent impact	Number of students on projects either hired or interned by the company annually

services, or process; and the number of hires or interns who join the company due to these engagements (Table 7.6).

7.8   ESTABLISHING MEASURES OF SUCCESS

During 2012, Schlumberger conducted a pilot study that evaluated the quality of new hires and science and technology research collaborations and the perceived (or measurable) impact on Schlumberger and our energy sector for each of the institutions included in the study. The intent was to better understand how well our university ranking schemes have performed in the previous 5-year cycle and enable us to create a more robust and sustainable results-based set of measures for university selection criteria.

After the pilot study, Schlumberger embarked on the following steps in relation to the criteria:

Selecting: With the recommendations of management and HR—as well as outside consultancy and market research organizations, such as CEB

Corporate Leadership Council, APQC, and Forrester—we selected a set of criteria for ranking academic institutions that we deemed would best fit with our corporate goals and values and, when available, we adopted results-based criteria validated by published industry studies.

Validating: We selected a representative set of employees and universities with which we have established collaborations. We analyzed the resulting data against time and originating institution. For example, we reviewed the performance of university alumni and that of ongoing collaborations that led to advancing science and technology relevant to our portfolio of products and services. We also considered how best to weigh and present this data to highlight differences and rankings by using a scorecard approach.

Benchmarking: We compared the validated results-based ranking system and criteria with published industry ranking systems, including Shanghai World (and National) Ranking, the Times Higher Education (THE), and QS. The benchmark focused on identifying the most relevant criteria for evaluating academic institutions that produced the best results over the past 5-year cycle, which narrowed the selection considerably.

Analyzing: We analyzed the benchmark results to arrive at a definitive set of common criteria for ranking universities, both for collaborations and for recruiting. During the fourth quarter of 2012, we conducted reviews with select operating regions and technology centers in order to promote the use of this set criteria.

Measuring: Finally, we recommended to the business and technical leadership team a scorecard for measuring the impact of applying the criteria with the flexibility to adapt it, within a set of guidelines, to their specific function or geography in the organization. We also made recommendations for more effective data capture, data mining, data analytics, and reporting of results across the corporation and at a regional or local level.

It is critical to acknowledge and take into full consideration the maturity and readiness of the organization to embrace change, adopt corporate guidelines, and adapt to established processes and culture regarding engagement with the academic sector. The Schlumberger corporate culture has transcended geographies and has clearly been an advantage and a key enabler of rolling out a global set of university relations programs, with corporate oversight and regional/local management. For corporations, like ours, rolling out global programs and continuously measuring their success has been a journey that will undoubtedly require executive buy-in and oversight.

7.9 EXECUTIVE OVERSIGHT IN ACTION

After defining the criteria and establishing a scorecard for the key functional teams, we established a set of processes that ensured quality assurance with the direct engagement of upper management. In order to sustain this executive oversight and engagement, we conduct regular reviews with the leadership team accountable for the success of university relations in their functional areas.

For example, we conduct annual working sessions with the presidents of operational areas to review the results versus objectives within their areas. The reviews are quite structured and include an overview by the corporate director of the overall company results and directions for university relations; a summary of the operational area results presented by the HR team covering recruiting-related activities over the past year, the past 3−5 years, and a preview of what is to come in the following year.

The results focus on how well the area-selected universities have performed with respect to the set of KPIs. These KPIs include the efficiency and performance of the recruiting team, that is, the ability of recruiters to engage and acquire the talent needed by the operational units over the past year (ref. Table 7.2), and how well the recruits hired over past 3−5 years have performed on the job (ref. Table 7.3).

Presidents of operations provide insights about the business and the impact university activities have on their unit's performance across the area. Following that, the corporate and area management decide whether to retain the selected universities for the area and might include adding a high-performing institution, removing a low-performing one, reassigning Ambassadors to the top performing universities, or filling vacant key University Relations positions. Finally, the Corporate Executive Vice President of Operations reviews, recommends revisions, and ultimately approves of the decisions made at the area level.

Similarly, we hold structured reviews with the VPs of our technology functions, namely Research, Engineering, and Manufacturing. These reviews include the corporate director and the HR team that reports to the technology function. In addition to reviewing the results related to talent acquisition for that function, the VPs also evaluate the specific performance indicators. These indicators directly measure research activities and/or the transfer of intellectual property and technology from the university programs to our engineering and manufacturing teams across all of the corporation's product lines. Likewise, the VPs comment on results versus set objectives for the year, and the management team makes decisions related to university selections for the coming year based on technology directions as well as performance of the universities versus the indicators.

Schlumberger has had these processes in place since the establishment of the corporate University Relations role in 2012. Since then, the processes have been refined as we continue to learn more about the effectiveness of the measurements and the KPIs. We also revisit and fine-tune these KPIs to key influencers such as business conditions, technology demands, or generational trends. In addition, since 2012 we have enhanced our capability to provide measurements that are more accurate by better connecting our HR, technology development, and business process systems.

Overall, we continue to allow for refinements from our geographic and business segments. This has proven critical in selecting effective indicators that would better fit the business by taking into account variations in the level of education and research across boundaries. This becomes even more important when we are entering or developing business in a new location that does not have the option of providing local talent or technology. This level of flexibility is critical for a multinational global corporation that operates with a very diverse portfolio of technology and talent across multiple geopolitical systems.

Finally, it is worth mentioning that we are among the few corporations that have representatives of major universities on its board of directors and science and technology board committees. For example, since 2007 the rector of The Moscow Institute of Physics and the President of the Massachusetts Institute of Technology have been members of the Schlumberger board of directors.

7.10 LESSONS LEARNED AT SCHLUMBERGER

The design and rollout of the University Relations programs has been a didactic journey. The programs have undergone several refinements that resulted in changes in the selection criteria, the selected or designated tier-one universities, and the assignment of key contacts to these universities. Generally, the application of the corporate guidelines and utilization of performance indicators has directly contributed to retaining our leadership position among the top 50 global engineering and technology employers.

Business, technology, social and economic drivers, and trends have influenced refinements made to the programs over the years. This has led to changes both in the profiles we wish to recruit and retain as future leaders of the company and in the technology we need to develop for our products and services over the coming years.

During this process, we have learned several lessons along with our university partners. The most prominent of these is that corporations and universities that seek to establish lasting and successful relations must build their programs upon the principles of partnership and account management, with clearly stated benefits for both partners.

Along our journey, we lost some partners and gained or regained others based on how they lived up to their commitment to the partnership. This directly relates to the influence that collective investments have had in developing a better "product" for our industry sector in reference to graduating talent and innovative outcomes in sciences, engineering, and technology, which is critical to Schlumberger as a provider of technology and services to the energy sector.

For example, we have terminated a university partnership because its engineering graduates were not a good fit to the profile of our "field" (operational) engineers. Our operations require an individual who is keenly interested in the "service" sector and who welcomes the potential of a mobile career that would take one to far-flung global locations that are quite different from a familiar local environment. Monitoring and analyzing attrition from year one through year three led to this institution losing its preferred status. However, the very same metric has been included in a renewed plan with different tactics to rebuild the relationship and turn the results around in a period of 3 years.

Similarly, we have terminated research and development agreements due to an inability to produce meaningful results over a reasonable period of time that is commensurate with our ability to compete in the energy sector's technology markets.

During the last few decades, the energy sector has undergone many market highs and lows. We learned to adapt, adopt different measures, and adjust our KPIs to account either for an accelerated rush to acquire talent and technology or for a severely sluggish hiring of talent or the development of novel sciences and technology. During the downturn that began in 2014, we witnessed the migration of many university programs away from the energy sector. In the interest of retaining and further developing our relationships with leading STEM universities, we adopted a longer-term view and engaged with programs that typically contributed to or were funded by other sectors, such as automotive, aviation, defense, and health. We believe that cross-pollination between sectors is a healthy measure of the industry–university relationship.

Similar to "living entities," corporations undergo transformations throughout their lifetime that are independent from their responses to market conditions. A recent corporate initiative at Schlumberger related to an internal transformation of our company has focused on technology innovation, reliability, efficiency, and integration. In response, university relations initiated several efforts with the operational and technology groups to ensure that all of our programs continue to serve the future needs of the corporation for talented profiles and novel sciences, engineering, and manufacturing. Evaluating the results of our University Relations activities over time will reveal the influence this has had on our selection of university partners and on our investments in research and technology programs at these universities since the launch of our internal transformation. In tandem, we are refining the set of measures to ensure the successful impact of university relations programs on our performance as a corporation.

7.11   CONCLUSION AND RECOMMENDATIONS

University Relations remains an important aspect of our corporate identity in Schlumberger. The executive sponsorship and corporate leadership have set high goals and expectations so that the programs will continue to directly contribute to the performance of Schlumberger as a leading technology company in the oil and gas sector. With that, it is critical that we continue to monitor and measure the success of the university relations programs, individually and collectively.

We have set up a framework that has delivered clear performance, placing us among top 50 global employers over the past few years. This framework has built-in the adaptability and flexibility, the performance-based measure and indicators, and the governance and executive oversight. Such attributes will undoubtedly sustain and grow the programs as leadership roles change hand and evolve. Given the structure Schlumberger has established and the power of the network surrounding our university relations programs, we are confident that we can adapt and continue to succeed even as the challenges facing our sector intensify.

I would like to leave the reader with an understanding that university relations programs are solid partnerships that industry and academia must constantly seek to nourish and grow, accepting that occasionally both partners may have to weed out programs that are no longer pertinent for either party.

In addition, I would like to remind the reader that there is no single recipe for success. Whatever framework a corporation establishes must align with its own corporate goals and values and the vision and strategic directions of its academic partners.

On this background, I would like to give the readers the following recommendations:

- Knowing that executive sponsorship and oversight are critical to the success of any University Relations program, ensure buy-in at highest levels and across technology developers and users within the corporate structure.
- Align the goals and objectives of the university relations programs with the company values, the business, and the technology roadmap.
- Adopt a targeted approach to selecting university programs that are best suited to provide the corporation with the talent and technology that are best aligned with the future; set criteria for selecting universities that serve all the functions of the corporation, e.g., operations, product development, HRs, marketing and sales, etc.
- Carefully select and adopt criteria to measure the success of a relationship with a university, with fairly regular reviews based on these measures, adapting to changes in business and technology; hold these reviews with business owners and technology leaders within the corporation as well as with the individual universities.
- Within the overall university relations program and based on the selection and measurement criteria, designate universities as strategic, assigning leaders to oversee the relationship, holding these leaders accountable to the successful outcome including talent and technology impact.

REFERENCES

Academic Ranking of World Universities. See http://www.shanghairanking.com/index.html

Al-Ashaab, A., et al., 2011. A balanced scorecard for measuring the impact of industry-university collaboration. Prod. Plann. Control 22 (5-6), 554–570.

American Productivity and Quality Center. https://www.apqc.org/.

APQC, 2012. Human Capital Definition and Key Measures. See https://www.apqc.org/knowl-edge-base/documents/60-develop-and-manage-human-capital-definitions-and-key-measures-pcf-versio

Berlin Principles on Ranking of Higher Education Institutions, Berlin, May 20, 2006. See http://www.che.de/downloads/Berlin_Principles_IREG_534.pdf

Corporate Leadership Council. https://www.cebglobal.com/human-resources/corporate-leader-ship-council.html

Engineering and Physical Sciences Research Council. https://www.epsrc.ac.uk/

Evelson, B., Schooley, C., November 7, 2011. Use HR Analytics to Optimize Talent Processes. Forrester Research. See https://www.forrester.com/report/Use + HR + Analytics + To + Optimize + Talent + Processes/-/E-RES60636

Forrester Research. https://go.forrester.com/

Global Climate & Energy Project (GCEP). https://gcep.stanford.edu/

Holder, D., 2012. Industry Helps Shapes Instructors' Lesson Plans; The American Oil & Gas Reporter. See http://www.aogr.com/index.php/web-features/exclusive-story/industry-helps-shape-instructors-lesson-plans

Mayer, D., May 8, 2011. College Rankings: "Where's the Outcome Measure?" CPSI. See http://www.collegeplanning.com/blog/college-rankings-where%E2%80%99s-outcome-measure

NACE Recruitment Survey, 2006. See http://www.nasrecruitment.com/docs/white_papers/Campus-Recruiting-Trends.pdf

Perkmann, M., et al., 2010. How Should Firms Evaluate Success in University-Industry Alliances? A Performance Measurement System. AIM Research.

Schlumberger Global Stewardship Reports. http://media.corporate-ir.net/media_files/IROL/97/97513/global_stewardship/reports.html

Sullivan, J., October 9, 2005. Best Recruiting Practices from the World's Most Business-like Recruiting Function, at https://www.eremedia.com/ere/best-recruiting-practices-from-the-worlds-most-business-like-recruiting-function-part-4/

World Bank Development Indicators. http://data.worldbank.org/products/wdi

FURTHER READING

Hammond, J., 2011. Hiring Creative Developers: 10 Questions You Should Ask Prospective Developers. Forrester Research.

Chapter 8

Evaluating Solid Long-Term University–Industry Collaborations: Lessons Learnt From Ferrovial's Strategic Cooperations

Ciro Acedo Boria, Manuel Martínez Alonso and Alberto López-Oleaga
Ferrovial, Madrid, Spain

Ferrovial Facts & Figures (Fiscal Year 2017)	
Company name:	Ferrovial
Headquarters:	Madrid, Spain
Annual revenues:	EUR 12,208 billion
Number of (R&D) employees:	95,978 (300)
R&D budget:	EUR 46.7 million
Average number of university R&D collaborations per year:	30
Industry branches:	Construction, Services, Airports, and Toll roads
Product examples:	Highways, viaducts, train and subway stations, water treatment plants, desalination plants, concession management, end-to-end solutions for cities and infrastructures (urban, transportation, industrial, and social and environmental infrastructures), airport operation, and air traffic control

Strategic Industry-University Partnerships. DOI: https://doi.org/10.1016/B978-0-12-810989-2.00008-4

8.1 INTRODUCTION

What is a key success factor when building disciplined long-term university—industry collaborations? What is needed to achieve win—win long-term university—industry collaborations?

Depending on their experience, each company would highlight the key success factor that they consider most important. From Ferrovial's point of view, the key success factor that has made the difference and that let us identify whether or not a relationship with a university was a success was being able **to monitor and evaluate the relationship performance during its development**.

Thanks to creating an evaluation and monitoring procedure, Ferrovial has been able to assess the university—industry collaboration alongside the collaboration development itself. Thus, this assessment and monitoring has granted us the opportunity to, first, pivot when a collaboration agreement was going out off the rails, and, second, gather enough information to make a decision about whether or not to renew the collaboration agreement.

First of all, in this chapter, we would like to present Ferrovial, a global company present in more than 15 countries. After a brief presentation of Ferrovial and its history, the chapter presents the strategic context for innovation, or why Ferrovial has a commitment to innovation as a tool for future success, and the Ferrovial innovation strategy, introducing how Ferrovial structures and manages its innovation strategy. Following that, the chapter sets out a few examples of university—Ferrovial collaborations.

After this introduction, the main text of the chapter follows, where we explain strategic success factors. First, explaining why we decided to build long-term collaboration agreements instead of short-term ones, second, how we built the monitoring and evaluation process and, finally, the challenges we faced when implementing the monitoring and evaluation methodology.

To conclude, the chapter showcases two successful examples of collaboration agreements between universities and Ferrovial. And, finally, the chapter ends with some conclusions, recommendations, and learnings from our side.

8.1.1 About Ferrovial

Ferrovial is a global comprehensive manager of infrastructures, which handles the complete asset cycle, from financing and design to construction, operation, and maintenance.

Ferrovial is one of the world's leading infrastructure operators and municipal services companies, committed to developing sustainable solutions.

The company has 96,000 employees and a presence in over 15 countries. It is a member of Spain's blue-chip IBEX 35 index and is also included in prestigious sustainability indices such as the Dow Jones Sustainability Index and FTSE4Good.

The company's activity is carried out through four business lines:

- **Services**: efficient provision of urban and environmental services and maintenance of infrastructures and facilities.
- **Toll roads (Cintra)**: promotion, investment, and operation of toll roads and other infrastructures.
- **Construction**: the design and construction of infrastructures in the areas of civil engineering work, building, and industrial construction.
- **Airports**: airport investment and operation. (Fig. 8.1).

Being a multinational company today, Ferrovial's history was written step by step: On 18 December **1952**, Rafael del Pino y Moreno founded Ferrovial in a loft apartment in central Madrid. The company originally focused on railway projects: it was created to execute a contract to mortise wood railroad ties for Renfe, the Spanish railroad company. In 1958, Renfe awarded Ferrovial the project to build the railway link between Las Rozas and Chamartín, in Madrid; it laid 30 km of track in 30 days. At the beginning of the **1960s**, Ferrovial had over 500 employees. The company expanded into constructing waterworks, roads, and buildings, and also moved into the toll road concession business. Ferrovial diversified into projects that were highly complex in both engineering and financial terms. Towards the end of the **1970s**, during the recession caused by the oil crisis, Ferrovial decided to explore opportunities in other countries. Its first international projects were concentrated in four countries: Libya, Mexico, Brazil, and

Toll roads

cintra

- Private development of transport infrastructure
- Managing 26 concessions in 109 countries, including 407 ETR in Toronto and the NTE and LBJ highways in Texas

Services

ferrovial
services

- Transport infrastructure maintenance
- Environmental services
- Services to the Natural Resources and Industrial sectors
- Facilities Management
- Services to Utilities

Construction

ferrovial
agroman

- Recognised worldwide for its design and construction capabilities in landmark projects in the areas of civil engineering, building, and particularly, large transport infrastructure
- More than 55 years' international experience in over 50 countries on 5 continents

Airports

ferrovial
airports

- One of the world's largest airport operators and investors
- 4 airports in the UK:
  - 25% stake in Heathrow
  - 50% stake in Aberdeen, Glasgow and Southampton
  - 90 M passengers in 2016
- Acquisition of Transchile, diversification of business in this area

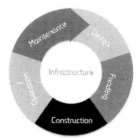

FIGURE 8.1   Ferrovial's business lines at a glance.

Paraguay. This constituted the first phase of international expansion in Ferrovial's history. During the **1980s**, Ferrovial played a very important role in modernizing Spain and making it more European after it joined what was then called the European Economic Community. The company was one of the key players in building the network of highways and access routes to big cities, and in expanding and modernizing ports, airports, and railways, as well as building new schools and hospitals. During this time, Ferrovial acquired Cadagua, a company specializing in designing, building, and operating drinking water and sewage treatment plants.

In **1992**, Rafael del Pino Calvo-Sotelo was appointed as CEO. By acquiring Agromán, Ferrovial positioned itself as one of Spain's largest construction companies. Ferrovial entered North America by obtaining 407 ETR, a Canadian toll road, under a 99-year concession. The company was floated on the stock exchange in 1999. In **2000**, Rafael del Pino Calvo-Sotelo was appointed company chairman. Ferrovial made important acquisitions during this decade: Polish construction company Budimex, services companies Amey in the UK and Cespa Spain, and the airport operator then called BAA, now Heathrow Airport Holdings. In **2013**, Ferrovial acquired Enterprise, a UK company specializing in services. In **2014**, the company acquired Glasgow, Aberdeen, and Southampton airports. Last, but not least, during **2016** Ferrovial purchased the Australian company Broadspectrum. This is a large services company working in various sectors, such as natural resources, energy, and transportation infrastructures. The company operates in Australia, and has a significant presence in the United States, Canada, New Zealand, and Chile. (Fig. 8.2).

Ferrovial's vision and values have evolved, adapting to modern times and to the culture of the various organizations within the group.

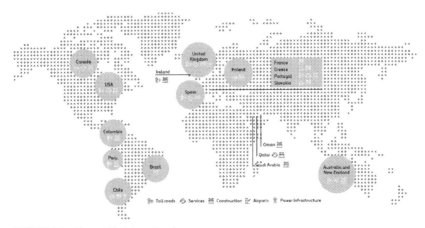

FIGURE 8.2   Ferrovial's international presence.

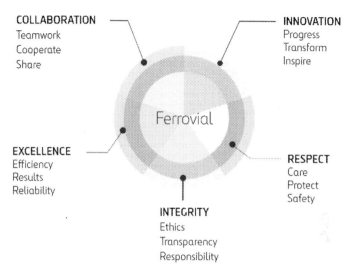

FIGURE 8.3   Ferrovial's corporate values.

Our vision addresses three questions about our activity:

Why? Shaping the future through the development and operation of sustainable infrastructures and cities.

How? Committing to the highest level of safety, operational excellence, and innovation.

What? Creating value for society and for our customers, investors, and employees.

Ferrovial's corporate values can be summarized in Fig. 8.3.
In the words of our Chairman Rafael del Pino:

Ferrovial has distinguished itself, above all, for its excellent professionals. Hard work and creativity centered on performance have allowed us to overcome complex challenges and to take advantage of opportunities, transforming individual skills into collective success.

Ferrovial, as a leading developer and operator in the infrastructure and services sector, will continue to shape the future of society with a continuous focus on talent, integrity, safety, excellence and innovation.

——Rafael del Pino,
Chairman

8.1.2 Strategic Context for Innovation

Several global factors are influencing Ferrovial's strategies related to construction, management, and operation of transportation infrastructures and municipal services. Demographic shifts such as population growth—primarily in emerging economies and in urban areas—and aging—primarily in developed economies—are fueling demand for a variety of social infrastructure and transport services, especially for new integrated services. The globalization of financial markets has helped to increase the number of financial institutions and new investors eager to fund infrastructure projects and related services. A greater number of citizens—i.e., the users of infrastructure services—has access to the latest technologies and uses them to engage with and comment on infrastructure services, leading to greater expectations regarding the nature of the service (e.g., greater transparency) and greater scrutiny of the quality of service delivery. Growing concerns about the environment, pollution, and the scarcity of natural resources are leading governments to seek solutions that are energy efficient and sustainable. Together, these factors are propelling governments throughout the world to redevelop and expand national infrastructure plans and to seek solutions that are integrated, environmentally sensitive, and used by increasingly digitally savvy citizens. Local authorities are also seeking expertise in selecting projects that make economic sense. This creates opportunities to offer new services, such as infrastructure planning services.

Greater demand for infrastructure development is fueling greater competition among infrastructure companies. Companies in the sector are striving to distinguish themselves by expanding and integrating their catalog of products and services with new activities such as energy efficiency. But service integration is challenging. Most companies in the infrastructure services industry operate as holding companies.

A second competitive force is the demand for innovation. Many customers—often cities or municipalities—include innovation as a criterion for selecting proposals. These entities want to satisfy citizens' demands for digitally savvy services. Citizens may seek updated versions of traditional services, such as the use of Radio-frequency identification (RFID) chips to improve the collection of trash from public garbage containers; or completely new services, such as free Wi-Fi in airports and the ability to easily report overflowing trash cans via mobile devices. Cities and municipalities are also eager to profit from the effective and efficient services enabled by digital technologies. With the recent hype surrounding the promises of Smart Cities, for example, many calls for proposals sought solutions that involved the Internet of Things. In preparation, Ferrovial discovered that the associated technology was not as advanced as or significantly more expensive than promoters claimed. Developing solutions that cover the interests of customers (to appear cutting-edge) and the interests of Ferrovial (to provide reliable and cost-effective services) is another source of pressure to enhance its innovation capabilities.

However, it is difficult to sustain any competitive advantage through innovation. Ferrovial assumes that when it releases an innovative service, it has only a limited time before competitors release similar services. As a result, Ferrovial senior management considers the ability to continuously innovate and improve on past innovations as essential to competitiveness.

8.1.3   Ferrovial's Innovation Strategy

Innovation is in Ferrovial's DNA. The main purpose of our innovation strategy is [to develop] new solutions that generate benefits for our businesses, in terms of new business models, new and better services for our customers and improved operational efficiency in our contracts.

—*Federico Flórez,*
Chief Information and Innovation Officer

As we explained, Ferrovial's strategy focuses on the development of complex contracts with high financing needs and the requirement for technological and innovative capabilities to respond to the challenges of society and generate value for its customers and users through sustainable and efficient solutions. Innovation, together with operational excellence and sustainability, is one of the pillars that supports Ferrovial's mission.

To foster innovation, Ferrovial is developing a plan with these objectives:

1. Foster synergies through support from the Executive Committee and by continuously identifying, designing, and developing tools and resources to support the innovation process.
2. Promote an innovative culture by encouraging employees to innovate.
3. Open innovation by seeking the best partners (e.g., universities, technology centers, and startups) to complement Ferrovial's capabilities and needs.
4. Create a common digital platform to share and enhance digital innovation.

From an **organizational** viewpoint, Ferrovial's innovation strategy plan is founded on three broad areas: (1) common governance to establish the open innovation model and take on challenges and opportunities, (2) an innovation community that seeks to identify relevant individuals and facilitate an appropriate cultural climate and, finally, (3) the necessary resources for development, such as information, financing, ecosystem and programs that support the model.

The **governance of innovation** is executed through the Innovation Committee that, led by the Chief Information and Innovation Officer, includes representatives from all the company's lines of business through its Directors of Innovation, together with key Human Resources functions. Their responsibility is to develop the innovation strategy, coordinate global programs, share information on individual projects and better practices, and contribute to deepening the culture of innovation.

Ferrovial has introduced an action program designed to encourage a culture of innovation throughout the organization that facilitates the identification and implementation of innovative solutions for businesses and clients using existing resources and centers in accordance with the strategy and priority areas identified. This program comprises actions such as organizing innovation days for management, a review of innovation responsibility in human resource policies (selection, evaluation, development, and compensation), training in creativity, innovation and entrepreneurship, and the introduction of innovation prizes for employees (Ferrovial Innovation Awards).

Among these four main areas, we will now focus in the third one, **seeking the best partners to complement Ferrovial's capabilities and needs**, which is the only area included under the scope of this chapter. Ferrovial develops an open innovation model, looking for the partners and collaborators that best complement each other to provide unique solutions to the challenges of each business unit. These challenges are identified according to the priorities set in the strategic planning process of the business units and **are reviewed every 6 months**. These challenges are managed and shared through the ecosystem underpinning Ferrovial's innovation policy, seeking to identify proof of concept, prototypes, and/or projects for their further development and implementation. The innovation strategy places significant **focus on implementation**, as it is one of the key indicators of its activity.

Thus, a key aspect of Ferrovial's approach to innovation has been open innovation—working with external parties to create new services, where universities and research centers are essential, as they are replete with knowledge, talent, and technology, and are breeding grounds for innovation. Those responsible for fostering innovation at Ferrovial do not believe that internal teams should be the only source of innovation, and believe that developing an innovation ecosystem around Ferrovial is a key strategic factor for fostering innovation.

To develop this strategy, close collaboration is critical with the different agents in the community where Ferrovial operates (administration, companies, entrepreneurs and startups, and universities and technological centers). Thus, Ferrovial has been creating an ecosystem of open innovation over the years, including the best external partners, such as universities, technology centers, and startups. Ferrovial considers that this is essential for complementing internal capabilities and identifying disruptive innovation.

From the Department of Open Innovation, Ferrovial continues to nurture and care for the ecosystem that is depicted below (Fig. 8.4):

An impressive figure is that Ferrovial managed **more than 100 innovation projects in 2016**, with a total **investment of 48 million euros**. Among them, four projects were in collaboration with Massachusetts Institute of Technology (MIT).

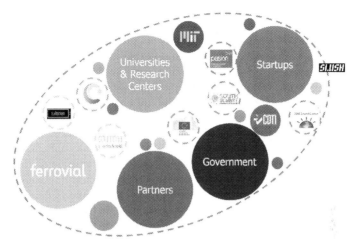

FIGURE 8.4   Ferrovial's open innovation ecosystem.

During the 2010—2015 period, an average of 20% of the innovation projects managed were collaborations with universities or research centers. In that period, Ferrovial invested 250 million euros to develop more than 600 innovation projects [for instance, 17 projects were developed in collaboration with MIT and 39 in collaboration with Center for Innovation in Intelligent Infrastructures (CI3)]. Last, but not least, more than 2500 employees were training in innovation skills and Ferrovial collaborated with more than 300 startups in that period.

Ferrovial has defined seven areas of interest in innovation on which it focuses its efforts:

- **Energy efficiency**: With the aim of reducing greenhouse gas emissions, helping to reduce energy costs and anticipating future regulations, projects are being developed in energy efficiency maintenance, monitoring, auditing, and optimization for buildings, reducing power consumption in public lighting, and implementing expert energy management systems.
- **Cities**: Projects are developed to meet the needs of the cities of the future. They are aimed at cutting costs and improving the population's quality of life by guaranteeing sustainable economic development.
- **Waste management**: In response to concerns regarding climate change and environmental sustainability, projects are underway to recover energy from waste, both as a partial substitute for conventional fossil fuels and as a solution to treat or eliminate the growing volumes of waste generated by the consumer society, as well as recovering materials from this waste.
- **Water**: Energy and process optimization, both in the field of seawater desalination employing reverse osmosis and in the purification of

wastewaters. For this, innovative technologies are incorporated and exist-ing water treatment processes are improved, while new ones are developed.

- **Innovative construction**: Execution of projects that improve the produc-tivity and environmental sustainability of construction activity in all of its areas.
- **Toll roads**: The main business lines include the optimization of traffic models, new payment methods, models to relate to and offer services to users, and solutions that increase operational effectiveness. By applying the latest technologies to infrastructures and vehicles, projects are being developed that are focused on: research using complex algorithms to operate managed lanes; deployment of lighter and more secure architec-tures for processing operational and financial data; remote management of toll plazas via applications on mobile devices; prototype toll systems using global positioning system (GPS) and mobile user interfaces; control of the management of critical assets; and the study of the elasticity of mobility.
- **Airports:** Optimization of real-time integrated management of the vari-ous assets and resources through sensor technologies or portable devices (wearables), improving the passenger experience within the airport, as well as the development of new business models and services.

Its aim is to position itself as a benchmark in Spain and around the world in the development of intelligent infrastructure products and services.

8.1.4   Ferrovial & Universities: It's All About Business

Ferrovial considers universities and technological centers a fundamental part of its strategy and ecosystem of innovation, taking into account the technical and engineering component of its activity, as well as the complexity of its developments and the expertise and knowledge they offer.

Ferrovial has built collaboration agreements with a wide range of univer-sities and research centers from Spain, Europe, and North America. For instance, the universities with which the group's companies have concluded agreements include: the Polytechnic University of Madrid (UPM), Alcalá de Henares University, Carlos III University of Madrid, and the Polytechnic University of Catalonia, among many others in Spain; the University of Surrey (United Kingdom), ALTO University (Finland), University of Birmingham (United Kingdom), University of Manchester (United Kingdom), and Newcastle University (United Kingdom), among many others in Europe; the MIT, University of Texas at Austin, Cornell University, and Stanford, among others in the USA and Canada.

Although in the next section, we will focus on Ferrovial's long-term rela-tionships with these centers, it is important to explain the general approach and framework employed in most of the collaborations. Thus, the process can be summarized as:

1. First, the capacities of each of the centers are identified, investigating as far as the research groups and departments that are of interest to Ferrovial. Ferrovial experts try to value these capacities according to the knowledge that may exist in the company and the experience obtained from past projects executed. The contracts and/or business units affected conduct this assessment.

2. Based on the challenges of each business unit, action lines are established with these centers, with the objective of identifying collaborative projects. This relationship is two way, and the projects must always be approved by the corresponding business unit.

3. The collaborations may have different forms:

   a. **Framework agreements for long-term collaboration**. This framework is developed below as a central part of this chapter.

   b. Specific projects with a defined scope, organization, deliverables, term, and cost. These projects are evaluated according to the degree of achievement of the objectives established.

   c. Participation in jointly funded public–private partnerships, which are evaluated the same as the previous point.

   d. Participation in programs to promote and accelerate entrepreneurship, with open calls focused on challenges within joint areas of interest: such as Madrid Smart Lab, Sheffield Smart Lab, Pasion IE, Global Futurizer, etc.

4. Biannual and coordinated by the Innovation Directorate, the evaluations of these centers are updated, according to the history of the executed projects. The evaluation is performed by each business unit and consists of:

   a. Assessment of the technical capacities provided by the university or research center.

   b. Valuation of dedication and involvement in joint projects.

   c. Individual evaluation of each of the collaborations, according to the achievement of previously defined objectives

5. During the Innovation Committee, managers put together projects and evaluations with the aim of making decisions for the future. These decisions may include:

   a. **Renew** the collaboration agreement with the university or research center if the evaluation is positive and the goals set have been met.

   b. **Modify**/adjust/revise the collaboration agreement when all goals are not being met or are not being adequately met.

   c. **Cancel** the collaboration agreement or make the decision to not renew it. In this case, the objectives have not been met, the dedication and involvement of the center is not adequate or the technical capabilities provided are not relevant to Ferrovial.

Following this process, Ferrovial plans to perform continuous and measured monitoring to adjust the capacities of the universities or research centers to the challenges and objectives pursued by Ferrovial, within a framework of collaboration and mutual benefits. We believe that it is only in this way that a mutual relationship of success and trust can be achieved between both parties.

As a final point of this introduction, we will briefly mention the indicators used in innovation management and that will be used for the subsequent development of the methodology used for the evaluation of the activity of technology centers and universities. These indicators are:

Volume of activity indicators:

- Investment
- Number of projects
- Number of staff trained in innovation
- Number of collaborations with universities and research centers
- Number of startups in portfolio

Indicators of evolution of innovation flow:

- Number of approved ideas
- Number of pilot projects started
- Number of pilot projects finished
- Number of pilot projects implemented

Expected and achieved benefits in the implemented projects:

- Economic benefits
- Branding/image benefits
- Strategic positioning benefits

8.2   EVALUATION AS A SUCCESS-FACTOR IN LONG-TERM UNIVERSITY-INDUSTRY COLLABORATIONS (UICS) COLLABORATION AGREEMENTS

8.2.1   Why Long-Term Collaboration Agreements?

After explaining the general innovation process and, in particular, relations with universities, we will focus on the long-term stable agreements that are developed within Ferrovial that seek working relationships with global and multiyear goals and set strategic research fields. Those research fields will always be in line with the seven areas of interest in innovation previously mentioned. However, the research fields could be defined in a more specific way, focusing, for instance, a new technology applied in one of the seven areas of interest for Ferrovial. As an example, those research fields may include:

- Energy efficiency
- Cities: Transportation and urban mobility

- Cities: Efficiency and improvement of urban services
- Water + Waste Treatment: Water desalination and waste treatment
- Toll roads: Digital technologies (i.e., Big Data) applied to infrastructures
- Innovative construction: 3D printing applied to construction
- Emerging technologies impact (i.e., drones, artificial intelligence) applied to Ferrovial's innovation areas of interest.

These strategic research fields must always be of application in the seven areas of interest in innovation set out earlier, namely: city energy efficiency, waste treatment, water, toll roads, and airports and innovative construction.

In turn, these long-term agreements seek the creation of mechanisms to jointly identify new challenges and projects in accordance with the university's capabilities and the needs of Ferrovial's business units, the development of projects of interest according to the defined areas and objectives, the development of an innovation ecosystem around these agreements (including administration, companies, and entrepreneurs), the dissemination of results and, finally, the measurement and monitoring of those results.

Among the collaborations that Ferrovial has led and continues to carry out in this area, these agreements merit mention:

1. Agreement with the MIT (USA) to develop innovative projects addressing infrastructure energy management and mobility of the future.
2. The CI3 (Spain), is a foundation established in Spain, between the regional government of Castile-La Mancha, the University of Alcalá de Henares and Ferrovial, according to the triple helix model proposed by Etzkowitz and Leydesdorff in 1966 as a three-component system (university, enterprise, and government) creating wealth together through a common project. The aim of this collaboration is the development of information technologies applied to infrastructure management.
3. Santander City Lab (Spain) is the research center formed by the Santander City Council, the University of Cantabria and Ferrovial following the triple helix concept as well. The Santander City Lab (known as the Research Centre for Smart Cities in Santander—CiCiS per its Spanish acronym) is working to define analytical models that will enable us to improve the efficiency of the provision of services through the intelligent use of urban information.
4. UPM. Ferrovial collaborates with the UPM with the objective of finding solutions to Ferrovial's challenges with the support of the researchers and spin-off startups from this university.
5. Manufacturing Technology Centre (MTC). This collaboration agreement makes it possible to bring together Ferrovial engineers and technology leaders with MTC engineers to discuss their business and technology needs and automation challenges in an open forum with a favorable environment. This gives them the ability to discuss with colleagues and experts across groups and across lines of business, while in dialog with MTC experts who can catalyze the ideas into reality. This agreement aims to inform

Ferrovial engineers of the latest technologies available from Industry 4.0, advanced automation and inspection and, in particular, additive manufacturing and how these may fit with Ferrovial's current challenges.

6. Agreement with Cornell University (USA) to endorse the Cornell Program in Infrastructure Policy and boost research and knowledge in transportation policy.

7. Agreement with McGill University (Canada) and, in particular, with McGill's Department of Civil Engineering and Applied Mechanics, in order to pursue a research collaboration under Mitacs (Accelerate program) and/or Mitacs (Elevate program) for social welfare analysis of road capacity expansion options.

We will now explain the first two examples in detail, although the relationship approach always follows this same process:

1. Definition and signing of a collaboration protocol and framework agreement.

2. Identification and collection of the objectives pursued, definition of a general action framework, as well as identifying other issues related to intellectual property and commercialization of the results that will be obtained under the collaboration agreement.

3. Governance of the agreement, at a general and project level.

4. Generation of follow-up reports and deliverables.

5. Identification of key performance indicators (KPIs) and monitoring the established metrics for evaluating the collaboration agreement.

As mentioned in Sections 8.2.4 and 8.2.5, we will explain the collaboration agreement with MIT in detail, as well as the agreement with the University of Alcalá de Henares to create the Center for the Innovation of Smart Infrastructures (CI3).

8.2.2 Success Factor: Monitoring and Evaluation of Collaboration Agreements

We have mentioned what, in our opinion, is the most beneficial kind of collaboration between universities and research centers or industry: to set up long-term collaboration agreements between the university and research center and Ferrovial.

But, why is it necessary to set up a successful and disciplined long-term collaboration agreement? What is the success factor? From Ferrovial's experience, it is extremely helpful to develop a structured methodology that facilitates the process of monitoring and evaluation of these collaboration agreements. Thanks to creating an evaluation and monitoring procedure, Ferrovial has been able to assess university–industry collaborations, in parallel with the collaboration development itself.

The aim of the monitoring and evaluation process is to:

- Keep the company posted about news about the collaboration.
- Assess if the collaboration is meeting the goals set at the beginning.
- Facilitate internal communications with the partners involved in the collaboration.
- Assess the status of the collaboration.
- Support the decision of canceling, modifying, or renewing the collaboration agreement.

In this monitoring and evaluation process the following internal bodies are involved, which have these roles and are made up of these company representatives:

- The **Collaboration Committee's** task is to assess the status of on-going projects and monitor if the results are meeting the previously established project goals as well as evaluating the capacities and dedication provided by the university and research center. The Collaboration Committee is formed by the Ferrovial representatives directly involved in the collaboration agreement, which include the people responsible for the collaboration agreement, representing both the Innovation Department and the business units, and the different project managers in charge of the current project under development within the agreed framework. It meets quarterly.
- The **Ferrovial Innovation Committee** assesses if the global goals are being met and whether the benefits resulting from the collaboration are worth the effort put in by Ferrovial. The Innovation Committee meets biannually and is formed by the Ferrovial Innovation Director, the Innovation Directors and managers from the different business units, and the party responsible for the collaboration agreement, who acts as the Collaboration Committee spokesperson. The Ferrovial Innovation Committee makes the decision to cancel, modify, or renew the collaboration agreement, using the information gathered by the Collaboration Committee.

Both, the Collaboration Committee and the Innovation Committee will fill out the Collaboration Agreement Monitoring Template (please, see Annex I). This template will be used to follow the progress of the collaboration agreement and will to support making and reporting the final decision concerning the collaboration agreement.

8.2.3   Challenges in Implementing the Monitoring and Evaluation Methodology

There are a few challenges that threaten the implementation of a monitoring and evaluation methodology. Correct implementation of this measure is crucial for taking advantage of its outcomes. What are the main challenges a big corporation might face? Usually, when trying to implement a similar methodology, corporations struggle with a wide range of difficulties. For instance, many companies lose their focus. It is highly recommended to **clearly set the focus** and goals pursued by the agreement by setting business challenges, priorities, and needs, and sharing them with the university. If they are not set at the very beginning, collaborations tend to disperse and lead to a waste of resources and time in the end. Second, it is important to **involve the right people** in the different committees and boards. Initial assessments must be performed by the people who are in direct contact with the university and research center and who are actually monitoring the project being developed under the collaboration agreement framework. The methodology must be based on real facts and figures, which can only be provided by the people with access to them. Therefore, it is important to have all the people on the Collaboration Committee who can provide data straight from the source. Including all the right people will assure that all the information can be collected that is necessary to evaluate the collaboration agreement. Moreover, collecting the opinions of all the stakeholders involved will prevent you from making a decision that could be detrimental to some of them. In parallel, the representatives involved in the Innovation Committee, which will make the final decision at the end, must be able to look at the big picture. Canceling, modifying, or renewing the collaboration agreement should not be a decision made by people in direct contact with the projects being developed. This could adulterate the decision-making process. Another example that can undermine the collaboration between both parties is wasting time. **Being rigorous about planning meetings** is mandatory to ensure the smooth development of the collaboration. The methodology should be developed as it is. Delays or cutting corners will be detrimental to the whole monitoring, evaluation, and decision-making process. The different committees must stick to the planned agenda and meet with the stated frequency. This is even more important when both the company and the university are located at such a physical distance that time zones become another player at the table, as is the case with MIT and Ferrovial. Thus, being precise can help us to avoid unnecessary tension.

Although it may sound obvious, **freeing the necessary resources** is essential and primarily affects companies. It is a fact—especially with large corporations—that a huge workload is handled on a daily basis. Thus, executives and high-level managers are usually very possessive with their limited resources and reluctant to take part on different committees that will use up some of their time. Although this is understandable, for the sake of well-implemented methodology, high-level managers must allow the required employees to spend the time they need to participate on different committees and provide any information that may be requested. Another very common source of misunderstandings among parties is communication. **Communicating decisions properly**, in particular, when making a decision such as modifying or even canceling the collaboration agreement, is not easy to achieve and should be planned, and cannot be left to fate. A complete communication and dissemination strategy is necessary to avoid misunderstandings and negative feelings. Decisions resulting from the monitoring and evaluation methodology should be properly explained to the concerned people within the company and university, revealing the facts collected during the monitoring and evaluation process that support the decision made. Moreover, the people in charge of communications should be appointed in advance from the very beginning, assigning these roles to the appropriate individuals, not only due to their communication skills but also depending on their position and relevance in the collaboration agreement organizational chart.

Last, but absolutely not least, **be patient**. Long-term collaboration agreements do not produce their most important results in the short-term. Carrying out a disciplined monitoring and evaluation process is essential for the success of the long-term collaboration, but decision makers must take into account the long-term characteristics of the agreement and bear in mind that the metrics and KPIs must be tailored and evaluated according to the timeline of the collaboration development. For instance, the MIT and Ferrovial collaboration agreement could have been viewed as unsuccessful according to some KPIs if we looked at them after the first year. However, some KPIs were set to assess in the long-term and others were set for the short-term. Some managers tend to be impatient and look at the long-term KPIs as if they could be validly assessed in the short-term. This is a poor practice that can lead to canceling projects that—with some patience—can end up being really successful.

8.2.4   A Successful Example: MIT Energy Initiative (MITEI)

8.2.4.1   Agreement and Governance

In 2010, Ferrovial and the MIT signed a 5-year agreement to join the MIT Energy Initiative (MITEI) and to support a range of critical research projects to help to transform the world's cities and support the critical infrastructures of the future.

Established in September 2006, the MITEI is an Institute-wide initiative designed to help to transform the global energy system to meet the needs of the future and to help build a bridge to that future by improving today's energy systems. The MITEI program includes research, education, campus energy management, and outreach activities that cover all areas of energy supply and demand, safety, and environmental impact.

"Innovation in infrastructure development will play a vital role in the upcoming decades because of the major changes that we face," said Rafael del Pino, Chairman of Ferrovial. "Therefore, it is in our interest to join forces with MIT, a world leader in innovation, to participate in and lead the transformation of cities and infrastructures."

Through this collaboration, Ferrovial became a Sustaining Member of the MITEI and allocated 5 million dollars to support a portfolio of research projects at the institute that met the company's strategic needs, in parallel with advancing critical scientific and technical understanding to meet the world's energy challenges.

Susan Hockfield, former MIT president, said: "Ferrovial's interests in the fields of smart infrastructures, transportation, and energy efficiency in buildings and cities are a perfect fit with MITEI's priorities. MIT offers breadth and strength in all these areas through its departments and schools, and we are looking forward to meshing our multidisciplinary talent with Ferrovial's strategic interests."

Ferrovial joined the Governing Board and, on a rotating basis, the Executive Committee of MITEI. In addition, Ferrovial personnel were designated as project heads to work alongside MIT researchers in managing project execution, which facilitated the exchange of knowledge between the two organizations.

As a member of the initiative, Ferrovial participated in the MITEI seed fund program, supporting novel and early-stage energy research projects designed to find new pathways to help to meet global energy challenges. The company also supported two fellows at MIT, the Ferrovial—MIT Energy Fellows.

Professor Ernest J. Moniz, former Director of the MITEI noted, "Transportation, water, and other critical infrastructures are essential components of a sustainable and efficient energy future. As one of the world's largest infrastructure groups, Ferrovial brought a new and unique perspective to the MIT Energy Initiative."

Besides the Executive Committee and the Governing Board of MITEI, Ferrovial arranged a bilateral board with MIT to discuss the general progress of the research projects and define the strategic lines of investigation on a yearly basis. On the other hand, Ferrovial's Innovation Committee conducts an internal review of the status of the research projects every quarter.

Every 2 or 3 years, innovation managers from all Ferrovial's business units meet with MIT professors and researchers to review the portfolio of ongoing projects, as well as to explore new opportunities for innovation. As part of this face-to-face meeting, sessions are organized in key areas (i.e., entrepreneurship, mobility, and city management) and exhibitions of startups are held to make the most of the innovation ecosystem of Kendall Square. Speedstorming techniques are also employed, during which MIT researchers and Ferrovial professionals, through a chain format, interact with limited time to explore new interdisciplinary ideas and identify new collaborations.

8.2.4.2   Joint Research

Between 2011 and 2015, Ferrovial developed 10 projects that focused on critical areas of construction, cities, infrastructures, water treatment, waste treatment, and energy efficiency, among others. The results of these projects were positive for the business in terms of strategic positioning, economic models, and branding, leading Ferrovial to renew its agreement with the MIT for a further 5 years (until 2020), to continue supporting strategic research aimed at transforming cities and developing the infrastructures of the future.

"By renewing our agreement with the MITEI, we are entering into a partnership to develop energy innovation projects that benefit both the company and society," explained Federico Flórez, Chief Information and Innovation Officer.

Under the agreement, Ferrovial has supported research projects to increase its scientific and technical knowledge and face the new challenges. The projects for the first 5-year period were:

1. Building infrared (IR) scanning and retrofit prioritization based on energy return on investment
2. Key decision factors for toll road usage by trucks
3. Prediction of ground movements due to tunneling and their effects on adjacent facilities
4. Carbon footprint of wastewater treatment
5. Software automation for identifying the 10 most valuable energy service opportunities
6. Optimization of seawater reverse osmosis
7. Prediction of seasonal ground movements for expansive clay Subgrades and their effects on the serviceability of pavements
8. City light scanning optimization and remediation
9. Modeling of material separation systems
10. Real-time toll optimization based on prediction of demand and traffic conditions

For each project, both Ferrovial and MIT appointed an interdisciplinary project team formed by principal investigators and research assistants to define the project scope and deliver the defined tasks, who have engaged regularly throughout the project calendar.

In 2016, four new projects were launched.

The philosophy of this collaboration with MIT is open to identifying other possible areas of mutual interest. This outlook recently resulted in the partnership—with a diverse consortium composed of leading international companies—to conduct a study entitled "Mobility of the Future."

Ferrovial and MIT already have extensive research activities underway in many facets of mobility. For this study, an interdisciplinary project team (the team will be made up of economists, engineers, computer scientists, social scientists, and urban planners) will synthesize these different areas of research within a system dynamics framework.

8.2.4.3 Arranging the Collaboration: Monitoring Reports and Activity Metrics

As explained, the capacities of MIT and its research groups are very broad, and of interest to Ferrovial. With 300 + research centers and 3000 + faculty and research staff at MIT, targeting people and projects relevant to the company's research needs could be overwhelming. Therefore, the Institute's Industrial Liaison Program provides expert navigation of MIT's vast resources.

The Ferrovial Open Innovation Manager, with the help of an appointed Industrial Liaison Officer (ILO), has cultivated a strong, working relationship with MIT faculty and continuously monitors the latest lab news and research and technology developments to jointly design faculty interactions and to develop an action plan. The ILO is not only a veteran MIT insider, but is well-briefed on Ferrovial's needs and objectives, to perfectly advocate the company's research and strategic agenda on campus, quickly identifying and engaging the interest of relevant faculty. The ILO provides continuity and serves as the facilitator to move discussions along and work with both Ferrovial's representatives and faculty to enable mutually beneficial outcomes.

General objectives of the action plan are to:

- Prioritize interest areas of both Ferrovial and MIT
- Identify ideal company participants, stakeholders
- Develop objectives for Ferrovial−MIT interactions
- Schedule specific activities involving interactions with faculty researchers, labs, and centers
- Provide ongoing assessment, advice on next steps and follow-up to kick-off the research projects

The action plan calls for Ferrovial managers and researchers to visit the MIT campus several times a year, actively participating in a series of meetings with MIT experts.

In summary, the first stage is to connect Ferrovial's business units' challenges to MIT's expertise, talent, and technologies, and review these demands and capacities periodically. The benefits are strategic, economic, and branding.

The second stage is to frame each project interaction. The Ferrovial−MIT agreement is defined for a 5-year period to be renewed at the end. By definition, this is a framework for long-term collaboration regardless of the specific projects developed, but overall success obviously depends to a larger extent on the results of each of the research projects. The projects are evaluated according to the degree of achievement of the defined objectives.

Each research project has its own dynamics for follow-up, but mainly consists of monthly conference calls, meeting minutes, and brief reports or exchanges of information by email.

As stated, the impact of this collaboration also has a more far-reaching outlook and vision than just the research projects, as it provides the ability to participate in joint consortia with other leading companies, as is the case with the Mobility of the Future study and the seed fund program. Moreover, by being part of Kendall Square's innovation ecosystem, Ferrovial benefits from the entrepreneurial mindset and vibrant agents present in the area, as they are startups and VCs.

Quarterly, during Ferrovial's Innovation Committee meetings, managers update the status of each project, in order to adopt suitable measures to realign tasks to meet objectives. MITEI does provide a quarterly report on economic data.

Less frequently, on an annual basis the established Ferrovial−MITEI board reviews the priority areas of innovation and the progress of each project. And every 2−3 years a broader conference of professors, researchers, students, and Ferrovial innovation managers analyze the project portfolio and explore alternative areas of research.

Further, biannually and coordinated by Ferrovial's Innovation Directorate, the MIT agreement evaluation is updated. This evaluation is conducted by each business unit and consists of assessing the technical capacities provided, the valuation of the time allocated to the people involved, and the midterm results of the projects/studies/programs. The summary is explained and discussed at the Ferrovial's Innovation Committee along with the chief information and innovation officer (CIIO).

In addition, when the agreement was established, goals were defined and some indicators were set up to monitor their fulfillment, which would facilitate the decision-making and revision of the strategies. (Table 8.1).

8.2.4.4   Evaluating the Collaboration Agreement and Decision to Renew

As stated, the collaboration between the MIT and Ferrovial started in 2010. The initial agreement was for a 5-year collaboration.

The first decision made after signing was to appoint a party in charge of the collaboration agreement. This role would act as the contact between MIT and Ferrovial for managing issues. In order to monitor and evaluate the development of the collaboration agreement, Ferrovial created the committee that would take part in the monitoring process: the Collaboration Committee. The Collaboration Committee was formed by Ferrovial employees involved in the collaboration agreement. The committee would meet four times a year (quarterly) to assess the development of the collaboration agreement as a whole, but also the progress and the results of the different projects being carried out under the agreement. This committee was formed by senior managers as, for instance: Ferrovial's Quality & Environment Director,

TABLE 8.1 Goals and Indicators Set to Monitor MIT—Ferrovial Collaboration

Ferrovial—MIT goals	Indicators
a. To exercise the rights of the agreement and adequately use the resources allocated to develop 21st-century smart infrastructures, actively contributing to innovation knowledge by supporting, promoting, and facilitating the transfer of technology in Ferrovial infrastructures.	1. Number of innovation projects developed and implemented, studies and programs executed
b. To strengthen applied research in new technologies in the fields of transportation, water, cities, energy efficiency...	2. Number of fields of research covered
c. To effectively exploit innovation, through the creation and subsequent management of intellectual property.	3. Number of patents or exclusive rights
d. To identify future needs and early demands.	4. Number of reports of state-of-the-art or technological monitoring produced during the research projects
e. To make the most of MIT Sloan executive education and other nonformal and/or educational activities.	5. Number of participations in courses and/or external events held by MIT
f. To be an active agent to promote ecosystem innovation and entrepreneurship, and to publish some of the results to use such knowledge in other industries.	6. Number of startups (funded by MIT) reviewed 7. Number of articles published by Ferrovial and MIT
g. To establish collaborations with other public or private institutions for purposes similar to those included in these goals.	8. Number of collaboration agreements with third parties that could benefit from Ferrovial—MIT framework agreement; branding

MIT, Massachusetts Institute of Technology.

Ferrovial's R&D Director, Ferrovial's Technical Office Director, among others.

During the collaboration development, the Collaboration Committee monitored the project's results and metrics and collected feedback about the collaboration impact in Ferrovial's businesses. For example, Ferrovial's Quality & Environment Director stated that this collaboration agreement between MIT and Ferrovial "is a differentiating element in transformative projects and in the relationship with local administrations." In addition,

Ferrovial's R&D Director mentioned that "during the tender phase of the offer, we convey confidence to the client and, in the execution phase, reliability in the decision making process," thanks to this collaboration agreement. Last, but not least, Ferrovial's Technical Office Director added that this collaboration agreement "has given us access to a leading international department in the field of traffic and the prestige of collaborating with Professor Ben-Akiva, creator of the theory of the estimation of the values of time for models of assignment to networks."

Moreover, twice a year, the spokesperson on behalf of the Collaboration Committee briefed the Ferrovial Innovation Committee on the status of the collaboration agreement. When the agreement was facing its end, the Innovation Committee, in charge of making the decision to cancel, modify, or renew the collaboration agreement, reached the following conclusions: This agreement gives Ferrovial **access to a leading technological center** (talent, technicians and scientists, and knowledge). Although it is a complex environment and very different to the company world (researchers, graduates, and professors), its **flexibility helps to manage the agreement**. The **identification of suitable professors is critical** (company oriented, flexibility, commitment, and team). The collaboration agreement **strengthens the company image and positioning globally**. This agreement grants Ferrovial the **opportunity to develop transforming projects** with medium-long-term horizon. Efficient project management procedures and skills are key to ensure the collaboration success (scope, deliverables, deadline, resources, and implementation). Intellectual property rights (IPR) management has been identified as a potential risk, although today there has not been any issue, and conditions the selection of projects. It is definitely a **positive learning process for the company**. It is necessary to invest in resources and time to capture all the value offered by MIT through this Collaboration agreement.

Thus, led by these lessons learned, the Innovation Committee proposed to renew the agreement between MIT and Ferrovial. As a matter of fact, the collaboration agreement was extended for 5 more years.

8.2.5   A Successful Example: Center for the Innovation of Smart Infrastructures (CI3)

8.2.5.1   Introduction

The CI3 was founded in 2010 at the initiative of its three founders, the Castile-La Mancha regional government, the University of Alcalá de Henares, and Ferrovial (large corporation), following the triple helix model by Prof. Etzkowitz, which optimizes the links between the public administration, academia, and industry to improve the conditions for innovation in a knowledge society.

It was created as a nonprofit foundation with the aim of contributing to the encouragement, promotion, and development of ICT technologies applied to infrastructures and with the mission of becoming a national and international benchmark in the research, development, and innovation of products and services for advanced infrastructure projects, in both urban and interurban environments.

Based in the city of Guadalajara (Spain), the center executes numerous actions and projects with regional, as well as national and international, scopes, creating a privileged environment in Europe to promote the development of smart and ecoefficient projects for social uses.

8.2.5.2 Governance

The Foundation, according to its statutes, is structured in three bodies: the Board of Trustees, the Executive Committee, and the General Director. The Board of Trustees is the organ of government, representation, and administration that is responsible for ensuring the fulfillment of its foundational goals.

The Executive Committee is in charge of selecting and approving the projects that are developed at the Center for Innovation.

The General Director is the chief executive officer of the Center and is responsible for the regular management of the Foundation and for designing and coordinating the Center's strategic planning in accordance with the objectives set by the Board.

In the last 3 months of each year, the Board of Trustees approves and sends an action plan to the Protectorate, which reflects the objectives and activities to be developed in the following year.

8.2.5.3 Organization of the Center's Activities

1. Projects

 The foundation develops innovation projects under two types of funding resources:

 a. Projects financed with its own funds from the employers' contributions:

 The challenges raised by employers are analyzed, and those that can be addressed by the Foundation are identified.

 Once approved, a multidisciplinary team formed by CI3's own resources and specialized technological partners is formed, supervised by technicians assigned by the employer who raised the challenge and who participates at control meetings during the project's life.

 b. Consortium projects supported by national and international organizations.

 The Foundation is very active in submitting project proposals subsidized by both national and European organizations, taking part in the formation of the consortium, technical coordination, and preparation of documentation until its conclusion.

2. Technology transfer

One of the Foundation's objectives is to promote research and technology transfer between academia and business.

3. Technology monitoring

CI3 maintains a permanent state-of-the-art monitoring of the technologies that may be useful for the Foundation's and its patrons' interests.

4. Consultancy tasks for the administration and companies

CI3 consultants analyze, understand and design innovation strategies for third-party administrations and companies.

8.2.5.4 Monitoring Reports and Activity Metrics

The Foundation's character makes CI3 an organization whose value is measured by its capacity to bring benefits to society. Thus, it is important to allocate time and tasks aimed at evaluating and measuring the social impact generated by its activity.

When the Center was set up, foundational objectives were defined and metrics were set up to monitor their fulfillment, meaning that the objectives were transformed into quantifiable elements to verify the organization's progress over the time, as well as to predict its future evolution, which would facilitate decision-making and the revision of strategies. (Table 8.2).

TABLE 8.2 Goals and Indicators Set to Monitor CI3 Collaboration

Foundational goals	Indicators
a. To contribute actively to the design, promotion, development, fundraising, participation, and coordination of the projects that are promoted in the scope of intelligent infrastructures.	1. Number of innovation projects developed and implemented
b. To strengthen applied research in new technologies in the field of intelligent infrastructures, and contribute to the development of sustainable cities, assuming a commitment to society and the pursuit of its well-being.	2. Number of pilots in cities or infrastructures 3. Number of sustainable economic projects 4. Number of environmental projects 5. Number of social projects
c. To contribute actively to the innovation process by supporting, promoting, and facilitating the transfer of technology in the field of intelligent infrastructures.	6. Number of projects with universities

(Continued)

TABLE 8.2 (Continued)

Foundational goals	Indicators
d. To effectively exploit innovation, through the creation and subsequent management of intellectual property.	7. Number of patents or utility models 8. Number of licenses to patrons or companies
e. To identify future needs and early demands.	9. Number of reports of the state-of-the-art or technological monitoring
f. To develop training activities and other informative and/or educational activities.	10. Number of participations in courses and/or external events
g. To be a forum for reflection and debate between the public and private agents involved in the innovation process.	11. Number of forums organized by CI3
h. To establish collaborations with other public or private institutions for purposes similar to those included in these statutes.	12. Number of collaboration agreements with third parties 13. Number of national or European subsidized consortium projects

CI3, Center for the Innovation of Smart Infrastructures.

8.3 CONCLUSIONS/RECOMMENDATIONS

We cannot lose sight of what our end goal is: to build long-term collaboration agreements with universities and research centers, which are highly beneficial to both parties and generate products and/or solutions that, in the end, are implemented at Ferrovial's businesses. Bearing the success factor in mind, there are aspects that will ensure the feasibility of these agreements. They include:

- Clearly **set the focus and goals** pursued by the agreement by setting business challenges, priorities, and needs, and sharing them with the university. If they are not defined from the very beginning, collaborations tend to disperse, wasting resources and time in the end.
- It is important to **involve the right people** in the different committees and boards. Initial assessments must be carried out by the people who are in direct contact with the university and research center and who are actually monitoring the project being developed under the collaboration agreement framework. The methodology must be based on real facts and figures that can only be provided by the people who have access to them, straight from the source. Access to the right people will ensure collecting all the information necessary to evaluate the collaboration agreement.

Moreover, asking all the stakeholders involved for their opinions will pre-vent us from making decisions that could be detrimental to some of them. At the same time, the representatives involved in the Innovation Committee must be able to look at the big picture. Canceling, modifying, or renewing the collaboration agreement should not be a decision made by people in direct contact with the projects being developed. This could adulterate the decision-making process.

- Always hold **bilateral/matchmaking meetings**. If you want a relation-ship to be successful, it must be beneficial for both parties. You must find the fit to have a future together.
- Long-term collaboration agreements must be signed based on both **quan-titative and qualitative objectives** and a clear roadmap, stating a starting point and a destination where we want to go together.
- **Generate a climate of trust** between both entities, but also among all the people involved directly in the collaboration agreement, such as proj-ect managers and researchers.
- Once the collaboration framework is set, **do not delay in making deci-sions**. Starting the projects fast and start working as soon as possible facilitate meeting the established goals and metrics.
- **Being rigorous when scheduling meetings** is mandatory to ensure that the collaboration develops smoothly and to avoid unnecessary tensions. Delays or cutting corners will end up being detrimental to the whole evaluation process. The different committees must stick to the planned agenda and meet with the stated frequency. This is even more important when the company and the university are located at such physical dis-tances that time zones become another player at the table.
- **Communicating decisions properly**, in particular, when making a deci-sion such as modifying or even canceling the collaboration agreement, is not easy to achieve and should be planned. A complete communication and dissemination strategy is necessary to avoid misunderstandings and negative feelings. Decisions resulting from the monitoring and evaluation methodology should be properly explained within the company and uni-versity, revealing the facts that support the decision made. Moreover, people in charge of communications should be appointed at the very beginning, not only in light of their communication skills, but also their position and relevance in the collaboration agreement organizational chart.
- Last but not least, we highly recommend, first, **identifying the appropri-ate KPIs** to accurately measure the results obtained, and, second, the KPIs must be varied over the time, during the execution of the collabora-tion agreement. Hence, this should be an iterative process. **Be patient**. Long-term collaboration agreements do not yield their most important results in the short-term. A disciplined monitoring and evaluation process is essential for the success of long-term collaborations, but decision

makers must take into account the long-term characteristics of the agreement and bear in mind that the **metrics and KPIs must be tailored and evaluated according to the timeline of developing the collaboration.** Remember that **some KPIs are set to assess the long-term and others were set for the short-term.**

UNIVERSITY & RESEARCH CENTRE TEMPLATE   ferrovial

AGREEMENT CODE   (COMPANY-AGREEMENT-YEAR-NUMBER)

BUSINESS UNIT

SERVICES ☐   TOLL ROADS ☐   CONSTRUCTION ☐   AIRPORTS ☐

Company name	Agreement name

Business representative	Innovation representative

MAIN INNOVATION OR RESEARCH AREA

CITIES ☐	ENERGY EFFICIENCY ☐	WASTE TREATMENT ☐	WATER ☐
TOLL ROADS ☐	AIRPORTS ☐	INNOVATIVE CONSTRUCTION ☐	OTHER: _____

PURPOSE OF THE AGREEMENT

Description of the purpose of the agreement

Capacities & Technologies sought

ECOSYSTEM

University / Research Centre	Department / Area

University / Centre representative	Department / Area representative

SELECT THE OBJECTIVES APPLICABLE TO THIS AGREEMENT (at least 5)

OBJECTIVE	Weight*	Achievement (%)	Comments
1.			
2.			
3.			
4.			
5.			
TOTAL	100		

*Please allocate a weight to each objective taking into account that the total sum must be 100.

FUNDING

AGREEMENT INVESTMENT 2017 [................................] €   AGREEMENT DURATION

TOTAL AGREEMENT INVESTMENT [................................] €   FROM YEAR _____ TO YEAR _____

PENDING INVESTMENT [................................] €

FOLLOW UP LOG (status: On track*; requires adjustment*; failing to comply*)

Status	Date	Comments

*On track: The collaboration agreement is going well, all the objectives are being met and the development of the agreement is satisfactory.
*Requieres adjustment: Some of the objectives are being met but there are some deviations that should be fixed.
*Failing to comply: The objectives are not being met, the overall development of the project is not satisfactory at all.

RENEWAL DECISION (to be taken at the end of the collaboration agreement)

Decision responsible	Date

DECISION

RENEW ☐　　　MODIFY ☐　CANCEL ☐

CANCELLATION REASON

OBJECTIVES NOT REACHED ☐	ECOSYSTEM NOT RELEVANT ☐	LACK OF HR RESOURCES NEEDED ☐
DEDICATION & INVOLVEMENT NOT ADEQUATE ☐	CAPABILITIES NOT RELEVANT FOR FERROVIAL ☐	OVERDUE DEADLINES (week/month/year) ☐

Explain the decision according to the topics below

1. Objectives reached:

2. Capacities & Technologies provided by university or research centre:

3. Dedication & Involvement of university or research centre:

Chapter 9

Recommendations and Outlook

Lars Frølund[1,2] and Max F. Riedel[3]

[1]Aarhus University, Aarhus, Denmark, [2]Massachusetts Institute of Technology, Cambridge, MA, United States, [3]Siemens AG, Munich, Germany

The companies in this book give evidence to the change from an ad hoc approach to a more and more systematic approach to university engagement, and correspondingly, a professionalization of university relations. Against this background, and in long discussions with the authors of this book and many others, we have derived the five success factors that structure the book.

In the following, we synthesize the recommendations given across the book chapters and for each success factor. We then present the University Partnership Canvas[1] as a tool for companies (and universities) to assess and further develop a systematic approach to university—industry collaboration. Finally, we ask the question: What does the future of university engagement look like?

9.1 RECOMMENDATIONS

The research done in each chapter has helped us develop the 5 success-factors and has resulted in specific recommendations. This said, it is important for us to underline that each company should find its own way to drive university collaborations that fits their individual goals, industry sector, corporate culture, etc. There is no one-size-fits-all approach. Nevertheless, we can synthesize the recommendations for each success factor in the following way:

1. *Select the focus areas of your university partnerships in alignment with your business goals*
   a. Every topic or focus area for university engagement must be clearly linked with the corporate strategy to allow specific targets to be set. When creating this link, do not only include R&D, but also, for

---

1. See also Frølund, Murray, and Riedel (2018). The university partnership canvas is inspired by the business model canvas developed by Osterwalder and Pigneur (2010).

Strategic Industry-University Partnerships. DOI: https://doi.org/10.1016/B978-0-12-810989-2.00017-5

181

example, operations, product development, human resources, marketing, and sales.

b. Structure research fields for university collaboration cross-silo, so that university engagement becomes relevant for numerous departments and becomes a vehicle for internal collaboration. Achieve this by establishing a specific organizational entity, which includes those responsible for different business areas and functions like BMW's University Strategy Circle.

2. *Select your primary university partners in a systematic way*

a. Moving away from ad hoc collaborations often leads to the definition of tier-one strategic university partners. Select your strategic partners with established reputation in your focus areas and in strategically relevant parts of the world. More importantly, they should share your ambitions and the will to make the partnership a success for both.

b. Attract the best partners by offering access to in-house technology and infrastructure and by sharing strategic goals and deeper levels of knowledge. Rolls Royce's University Technology Centers are a good example for this approach.

c. Not all external innovation can or should be done with tier-one partners. Sometimes, certain universities are best suited for one but only one small research field, or for local talent acquisition. Do not make the mistake and prohibit this kind of collaboration just because it is not with a strategic partner. DuPont has even abandoned the strategic partnership concept in favor of a data-driven partner selection process.

d. For extended workbench projects, select partners case-by-case and based on expertise, technical equipment, and proximity. However, always consider working with one of your strategic partners, even if they are not *the* best but only *among* the best (for example, top three), since advantages like an existing master research agreement may outweigh slight disadvantages in expertise.

e. Both for strategic and ad hoc partners, be aware of spatial and cultural distances. To mitigate this, establish fast and transparent communication and don't underestimate the need for regular real (as opposed to virtual) personal contact between the project teams and executives.

3. *Select collaboration formats that match your focus areas and business goals*

a. Companies who successfully collaborate with universities deploy a wide range of collaboration formats which are constantly connected to the specific business goals in the innovation process—see the example of Novo Nordisk.

b. Strategic partnerships usually include a variety of collaboration formats under an umbrella that comprises a common vision, a clear topic focus, and a set of ground rules. The agreement should include business objectives, the duration of the partnership and budget, and a high-level research plan with milestones and stop/go or extension criteria. Grow the partnership further by integrating bottom-up proposals for new projects, but review proposals by clearly defined criteria to avoid opportunistic use of the strategic partnership. Use a high-level steering committee to steer the partnership, but structure collaborations so that decisions are made at the lowest appropriate level.

c. Jointly engaging in publicly funded projects (for example, through the European Commission's H2020 program) can serve well as a first step to get to know and evaluate partners for further engagement. Many consider this an even more important benefit of such projects than leveraging the funding, as the effort to prepare a proposal is relatively high (and not reimbursed) and the long-term commitment (usually for 3 years) should not be underestimated.

d. For contract research, it is important to have a specific research plan with clearly defined milestones and objectives to which the budget is linked. Agree on how to handle cultural differences, such as need to publish vs. need for confidentiality at the beginning of the collaboration. Of course, how to deal with intellectual property (IP) should be clarified upfront, but don't let contract negotiations delay the project start for too long, if not necessary. The project leaders should estimate the probability for generation of IP in the project. If this is low, it can be a good option to agree to negotiate IP ownership and licensing terms *not upfront* but only in the unlikely case that IP is indeed generated. If possible, ensure anchoring the project at a higher organizational level (sometimes difficult on the university side), to have a dispute solving mechanism in the collaboration.

e. PhD/Postdoc programs, as described by Novo Nordisk in their chapter, serve well as talent pipeline and to explore further collaboration with top-tier research institutes. Jointly select candidates for the PhD/Postdoc programs, with the final decision with the university supervisor. If the PhD/Postdoc is working with confidential data or in directly business-relevant projects, clarify upfront how to guarantee a thesis according to highest scientific standards, while at the same time keeping some information confidential. Focus the fellowship program to a few strategic partners to reduce complexity and resource demands and provide critical mass.

f. Invest in joint research infrastructure to create trust, long-term commitment, and a constant exchange of ideas and good practices as underlined by Rolls-Royce. Develop flexible "catch-all" contracts for colocation to cover the daily cooperation and also future, not yet foreseeable legal and IP issues, as IBM and ETH Zürich have done in their joint Nanotechnology Center.

g. Enrich the partnership with joint conferences, symposia, hackathons, idea competitions, and student mentoring. All of these are also helpful for talent search and recruitment.

4. *Have dedicated people, processes, and organization to support your university partnerships*

a. Management commitment is key. All strategic partnerships should be governed by a high-level steering committee with senior leaders from all partners to set the focus and balance various interests. Use crossfunctional steering committees to guarantee broad buy-in and internal alignment with other programs and thus maximize impact.

b. A management sponsor should lead the committee and be held responsible for the success of the partnership. This person should have personal commitment, passion for innovation, and a good internal and external network. When selecting the management sponsor, a balance between influence in the company and ability to commit resources to the partnership needs to be found—when in doubt prioritize engagement over rank.

c. Allocate a partnership manager to support the management sponsor and the daily running of a partnership, see the examples of Siemens and Ferrovial. Partnership managers should have a good understanding of the business goals, the focus areas of strategic interest to company, as well as basic knowledge about funding schemes, collaboration formats and their legal implication. To constantly invigorate the partnership, they should use their network in both organizations to create links between different projects and people.

d. To roll out a corporate-wide university program, top-level executive buy-in is needed. Consider modeling such a corporate-wide program like account management: Establish a central university relations unit (often situated in corporate R&D) to manage university collaborations and to oversee your partnership processes (including contract negotiation and recruiting). The partnership managers can either be employees of this unit (as for example, at Ferrovial, Rolls-Royce, or Siemens) or be part of the primarily involved R&D or regional units, with functional reporting lines to the corporate unit (as, for example, at BMW).

e. Dedicate a central cofunding budget to incentivize activities with strategic partners and to secure buy-in across the company.

5. *Regularly evaluate your university partnerships, using suitable key performance indicators (KPIs)*

a. Continuous evaluation should not "just" assess the health of a relationship, but lead to more targeted decisions and prioritized activities. For example, in both the Schlumberger and Siemens chapters, we can read about evaluations with unsatisfactory results, which lead not to the cancellation of the partnership but to revitalizing and improving it.

b. When assessing strategic university partnerships, take their long-term character into account when choosing and interpreting KPIs. For this, use a mixture of quantitative and qualitative metrics and consider both the past performance and prediction for future performance. Check that quantitative KPIs are automatically mineable from existing data or that the extra effort to collect the data is justified. Qualitative KPIs should incorporate the views of a variety of people, from researchers, to students, HR departments, and management.

c. If your company is operating in different business areas and countries you should allow adaptation of the evaluation template. In any case, review your evaluation criteria regularly to make sure that they still fit your business goals.

d. Initial assessments must be carried out by the people who are in direct contact with the university, based on facts and direct experience with the partners. Decisions based on the evaluation should not be done by project leaders, but by the high-level steering committee.

e. Plan how you communicate decisions to your partner, especially negative ones and appoint people in charge of communication.

9.2 THE UNIVERSITY PARTNERSHIP CANVAS

Much of this advice might not come as a surprise to the reader and some of it might even seem obvious. However, in our experience, most companies fail to follow good practices in at least one of the five areas. The reason is often that university collaborations are not prioritized in the company's strategic processes. Often, the company's way of dealing with universities has never been looked at on an organization-wide scale, and an overarching approach has never been defined in a systematic way. In some cases, certain people in the organization might be aware of improvement potential but lack a systematic way of identifying concrete measures and/or communicating them to upper management.

We thus asked ourselves how we can make the recommendations from this book more actionable in an organization. We aimed at creating a simple tool that would reduce the complexity of university collaboration and make explicit (and systematic) the relation between the success factors. Against this background, we have developed together with Prof. Fiona Murray from the Sloan School of Management at MIT the university partnership canvas (Fig. 9.1).[2]

---

2. For a more detailed description of the University Partnership Canvas and how to use it, please see Frølund, Murray, and Riedel (2018).

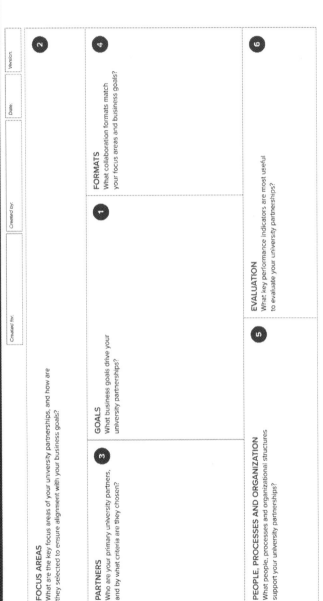

FIGURE 9.1 The University Partnership Canvas.

For this canvas, we turned the five success factors and the insight that university partnerships need to be tightly linked with the overarching business goals, into six questions:

1. What business goals drive your university partnerships?
2. What are the key focus areas of your university partnerships and how are they selected to ensure alignment with your business goals?
3. Who are your primary university partners, and by what criteria are they chosen?
4. What collaboration formats match your focus areas and business goals?
5. What people, processes, and organization support your university partnerships?
6. What KPIs are most useful for evaluating your university partnerships?

A company can use the canvas as a tool to *identify possible tensions in their current university engagement* between the business goals and the key focus areas, partner selection criteria, preferred collaboration formats, the existing organization of university relations, and the KPIs. Once the tensions are identified on the canvas, the natural next step is to define and implement solutions to overcome the tensions. A company may also use the canvas to explore the *impact of changing business goals* (for example, due to changing market situation, changes in the overall company strategy, mergers or carve-outs, etc.) on their existing university partnerships and against this background make timely decisions on what to change

For example, the stated goal of company managers might be to be exposed to new technology trends, business ideas and research-based start-ups. At the same time, it might be looking for talents with skills required for digitalization, for example, knowledge in machine learning or additive manufacturing.

However, the predominant collaboration format with universities might be contract research and publicly funded projects. Contract research is a "standard way" of industry—university interaction and a good match if the research goal and the milestones along the way are relatively well known. Participating in publicly funded projects can have several reasons, from leveraging funding, to evaluating partners to driving standards. But there are collaboration formats, such as idea contests, hackathons, or innovation boot camps, that are better suited to spark the imagination and creativity, are less resource-intensive and more flexible, and at the same time address a much larger pool of talents and ideas.

The partner selection criteria might focus on familiarity, excellence, and contract conditions, which are all important for the "standard" research cooperation that the company has been pursuing. But considering the goals and cooperation formats, the company should pay at least as much attention to the partner's entrepreneurial culture and a good access to a regional innovation ecosystem (RIE) through the university.

The company might also decide to introduce internal calls for research and innovation proposals, potentially combined with a crowd-funding approach. This way, unconventional or silo-spanning ideas might get attention, which otherwise would be lost in the hierarchical research planning process.

The KPIs currently used might be money spent for research projects with a university, funding leveraged, and students hired from that university. KPIs which measure the interaction (for example, number of events organized at the university, number of students, and faculty engaged) and the relevant output (e.g., number of relevant ideas generated, job performance of hires) might be harder to collect but would be much better suited to the company's goals and new collaboration formats.

An example of how the canvas could be used in this example to first identify tensions in the current university engagement approach and then to define possible solution to overcome the tensions is shown below. The arrows indicate a tension and the boxes indicate a possible solution (Fig. 9.2).

Besides serving as an assessment and development tool, the canvas can also be used as an internal communication tool and in discussions with university partners. In our experience, in communication with top-management such as CTOs, the canvas provides an effective tool to present a detailed assessment and suggest a way forward or even to codevelop a high-level assessment and jointly identify the major levers for improvement. In strategic discussions between partners, such as in a high-level partnership steering board, the canvas may also help to guide and structure the dialog and to make explicit the underlying goals and expectations of each partner. Naturally, although this book focuses on the industry-side of university—industry partnerships, the canvas can also be used by universities (in a slightly modified form) to assess and further develop their industry partnering strategy.

9.3 OUTLOOK: TOWARDS AN INNOVATION ECOSYSTEM APPROACH

How does the future of university engagement look like? We see today that large companies use substantial resources on embedding themselves in RIEs, like Kendall Square/MIT, Silicon Valley/Stanford, and Tel Aviv, just to mention a few. An innovation ecosystem cannot only be characterized by bilateral collaboration (governed by the master research agreement) between a large company and a research institution but by a much more diverse interaction with many more partners. We therefore see that additionally to joint research activities, companies sponsor innovation prizes, run hackathons, develop freemium business models (e.g., IBM's Quantum Experience which provides free access to one of the world's first quantum computers), and place people directly in the RIE to scout for new business ideas and/or talent.

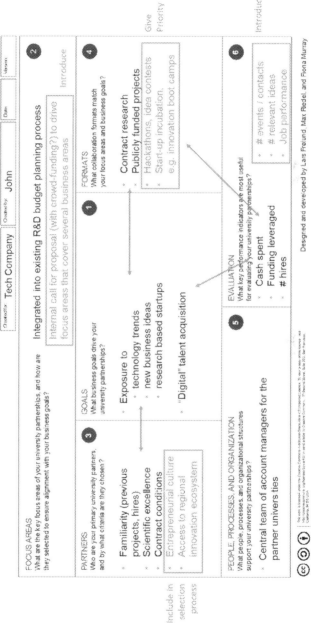

FIGURE 9.2 The University Partnership Canvas used to assess and further develop a university engagement.

This is also the trend that Karsten Keller and Rajiv Dhawan describe in their chapter on DuPont. They name it "Industrial Venture Collaboration":

The new model presents a much higher business impact approach for both, universities and companies. Industrial Venture Collaboration (IVC) is a new way to collaborate, which brings several advantages together. This involves a company working closely with its university partners to identify and mentor promising start-ups. The idea is for the company and university to work together early to provide guidance, people, labs, and other resources to drive the technology to faster commercialization. While money is important in an IVC, knowledge and access to large scale facilities and other resources found within companies are critical for a university-based start-up company's success (. . .).

On the organizational side, this means that the university relations unit is supplemented by technology and business scouts embedded in different RIEs around the globe, and for some companies, the unit for corporate venture now becomes an important integrated part of university engagement. Entrepreneurial culture and broad access to the RIE is now seen as key university selection criteria, side by side with familiarity and excellence. This can be seen in the evaluation where the traditional KPIs are supplemented with numbers of investments into start-ups and number of ideas (e.g., from hackathons or similar) that lead to new product features or business ideas. Recently, US companies have begun asking for First Right to Invest (into spin-offs from the collaboration) in the master research agreements side by side with Right of First Refusal (to acquire intellectual property rights).

We consider this RIE approach driven by digitalization an approach that *coexists* with the classic focus on bilateral collaborations. A way to explain this is to look at it through the lenses of two different speeds of the innovation: an innovation cycle of 3−6 years, and sometimes much longer as for example in the pharmaceutical or aerospace industries, and an innovation cycle of 6−12 months, driven by the fast pace of digitalization. Today, many companies experience the coexistence of these two different speeds of innovation in their product development. It is this coexistence that is translated into their university engagement. The product innovation cycle of 3−6 years correlates well with the goal of long-term development of new technologies and solutions, a primary focus on research excellence and the development of cocreated research labs, sponsoring PhDs and a contractual setup with Right of First Refusal at the core of the master research agreement. But this approach generally does not work for the innovation cycle of 6−12 months, it is simply too slow. Therefore, to have the right approach to the innovation cycle of 6−12 months the companies *simultaneously* focus on start-up scouting, running hackathons to find new ideas and talent, and seek to add a First Right to Invest in the master research agreement.

Innovation ecosystem
- Goal: Exposure to new technologies and business ideas through start-ups
- Partners selected by their access to regional innovation ecosystems (RIEs)
- Organization embedded in different RIEs

Strategic
- Goal: Long-term development of new technologies and solutions & talent acquisition
- Strategic partners selected by fit to overall company goals
- Centralized organization, reporting to senior management

Ad hoc
- Goal: Short-term, incremental problem solving
- Partners selected for individual projects, often based on familiarity
- No or decentral organization for university relations

FIGURE 9.3   Key characteristics of the ad hoc, the strategic approach, and the innovation ecosystem approach.

To summarize this three-step development in the field of university—industry collaboration, Fig. 9.3 illustrates the key characteristics of the ad hoc, the strategic approach, and the emergence of the innovation ecosystem approach.

In the process from an ad hoc to a more and more systematic approach to university engagement, the innovation ecosystem approach, driven by the all-encompassing digitalization, is the latest development that will most likely define university—industry collaboration in the years to come.

REFERENCES

Frølund, L., Murray, F., Riedel, M., Winter 2018. Developing successful strategic partnerships with universities. Sloan Manage. Rev. 59 (2), 71—79.

Osterwalder, A., Pigneur, Y., 2010. Business Model Generation: A Handbook for Visionaries, Game Changers, and Challengers. Wiley, New York.

Index

Printed in the United States
By Bookmasters